MW01615238

ART OF LIFE

MY BEST 100

KEN ROCHON, JR.

Art of Life – My Best 100

© 2018 by Ken Rochon, Jr.

All rights reserved. No part of this publication may be reproduced or transmitted in any form or by any means, electronic or mechanical, including photocopying, recording, or by any information storage and retrieval system, without the prior written permission from the publisher or the authors, except by reviewers who may quote brief excerpts in connection with a review in a newspaper, magazine or electronic publication. Contact the publisher for information on foreign rights.

ISBN: 978-1-949907-07-0

Printed in the United States of America

Dedicated to my son Kenny, the light of my life.

To my Dad for believing in me... it made all the difference.

To my Brother and Sister and all my nephews and nieces –
Andrew, Brendan, Caroline, KK, Matthew, & Stephanie.

To my wife Nelly for sharing this journey and
loving me unconditionally.

And most of all to my Mom who inspired me to believe
anything is possible. This is another tribute to you.

Life is a journey and memorializing it is a
gift to yourself and the people you love.

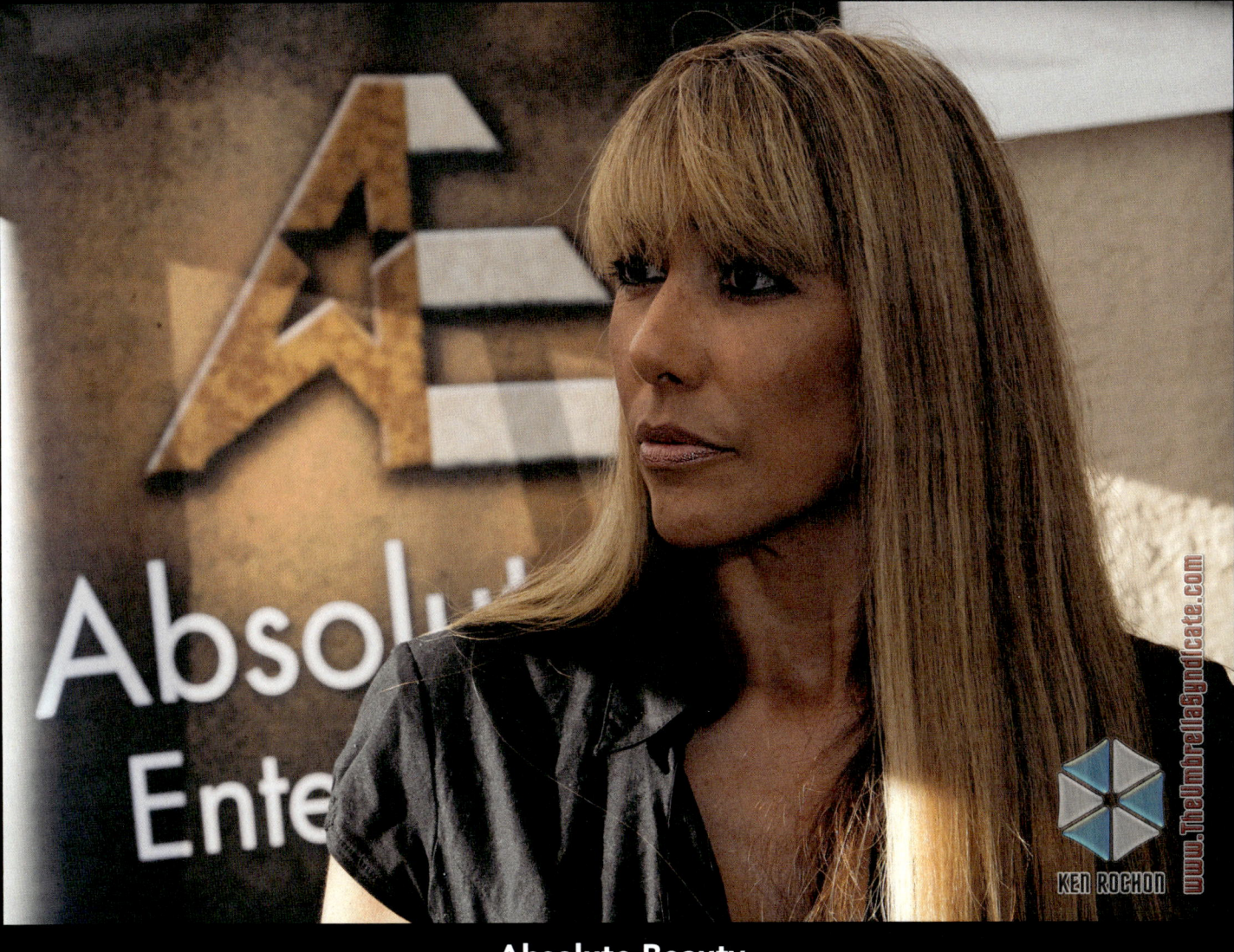

Absolute Beauty

www.TheUmbrellaSyndicate.com

KEN ROCHON

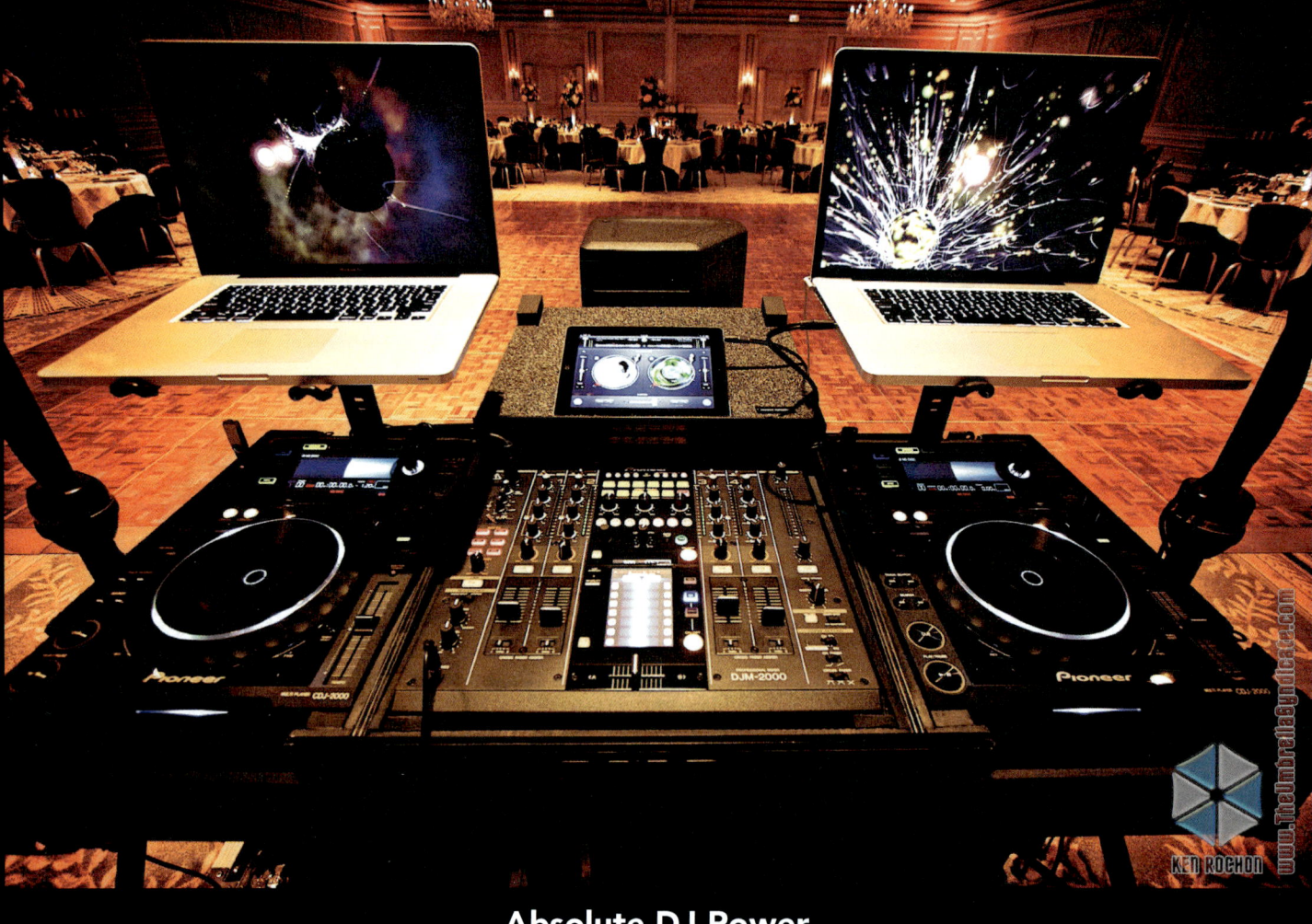

Absolute DJ Power

www.theUmbrellaSyndicate.com

KEN ROCHON

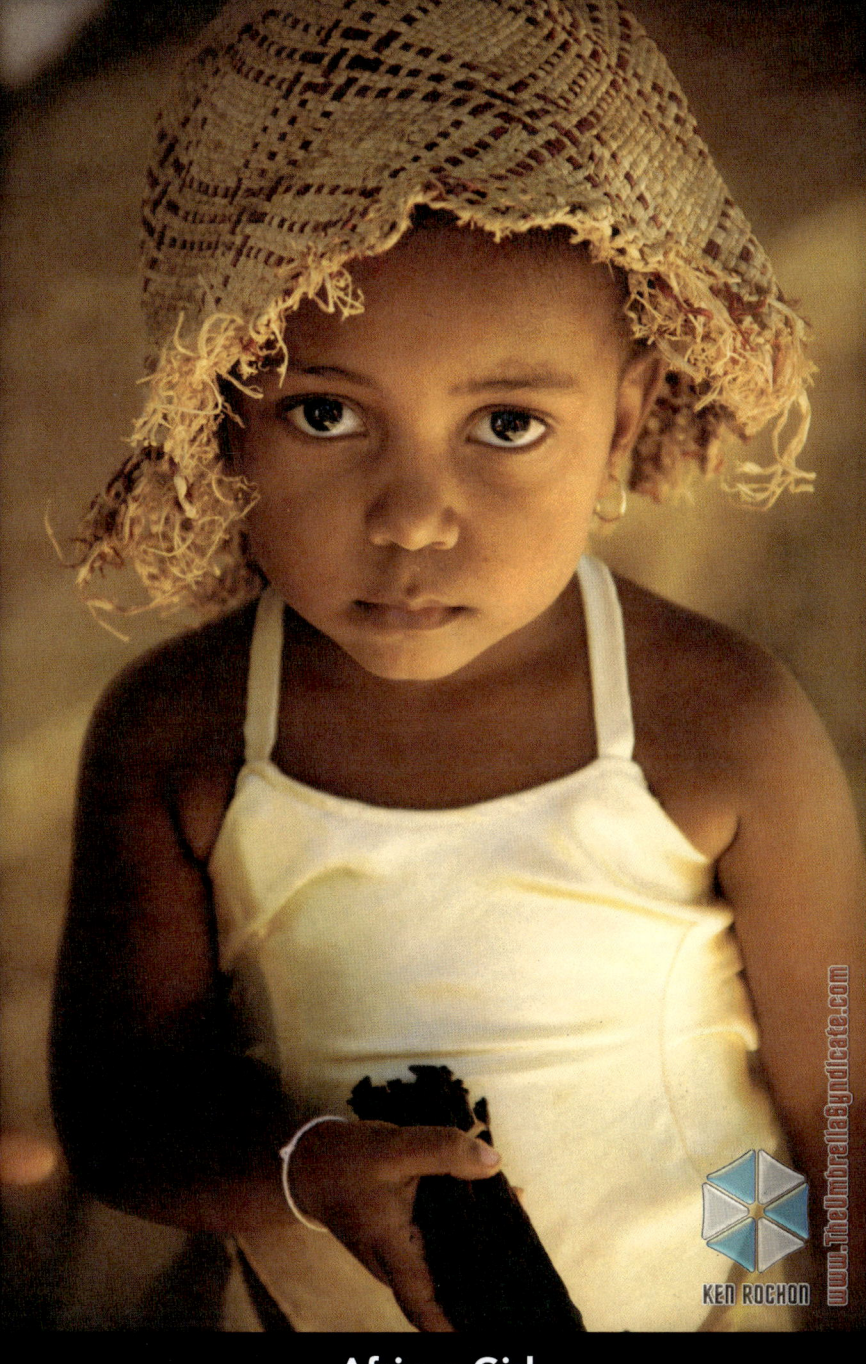

www.TheUmbrellaSyndicate.com

KEN ROCHON

African Girl

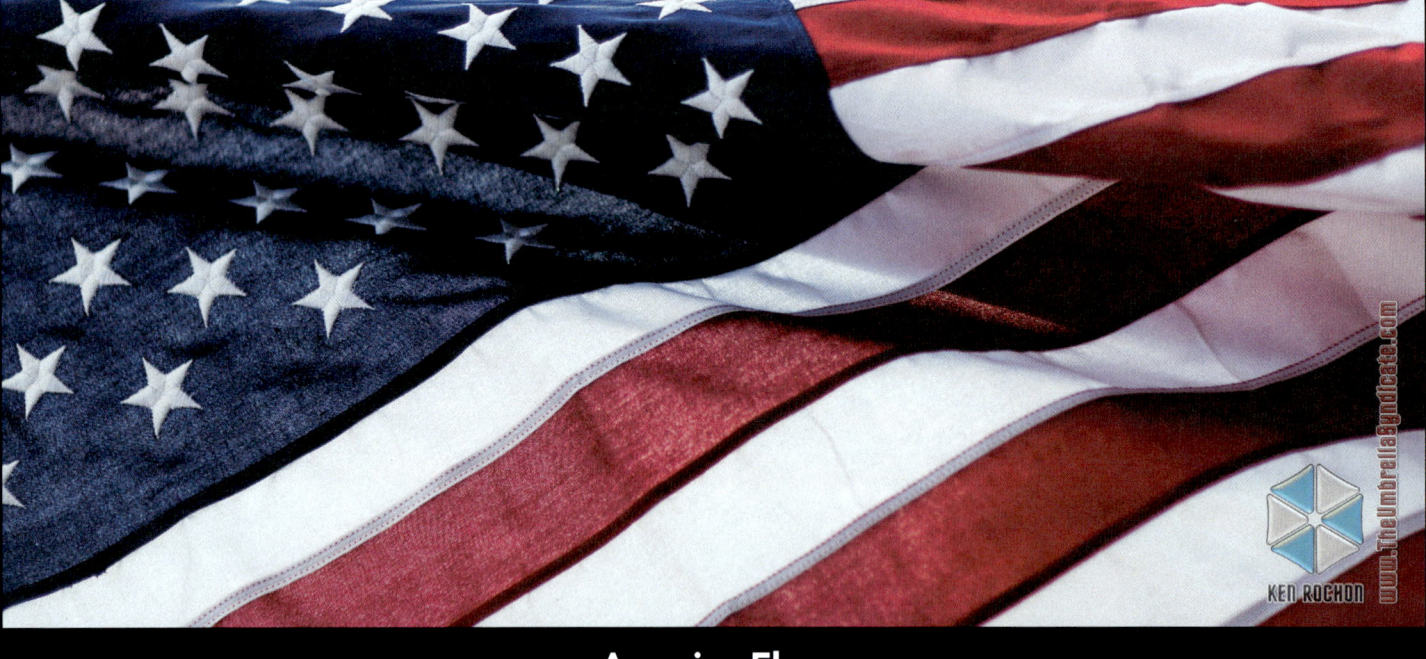

America Flag

www.TheUmbrellaSyndicate.com

KEN ROCHON

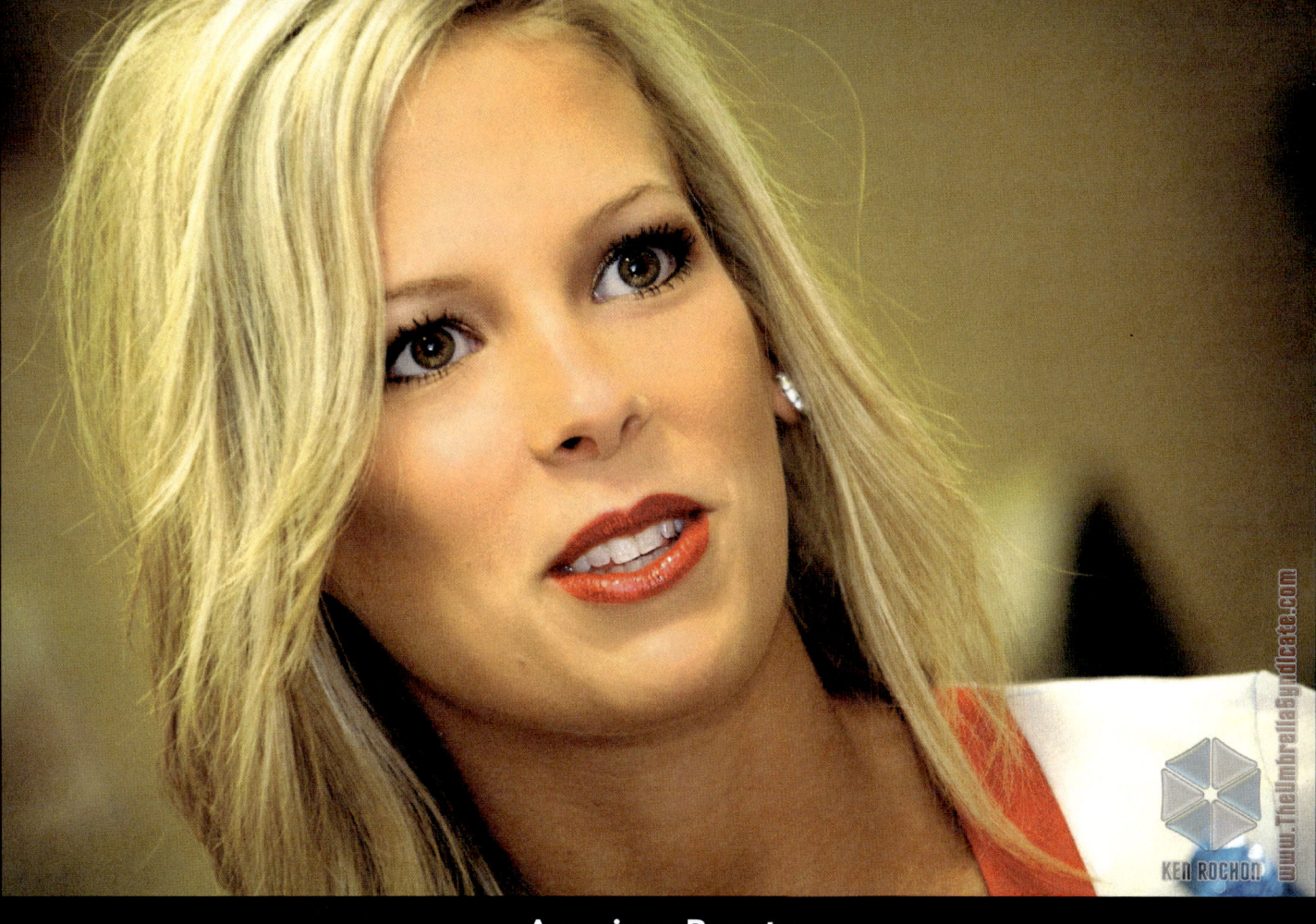

American Beauty

www.TheUmbrellaSyndicate.com

KEN ROCHON

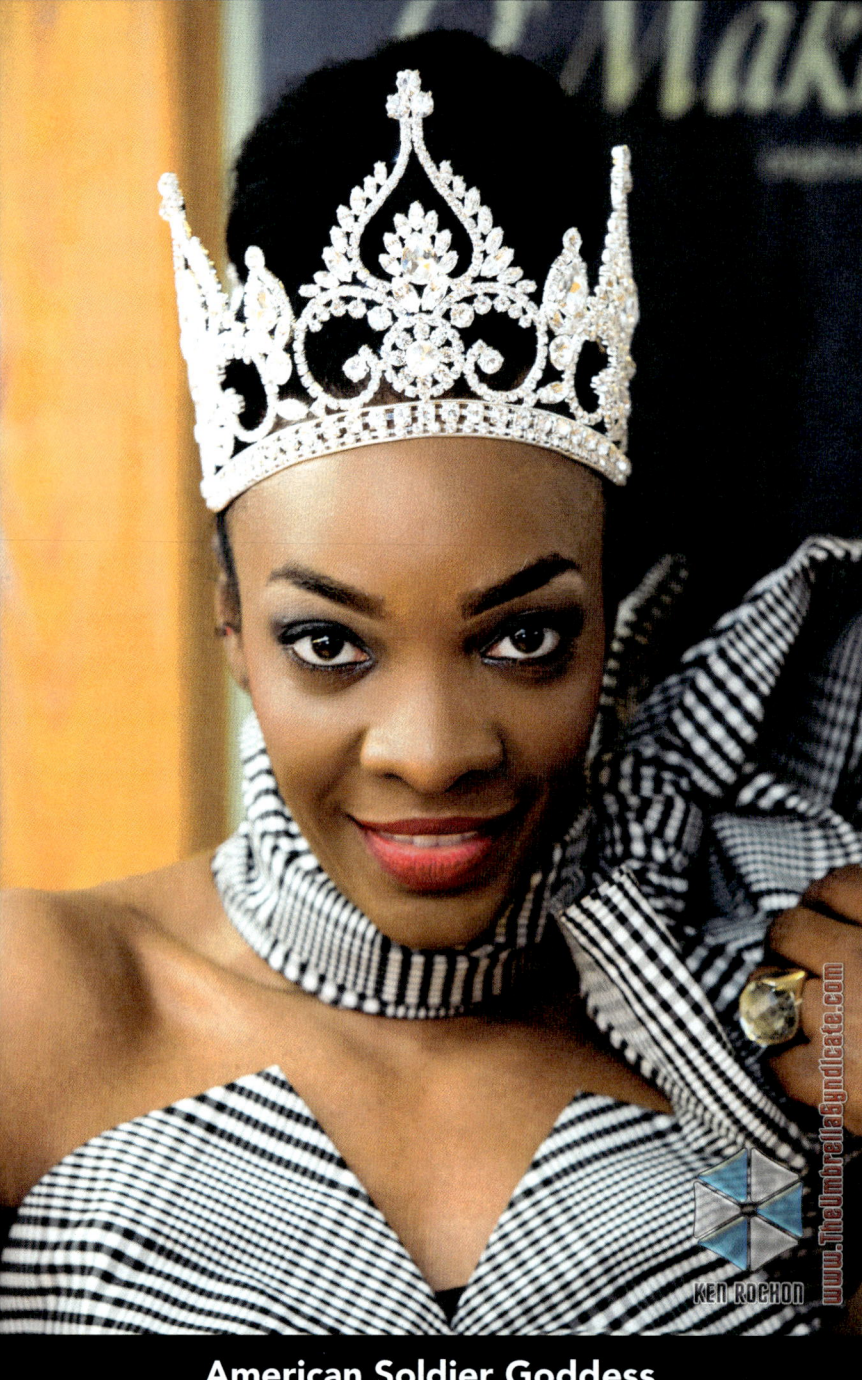

American Soldier Goddess

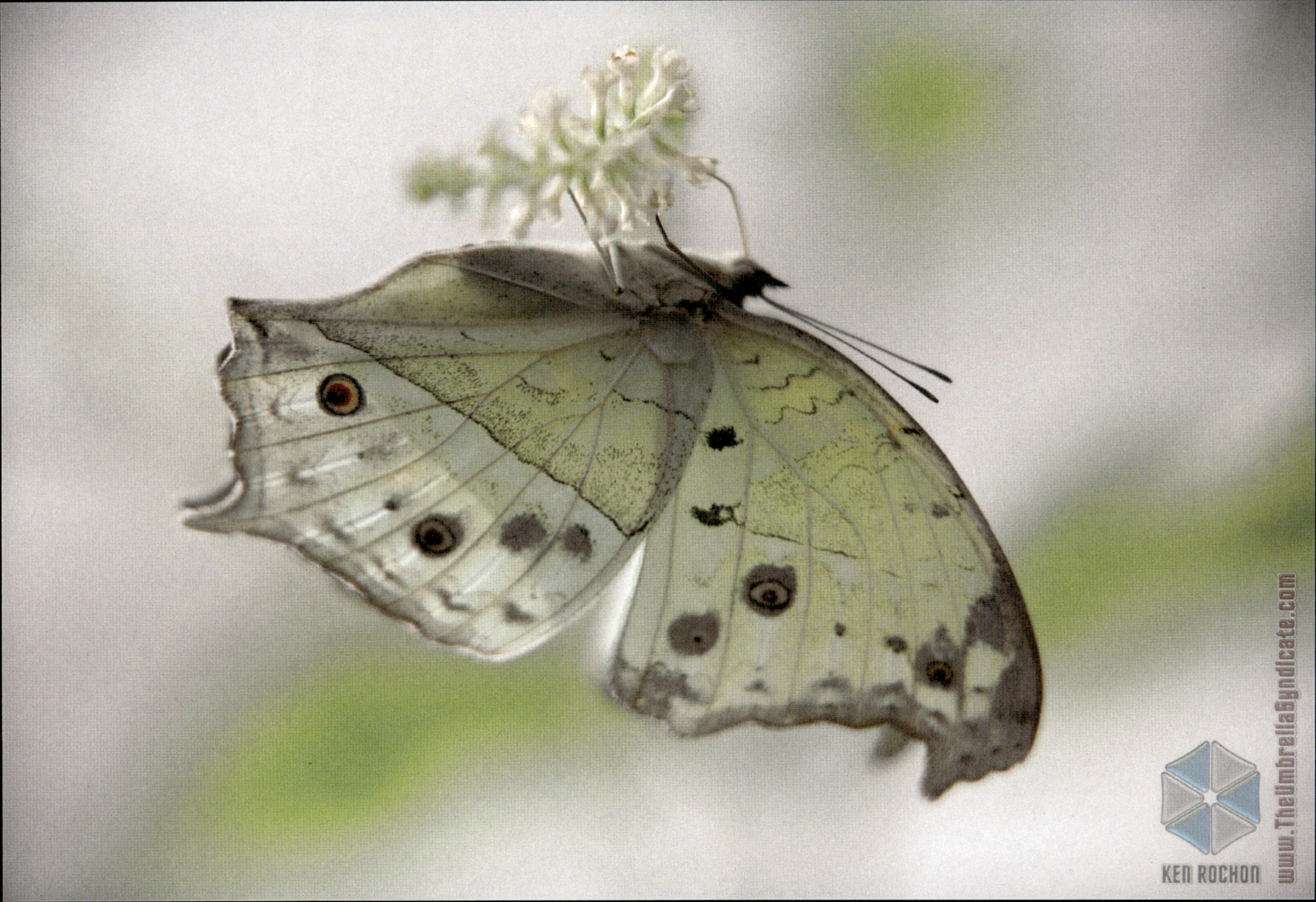

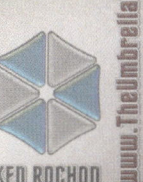

KEN ROCHON

www.TheUmbrellaSyndicate.com

Angel Butterfly

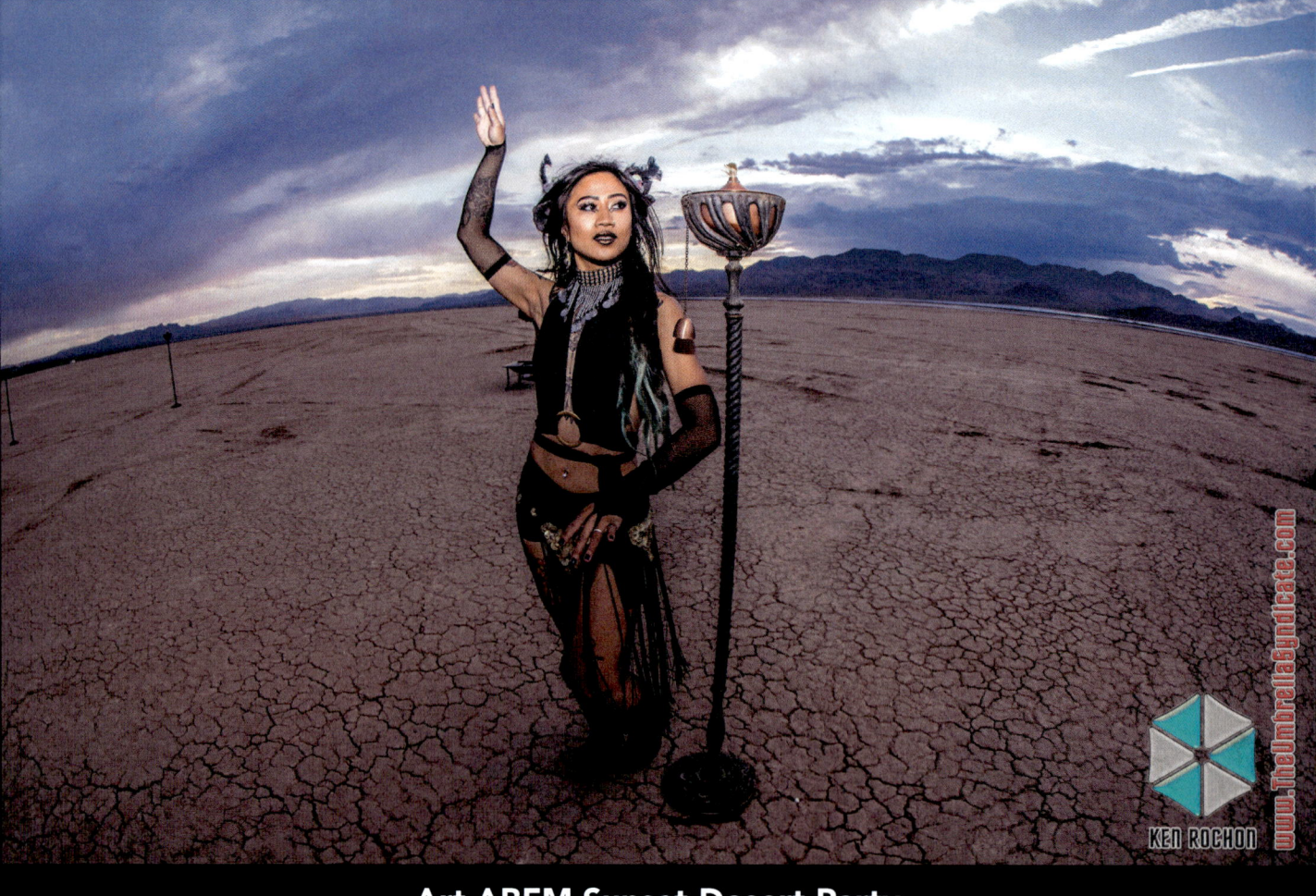

www.TheUmbrellaSyndicate.com

KEN ROCHON

Art ABFM Sunset Desert Party

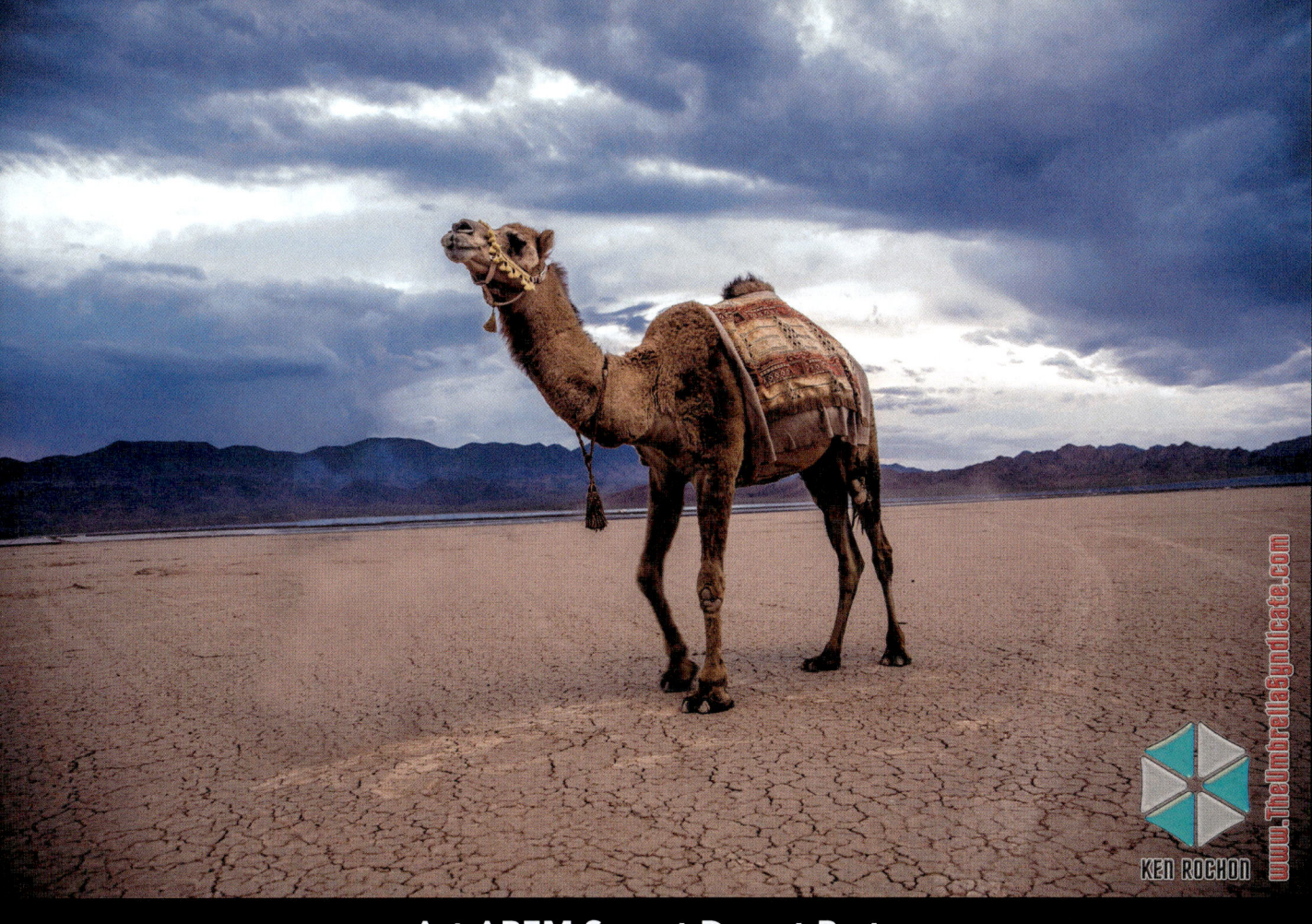

Art ABFM Sunset Desert Party

www.TheUmbrellaSyndicate.com

KEN ROCHON

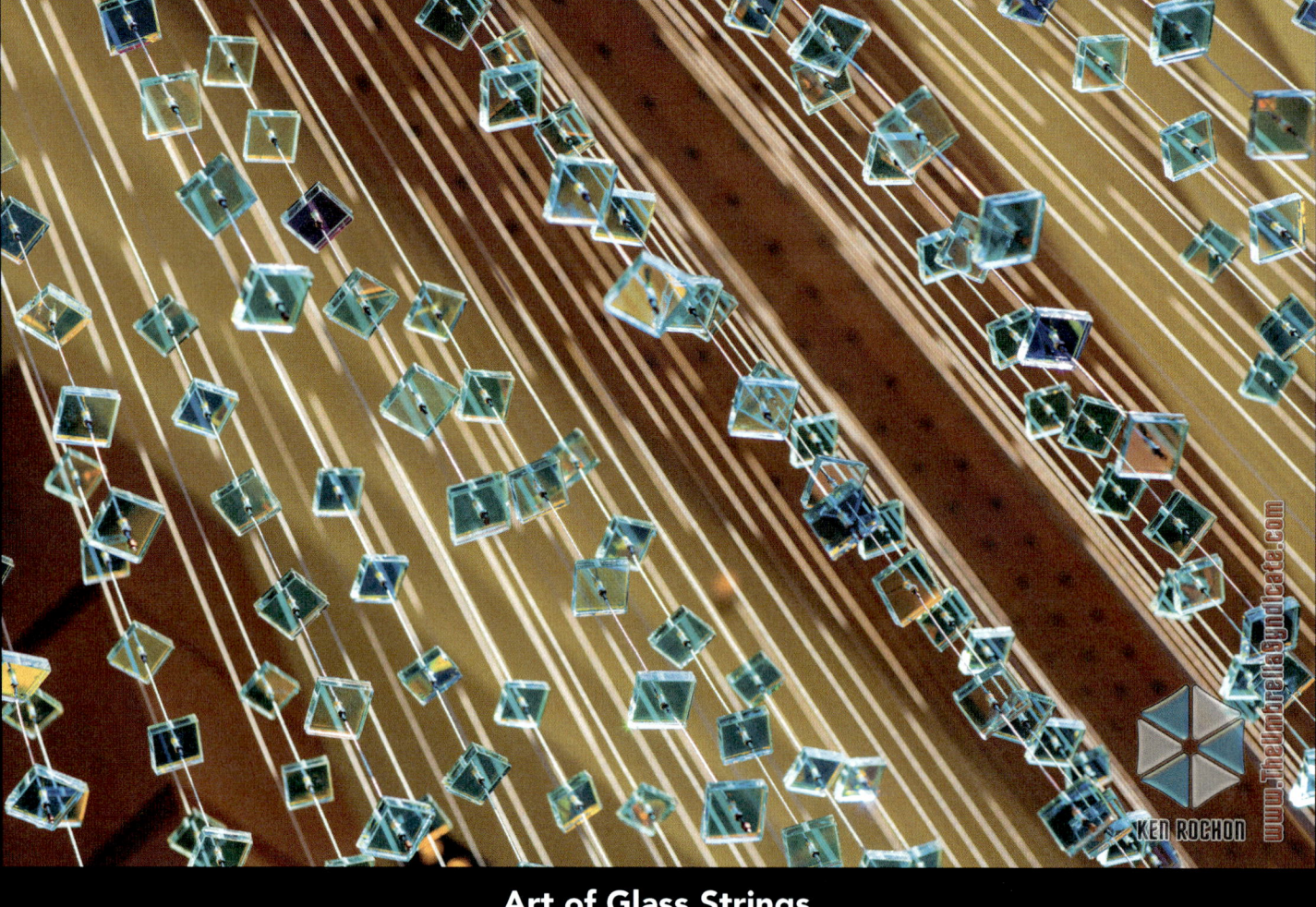

Art of Glass Strings

KEN ROCHON   www.TheUmbrellaSyndicate.com

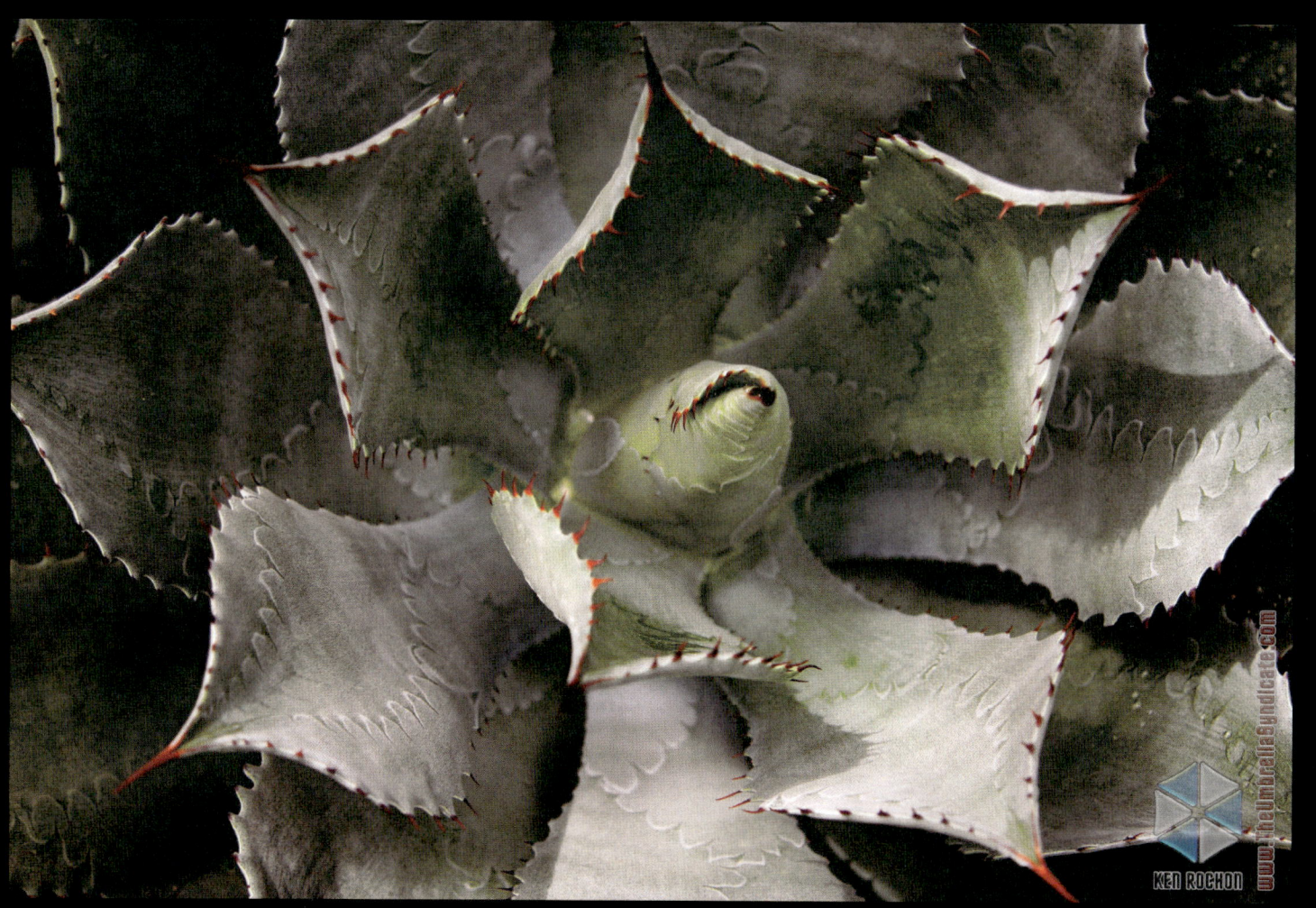

Art of Leaves

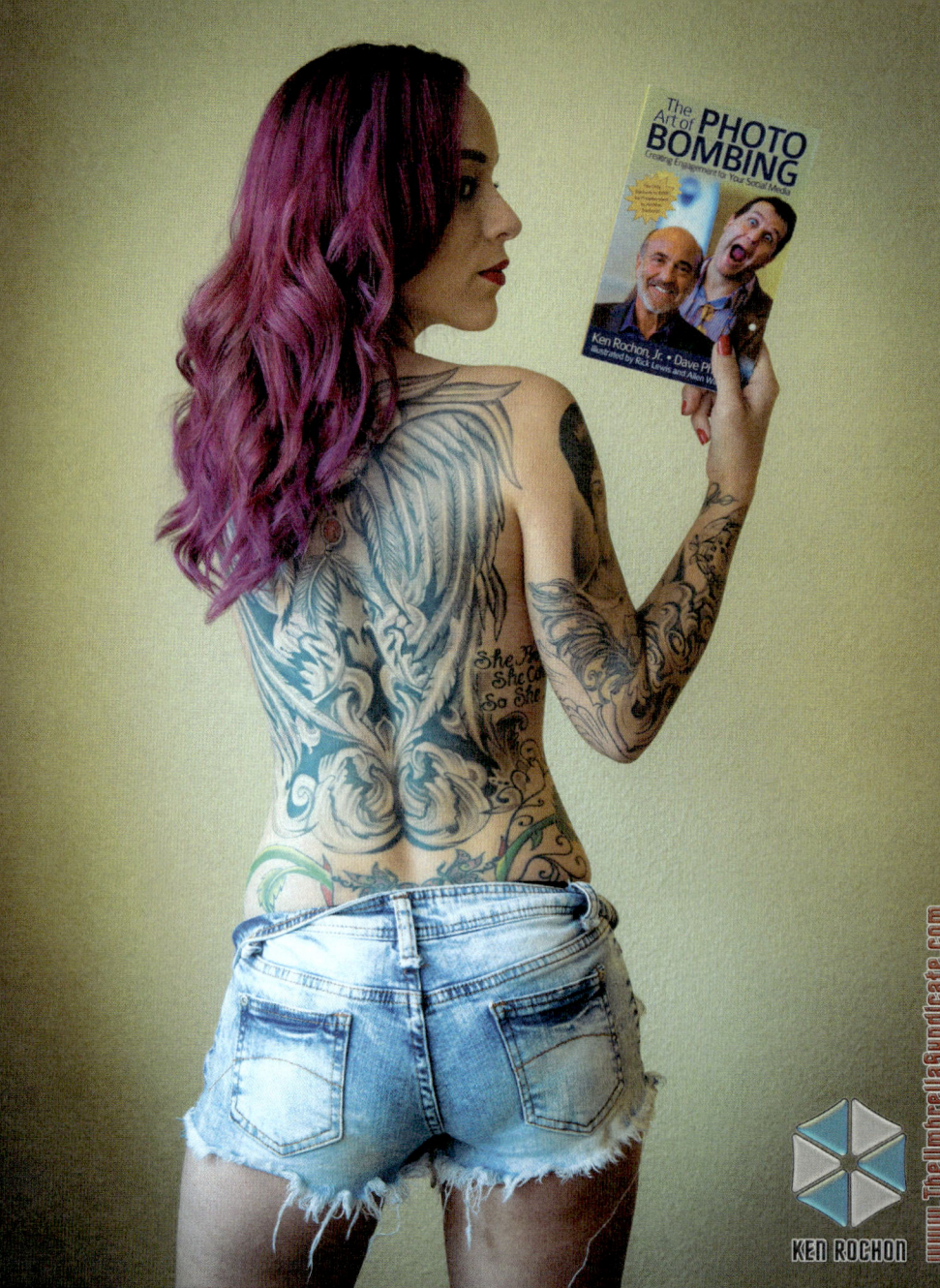

The Art of PHOTO BOMBING

Creating Engagement to Your Social Media

Ken Rochon, Jr. • Dave Ph...

Illustrated by Rick Lewis and Alan W...

She ...
She Co...
So She

www.TheUmbrellaSyndicate.com

KEN ROCHON

Art of Photo Bomb Book Tattoo

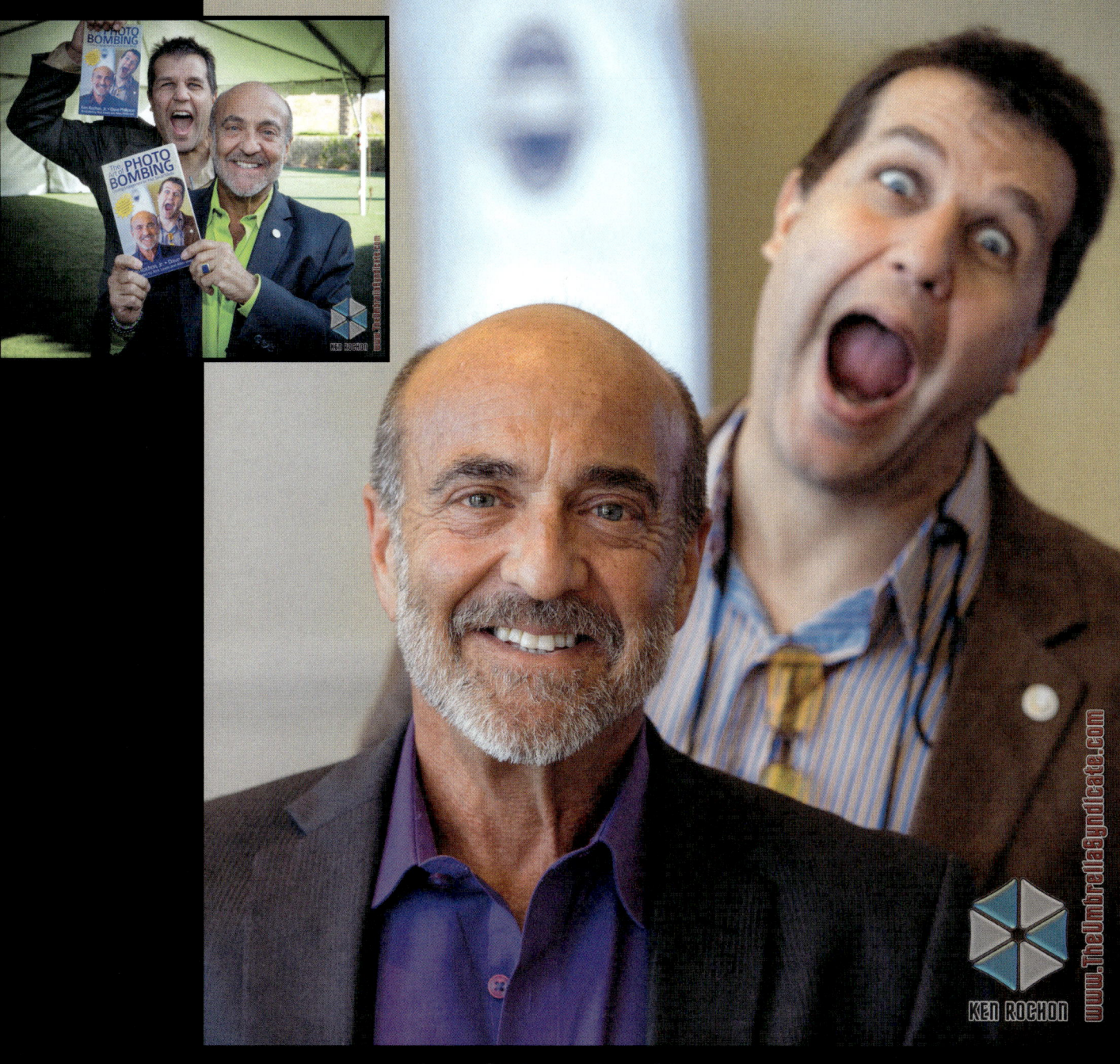

Art of Photo Bombing

www.TheUmbrellaSyndicate.com

KEN ROCHON

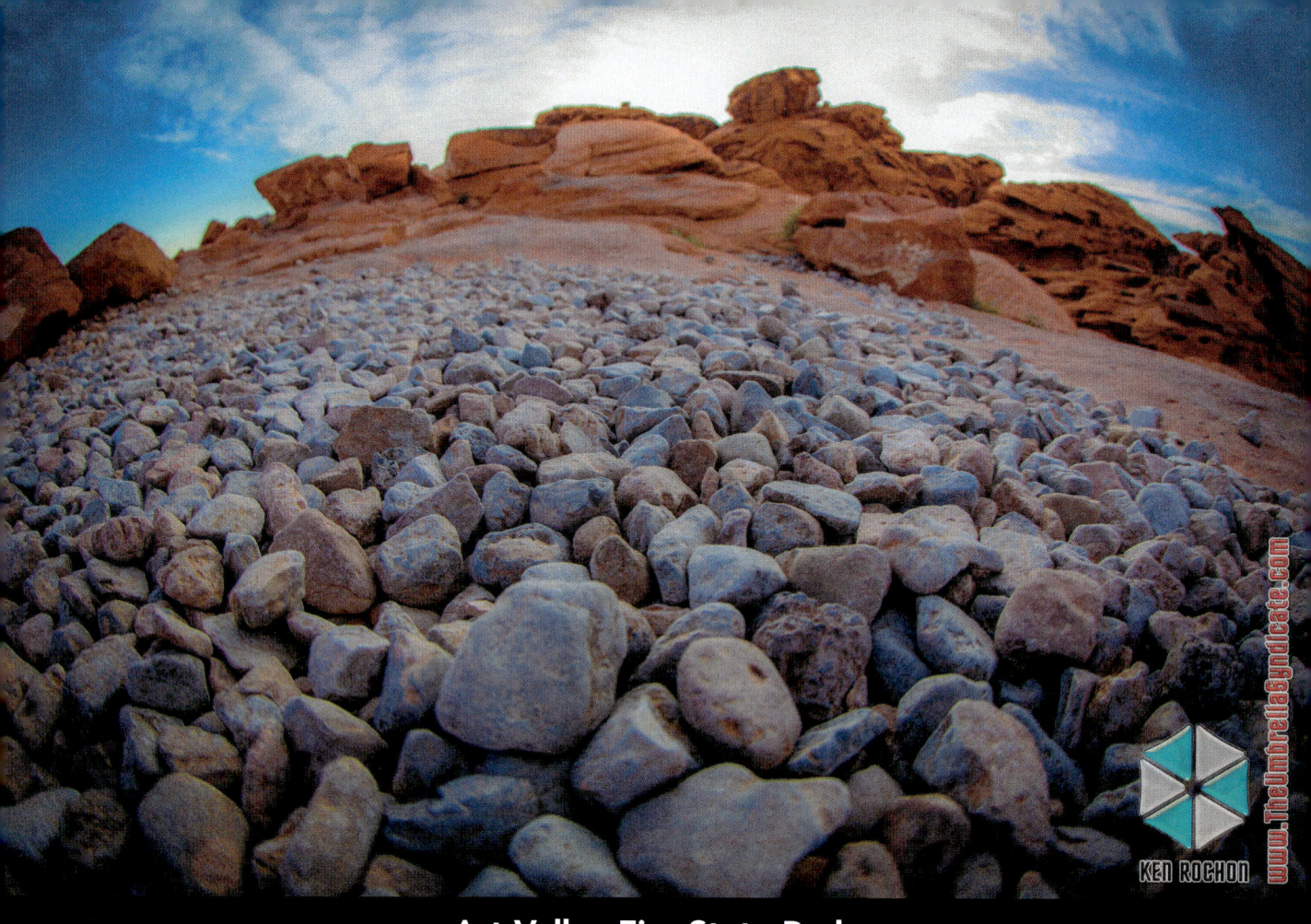

Art Valley Fire State Park

KEN ROCHON

www.TheUmbrellaSyndicate.com

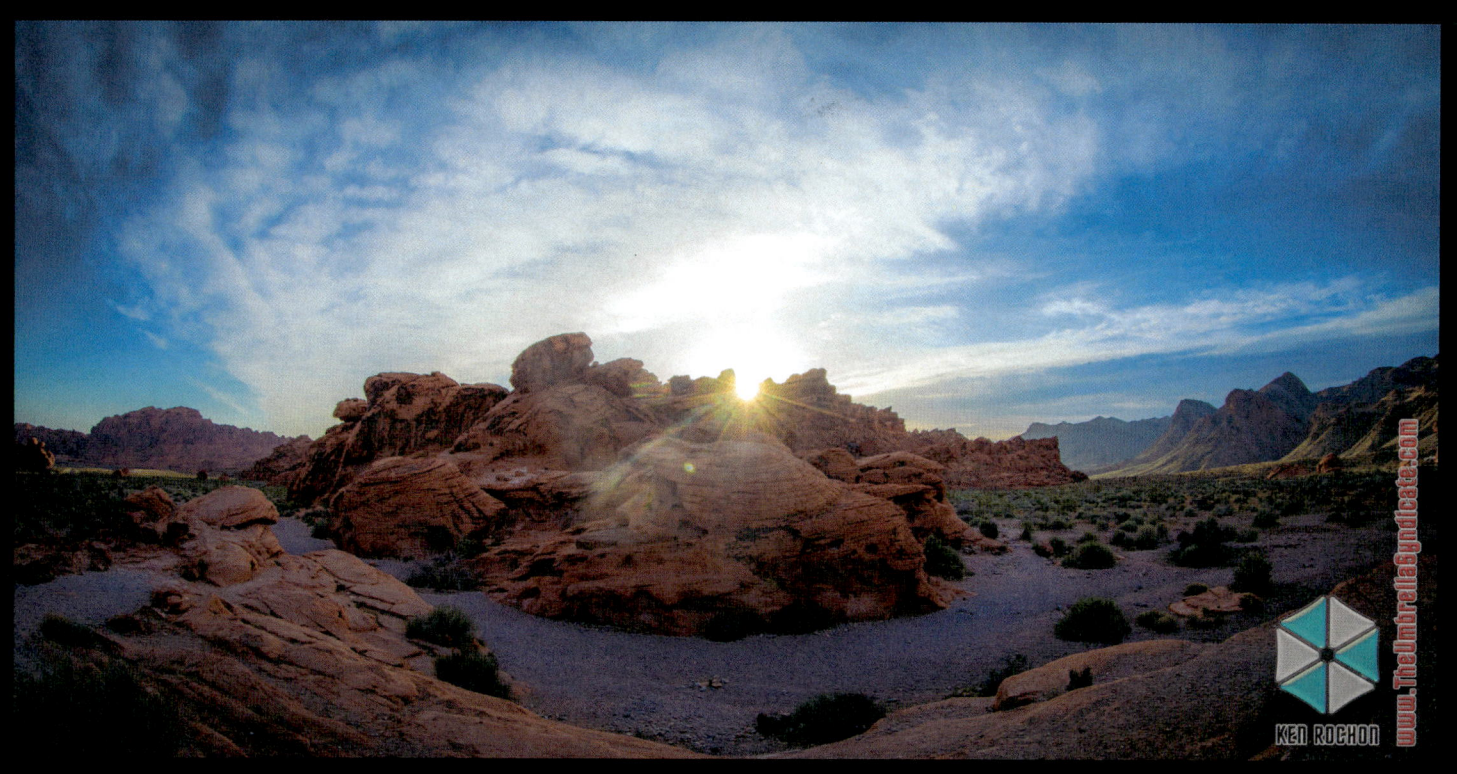

Art Valley Fire State Park

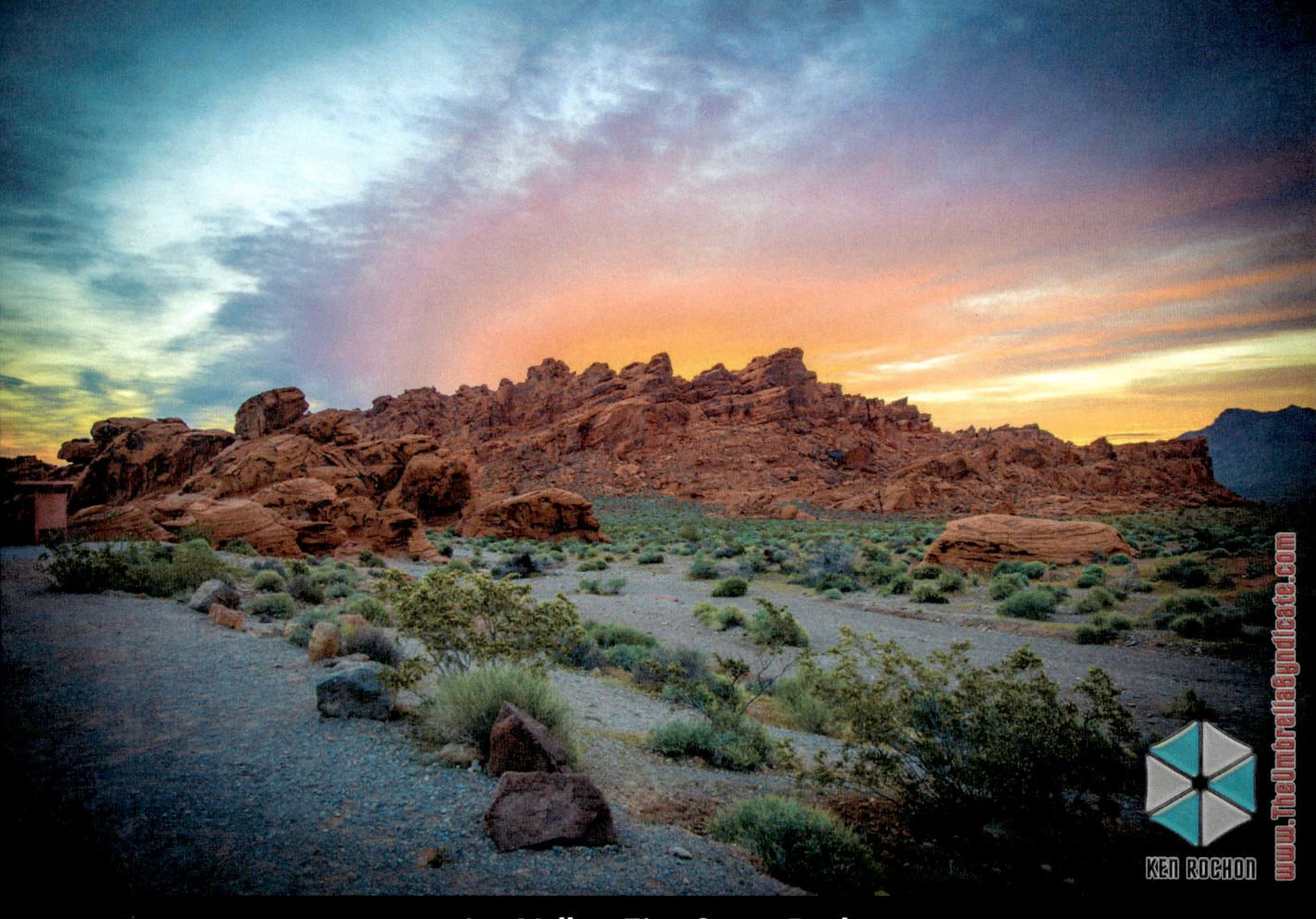

Art Valley Fire State Park

www.TheUmbrellaSyndicate.com

KEN ROCHON

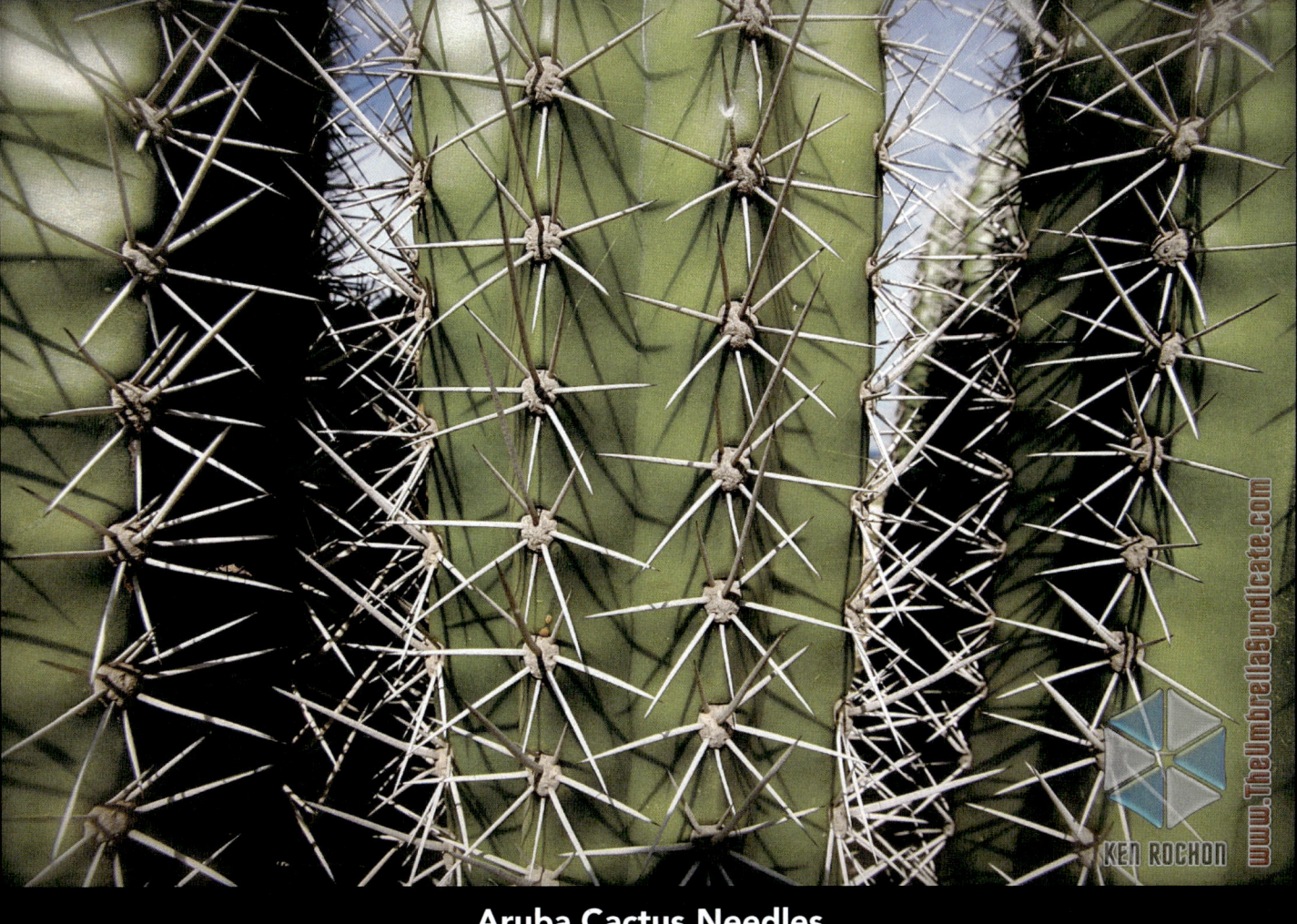

Aruba Cactus Needles

www.TheUmbrellaSyndicate.com

KEN ROCHON

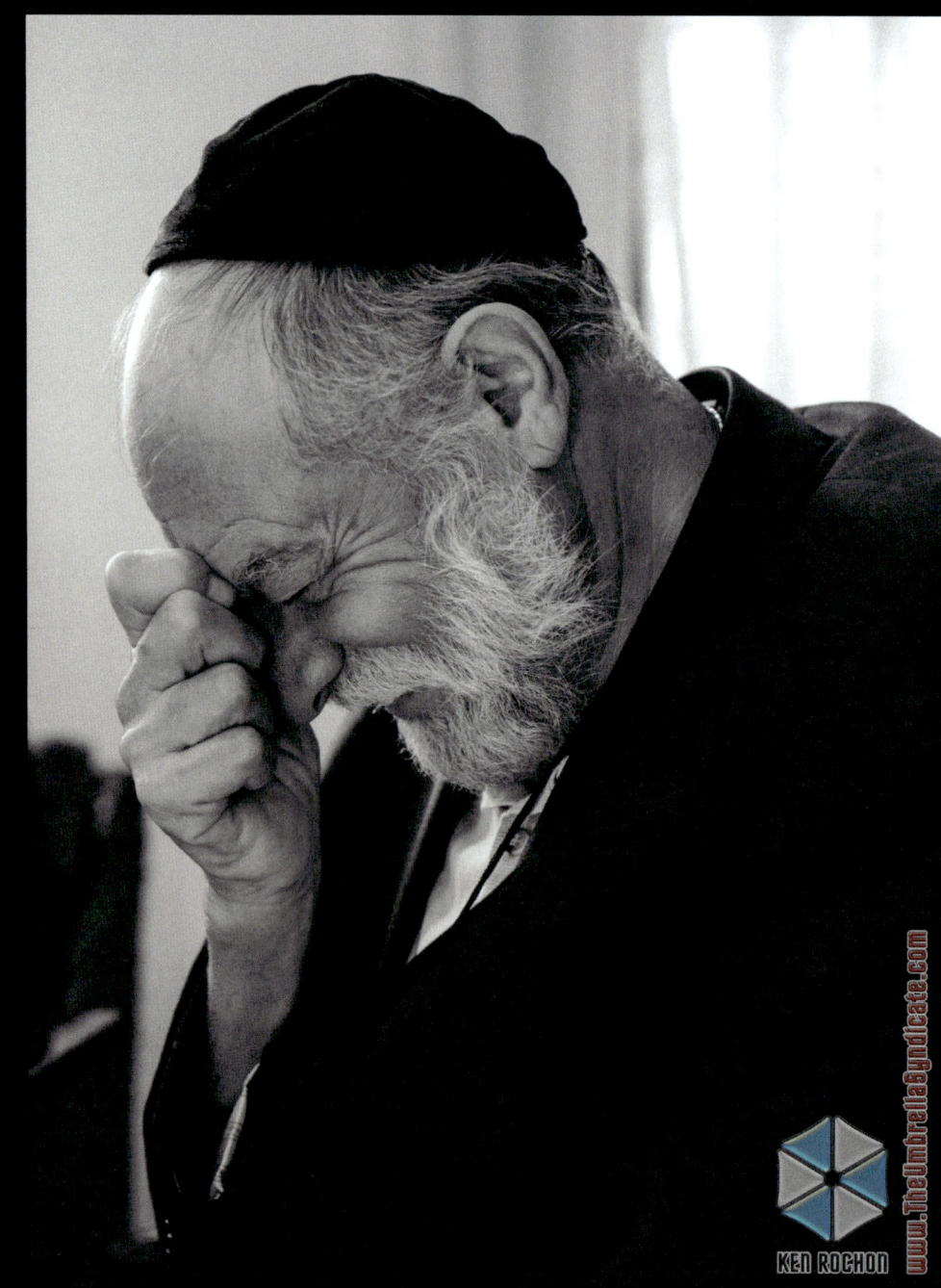

Barry Shore Joy

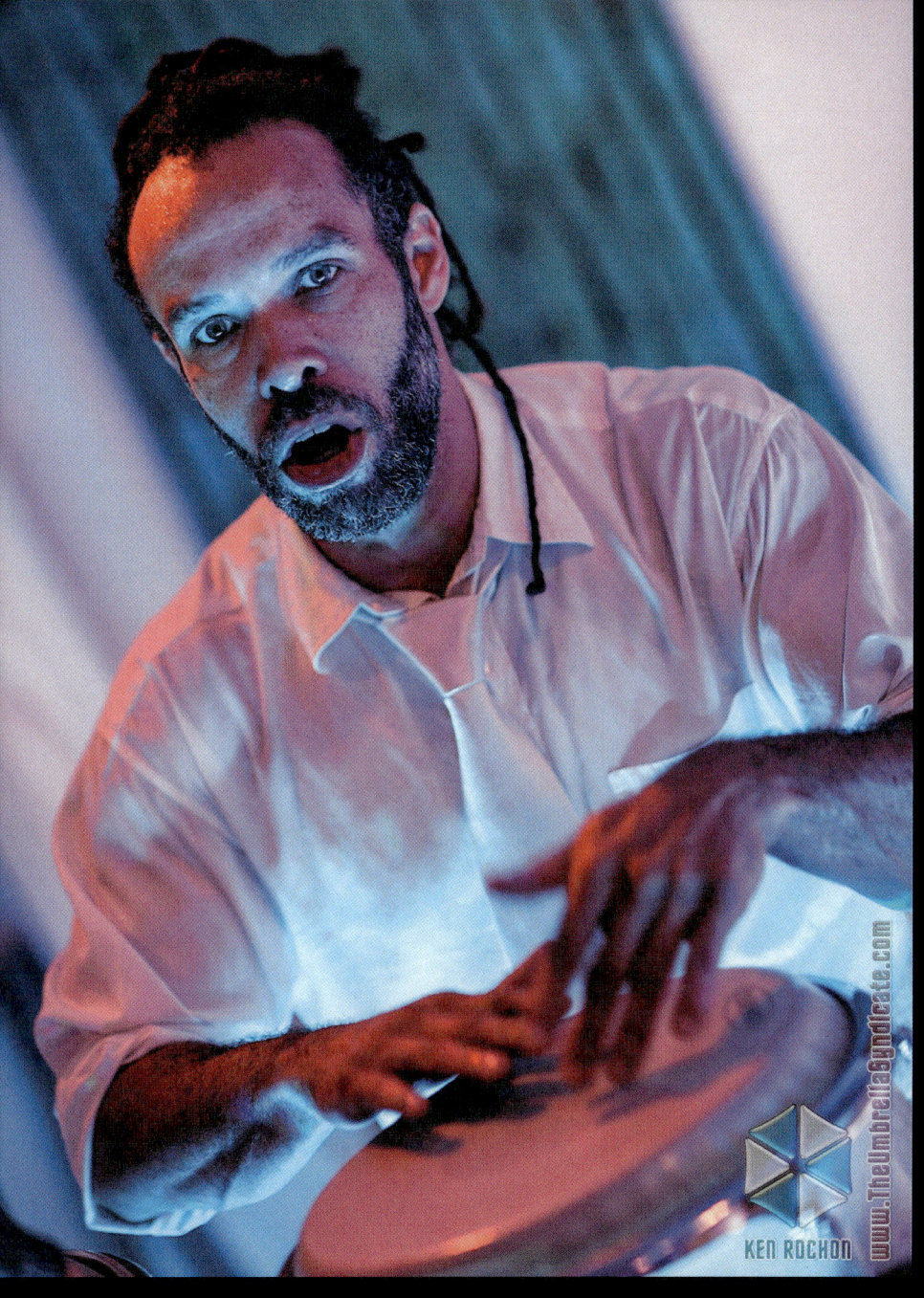

Beatto Wild Light

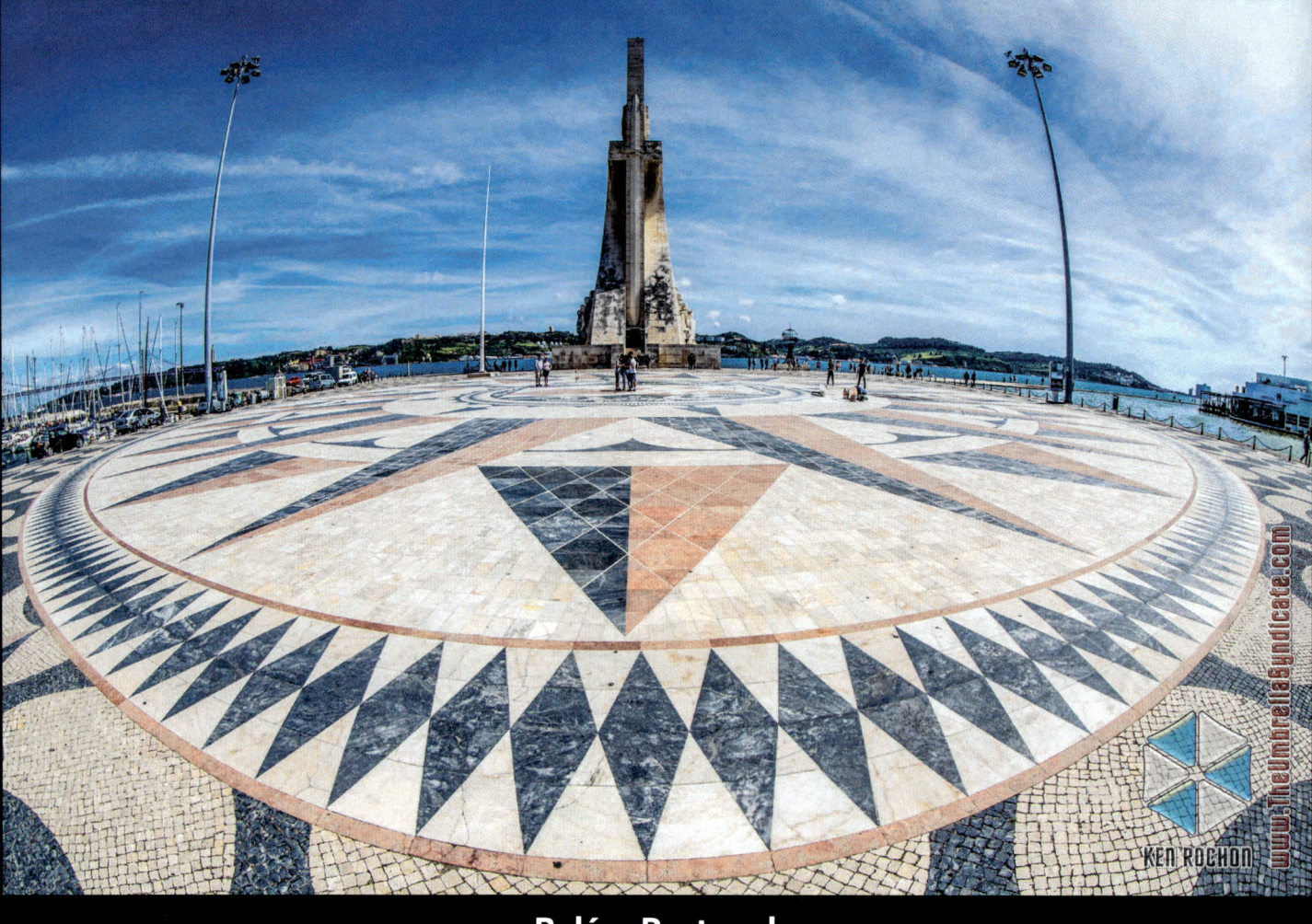

Belém Portugal

www.TheUmbrellaSyndicate.com

KEN ROCHON

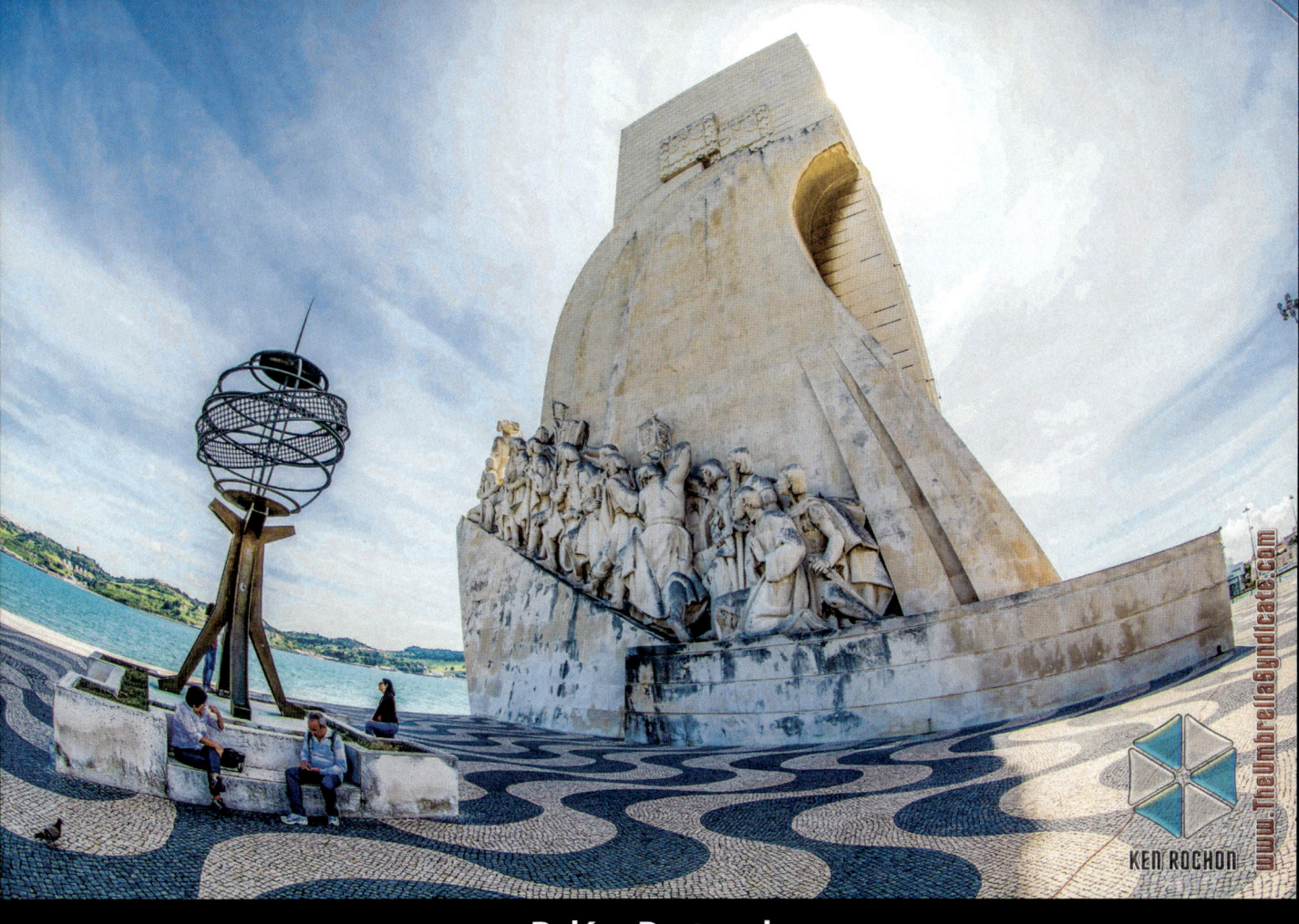

Belém Portugal

www.TheUmbrellaSyndicate.com

KEN ROCHON

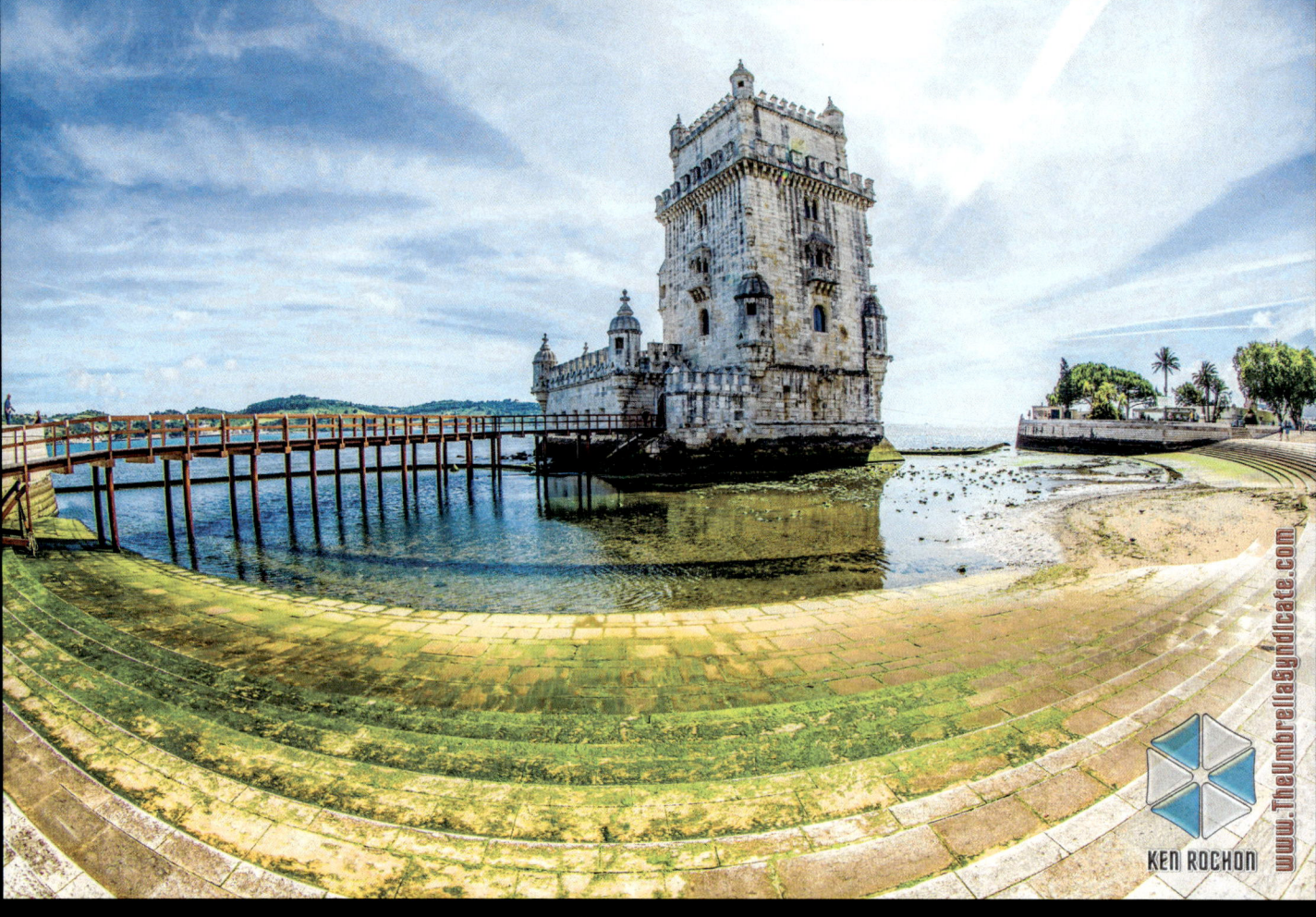

Belém Portugal

www.TheUmbrellaSyndicate.com

KEN ROCHON

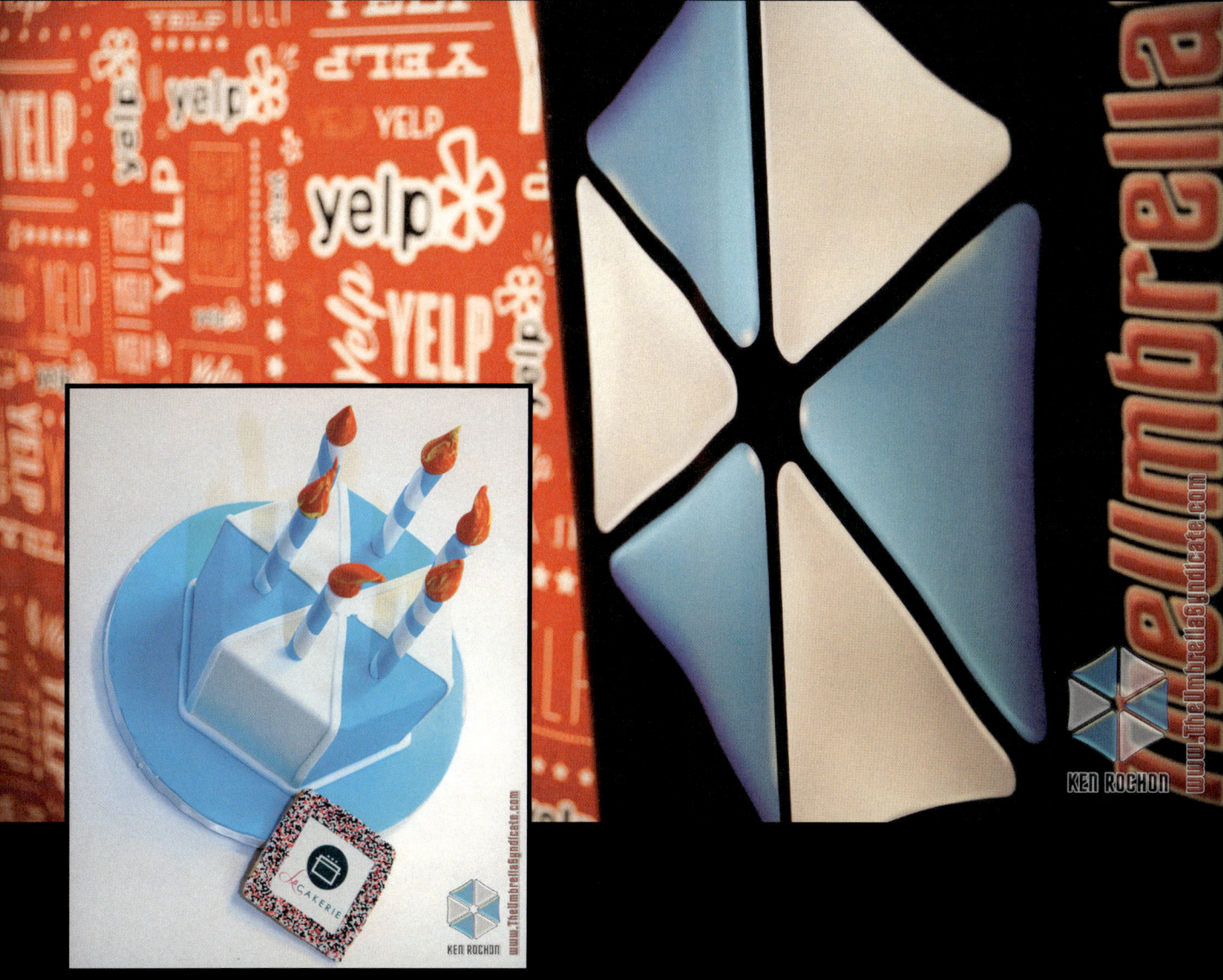

Brand Power

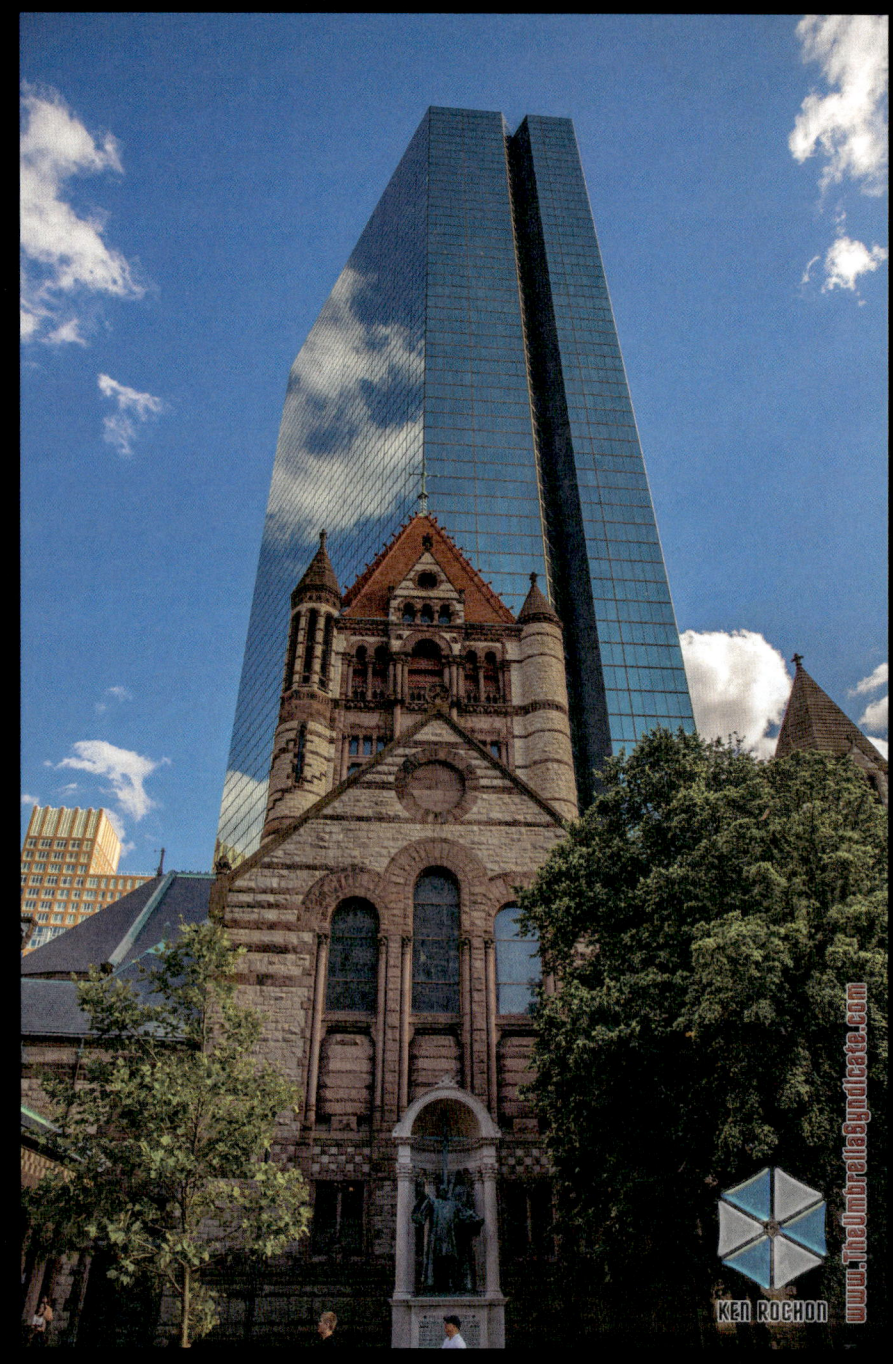

Boston Old New

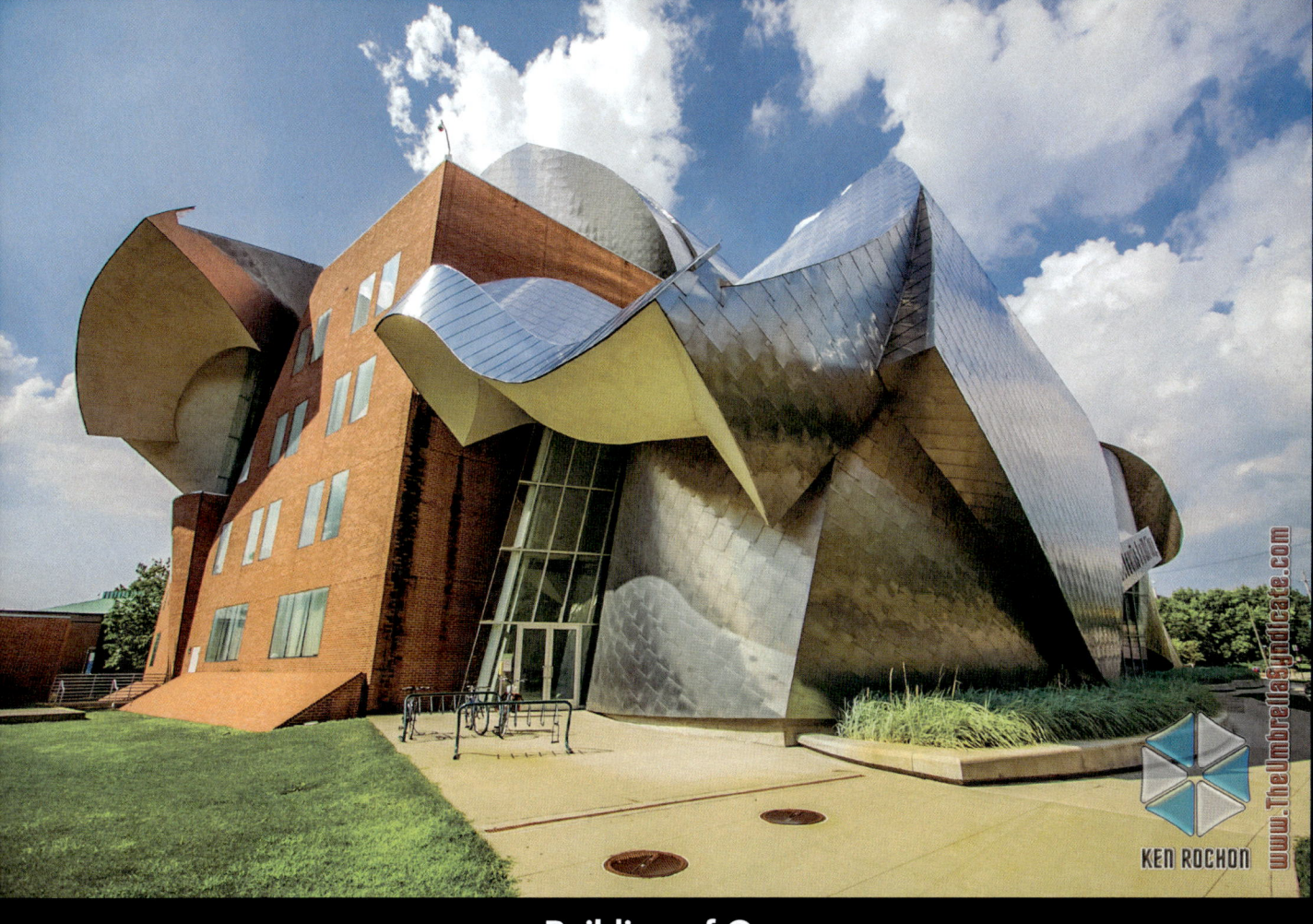

www.TheUmbrellaSyndicate.com

KEN ROCHON

Building of Oz

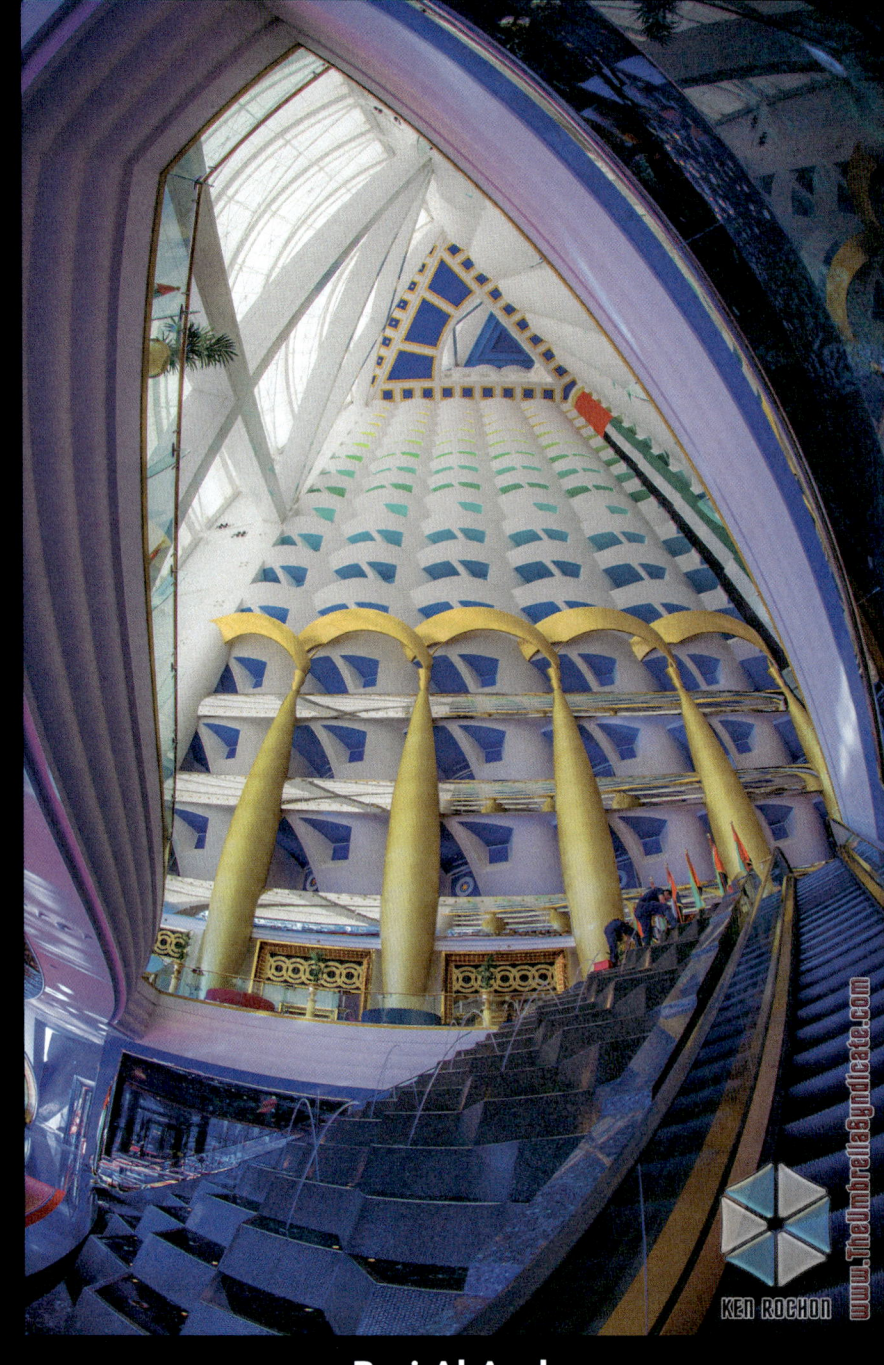

Burj Al Arab

www.TheUmbrellaSyndicate.com

KEN ROCHON

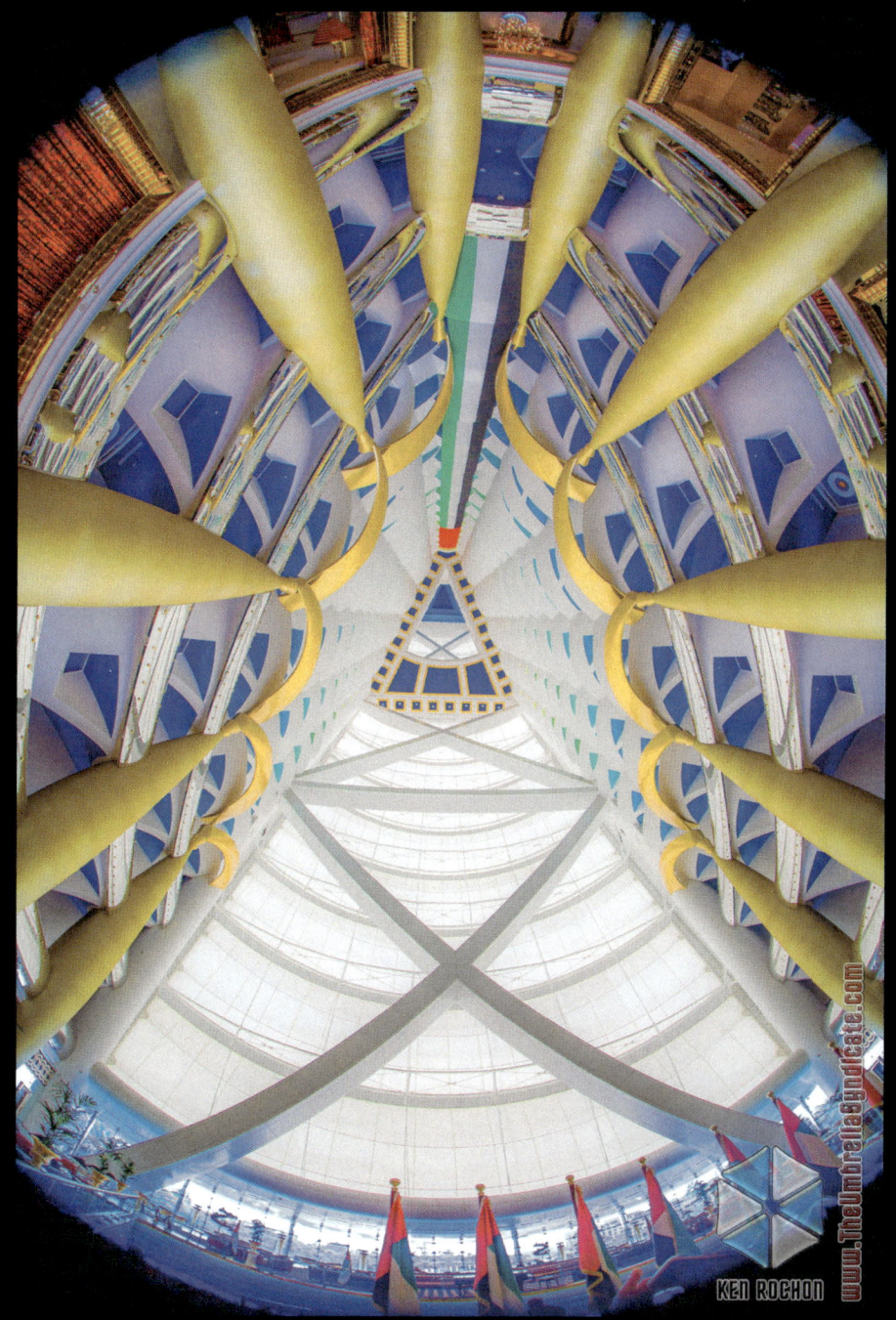

Burj Al Arab

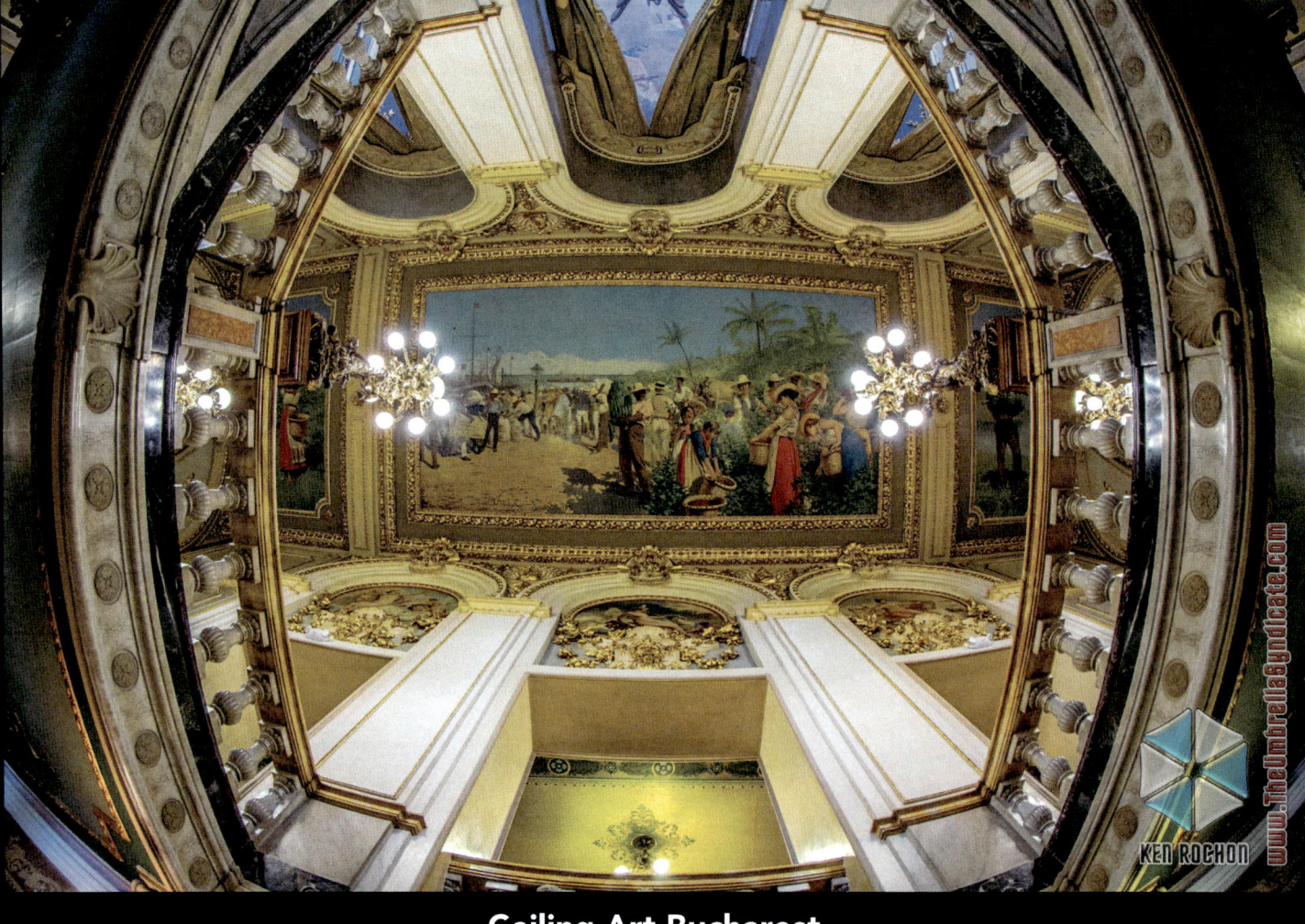

Ceiling Art Bucharest

www.TheUmbrellaSyndicate.com

KEN ROCHON

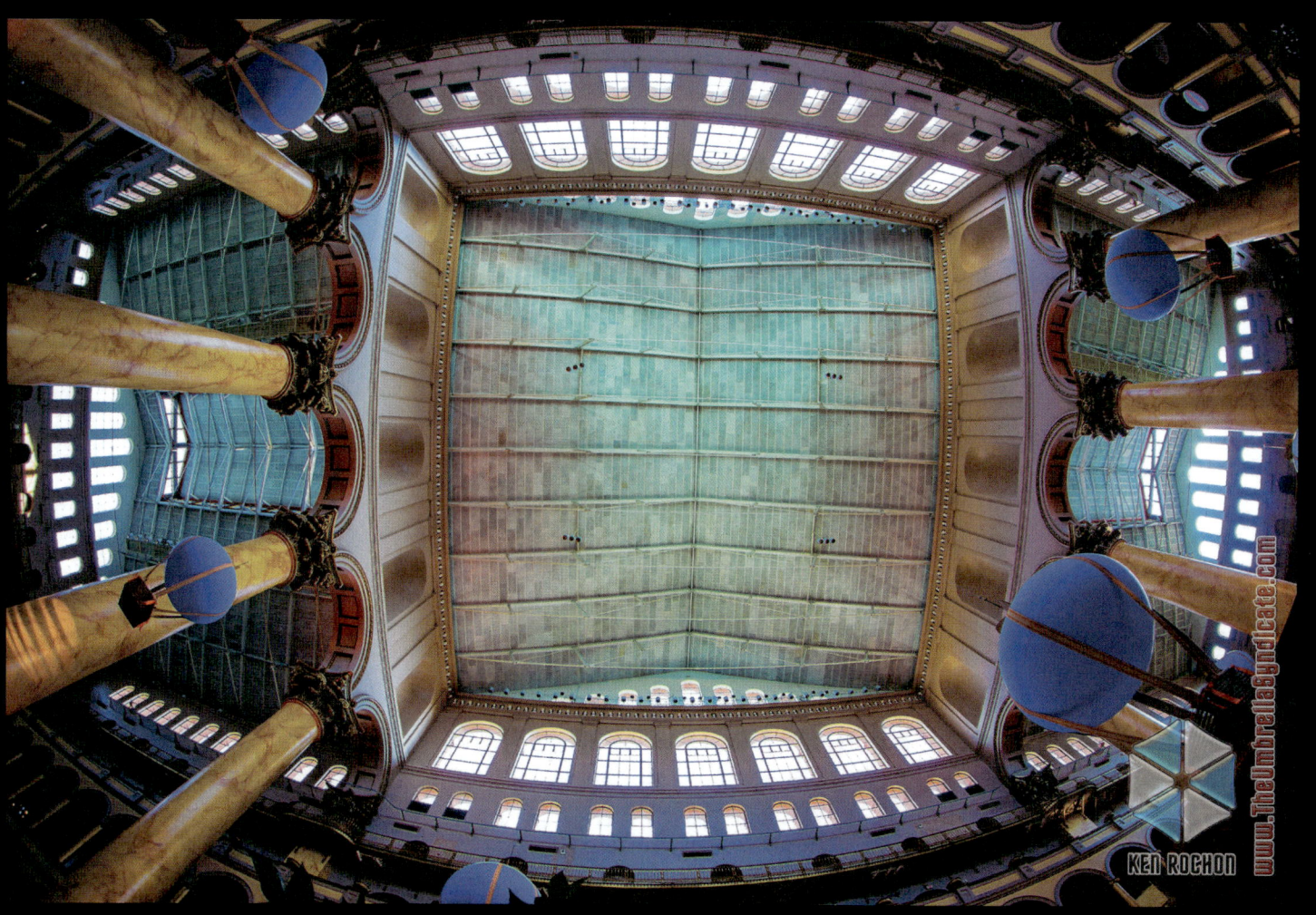

Ceiling of Color Columns

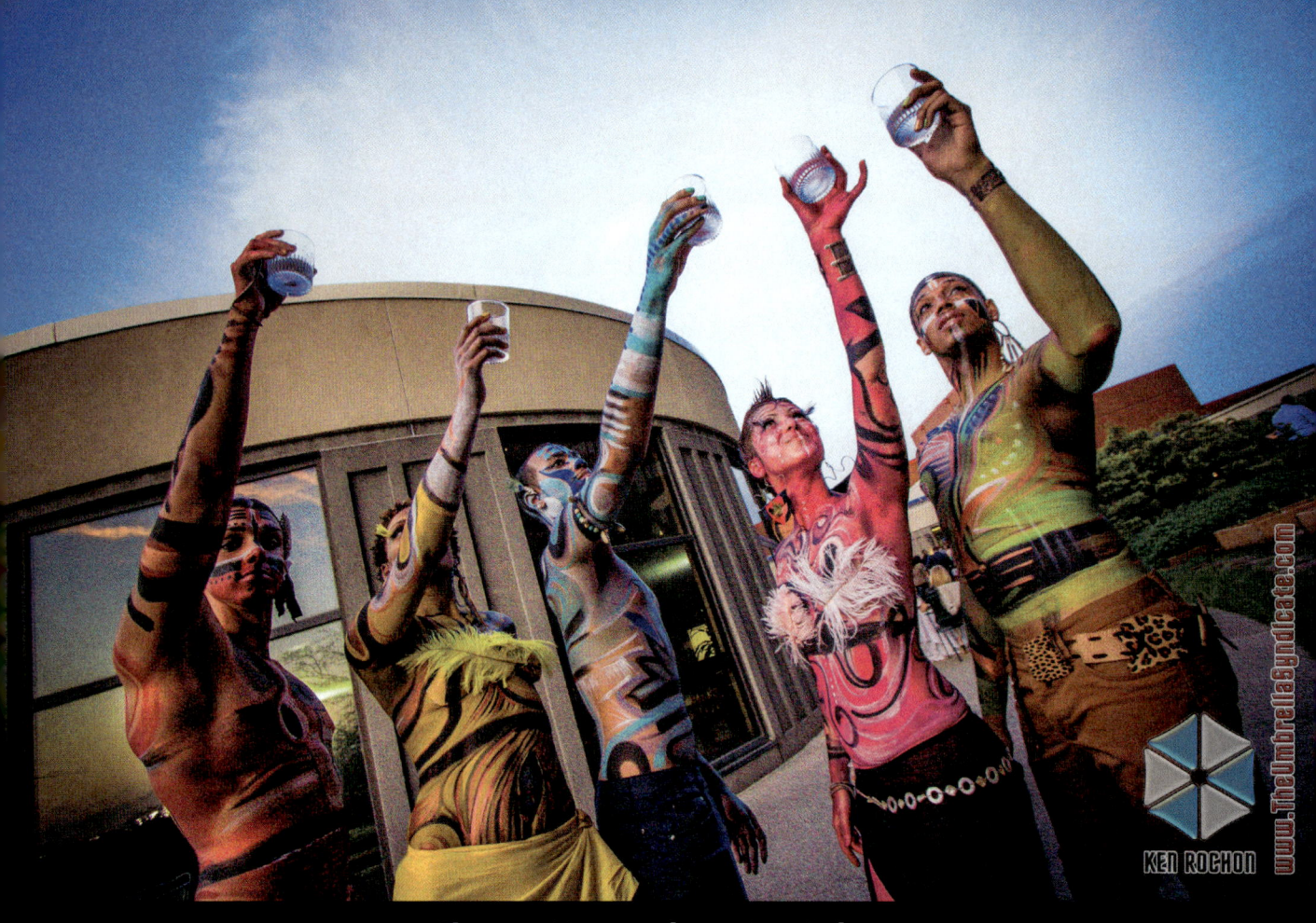

Charm City Body Paint Salute

www.TheUmbrellaSyndicate.com

KEN ROCHON

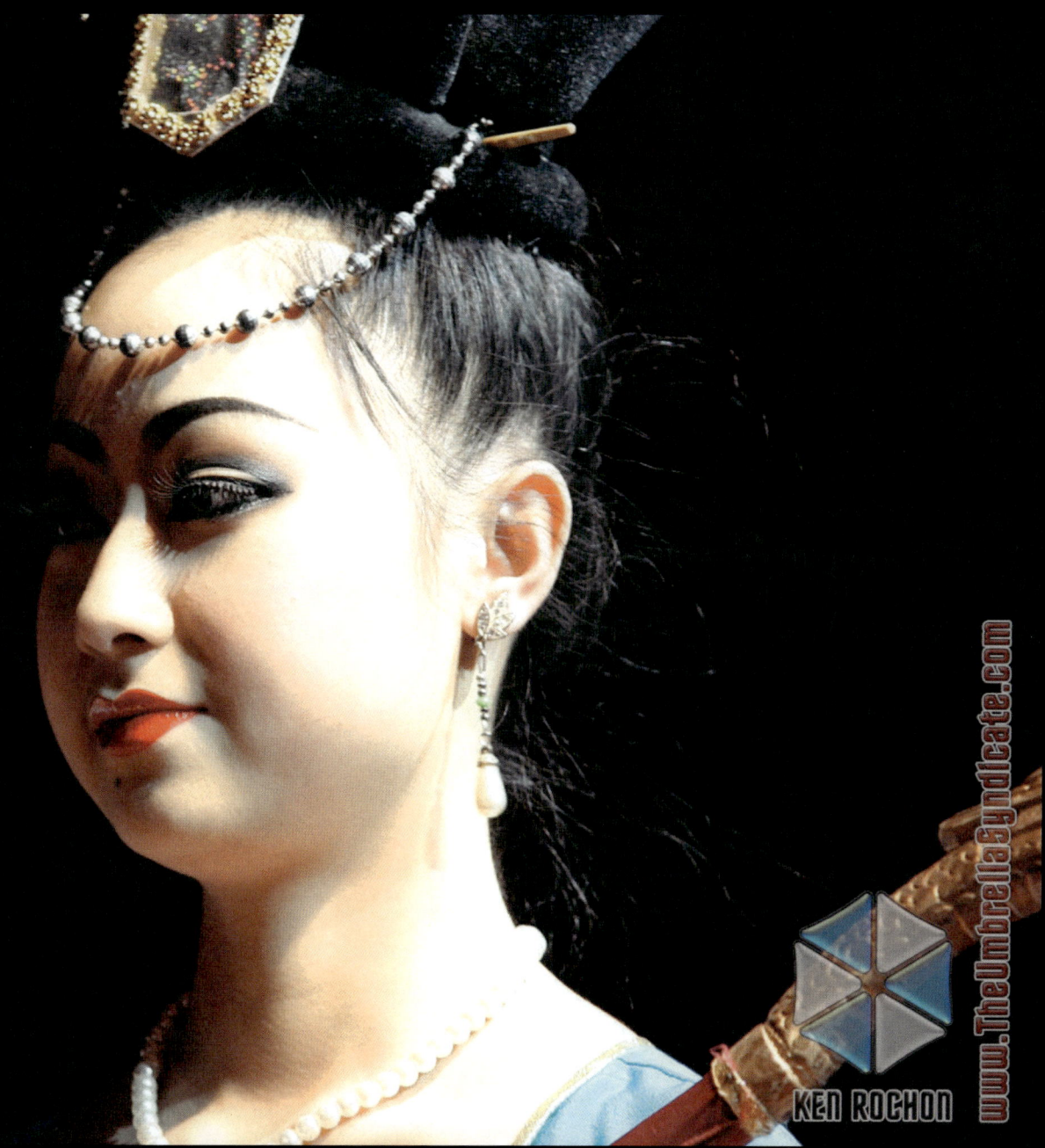

Chinese Performer

KEN ROCHON

www.TheUmbrellaSyndicate.com

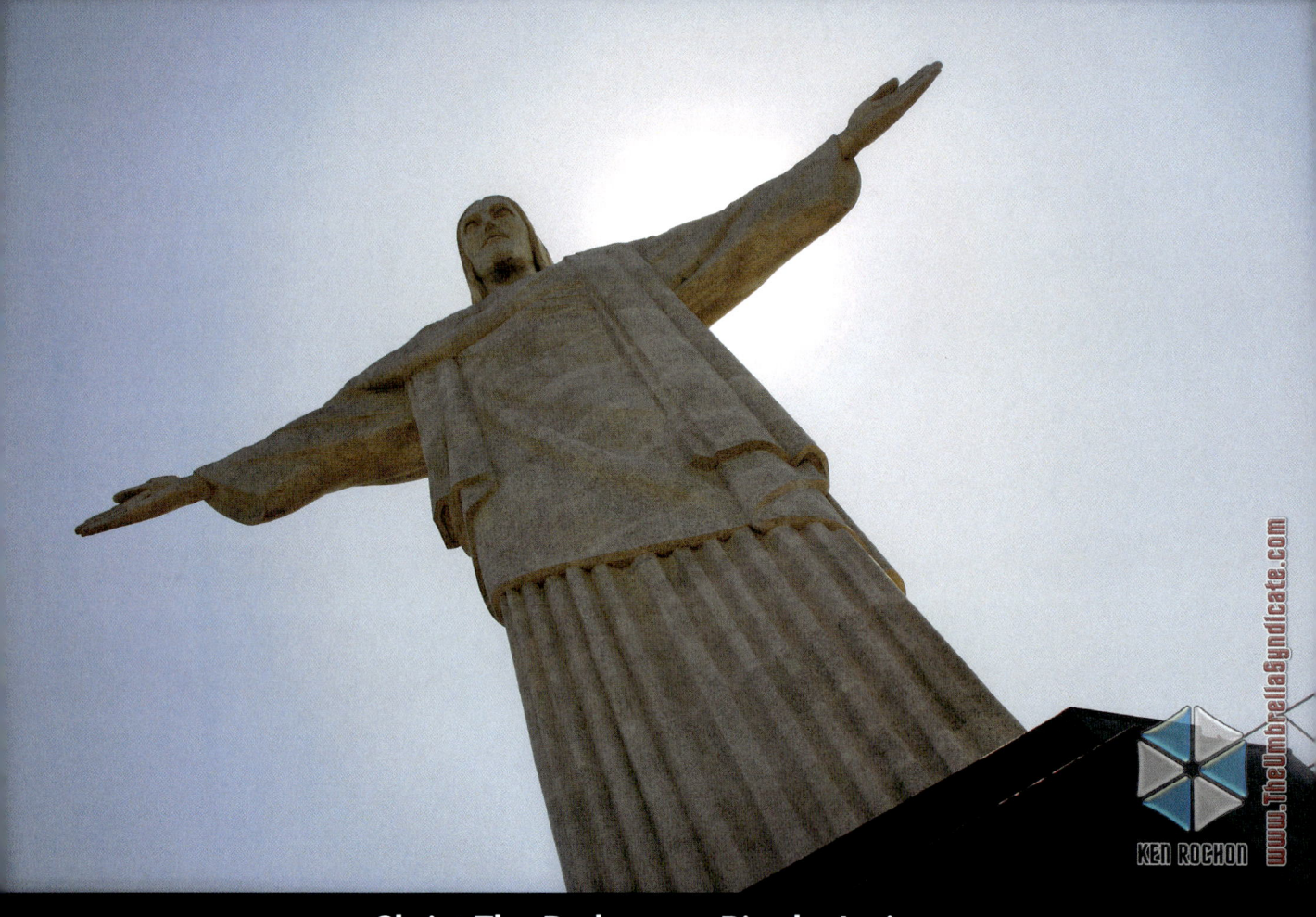

Christ The Redeamer, Rio de Janiero

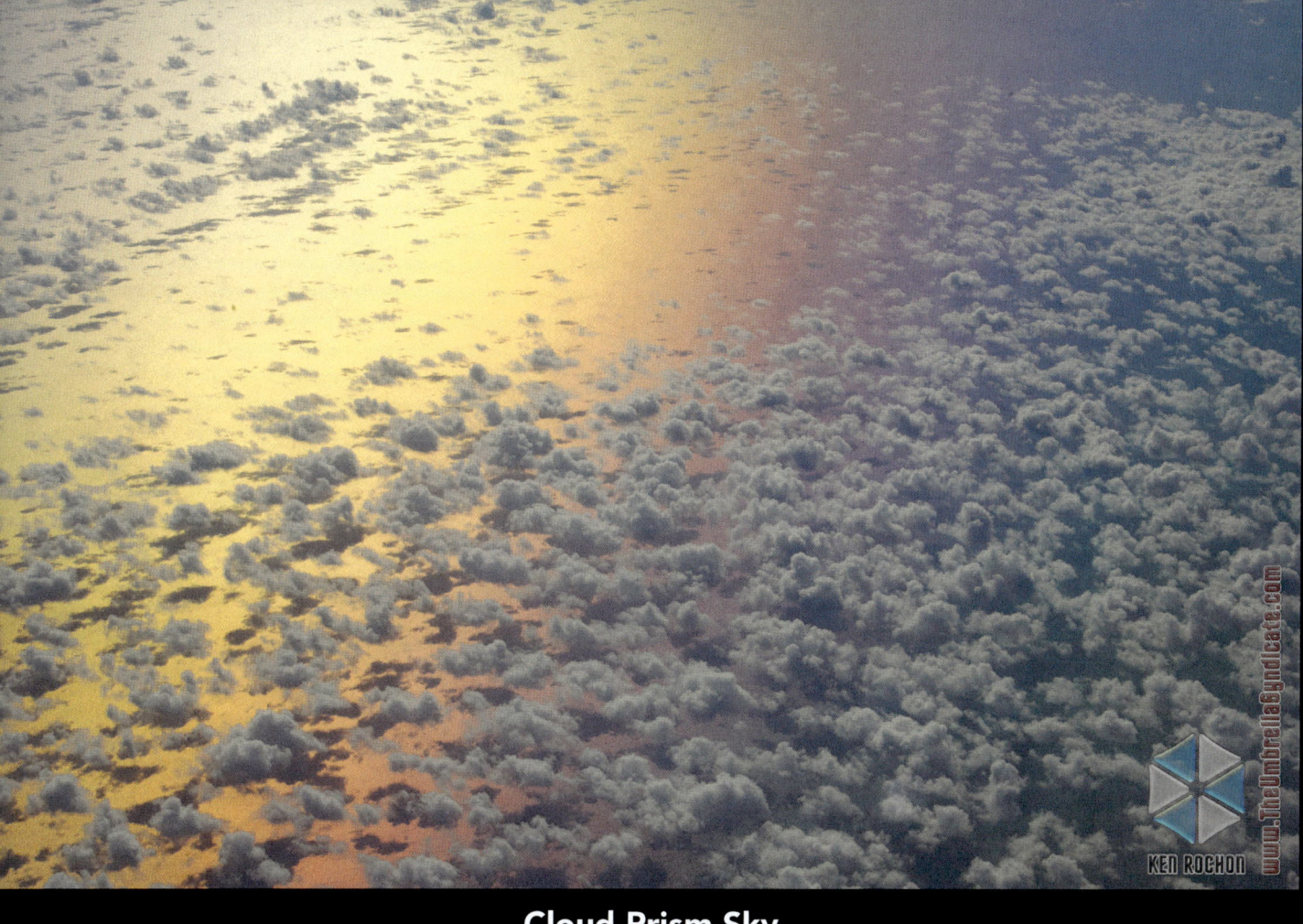

Cloud Prism Sky

www.TheUmbrellaSyndicate.com

KEN ROCHON

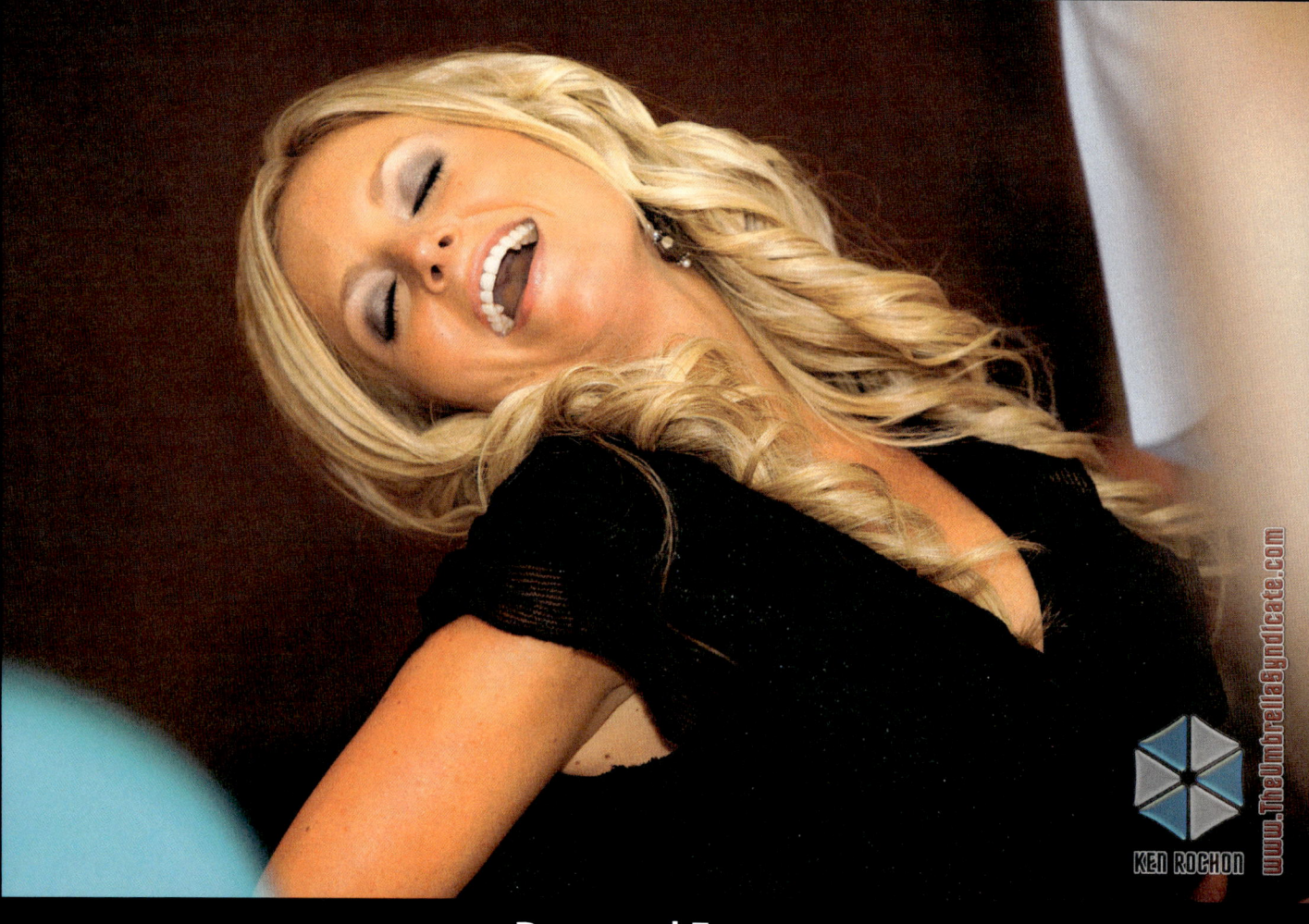

KEN ROCHON www.TheUmbrellaSyndicate.com

Dance and Forget

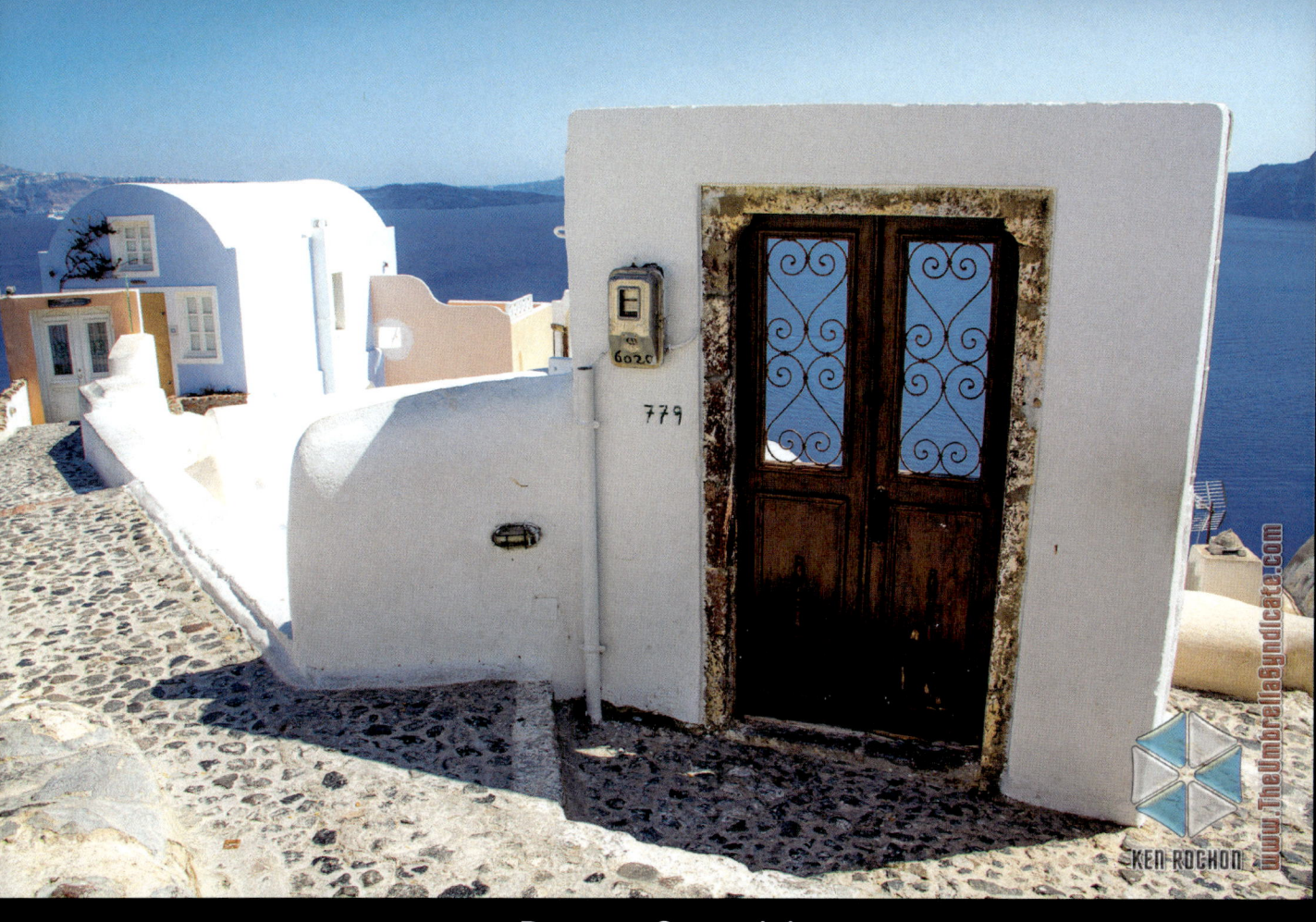

www.TheUmbrellaSyndicate.com

779

KEN ROCHON

Door to Santorini

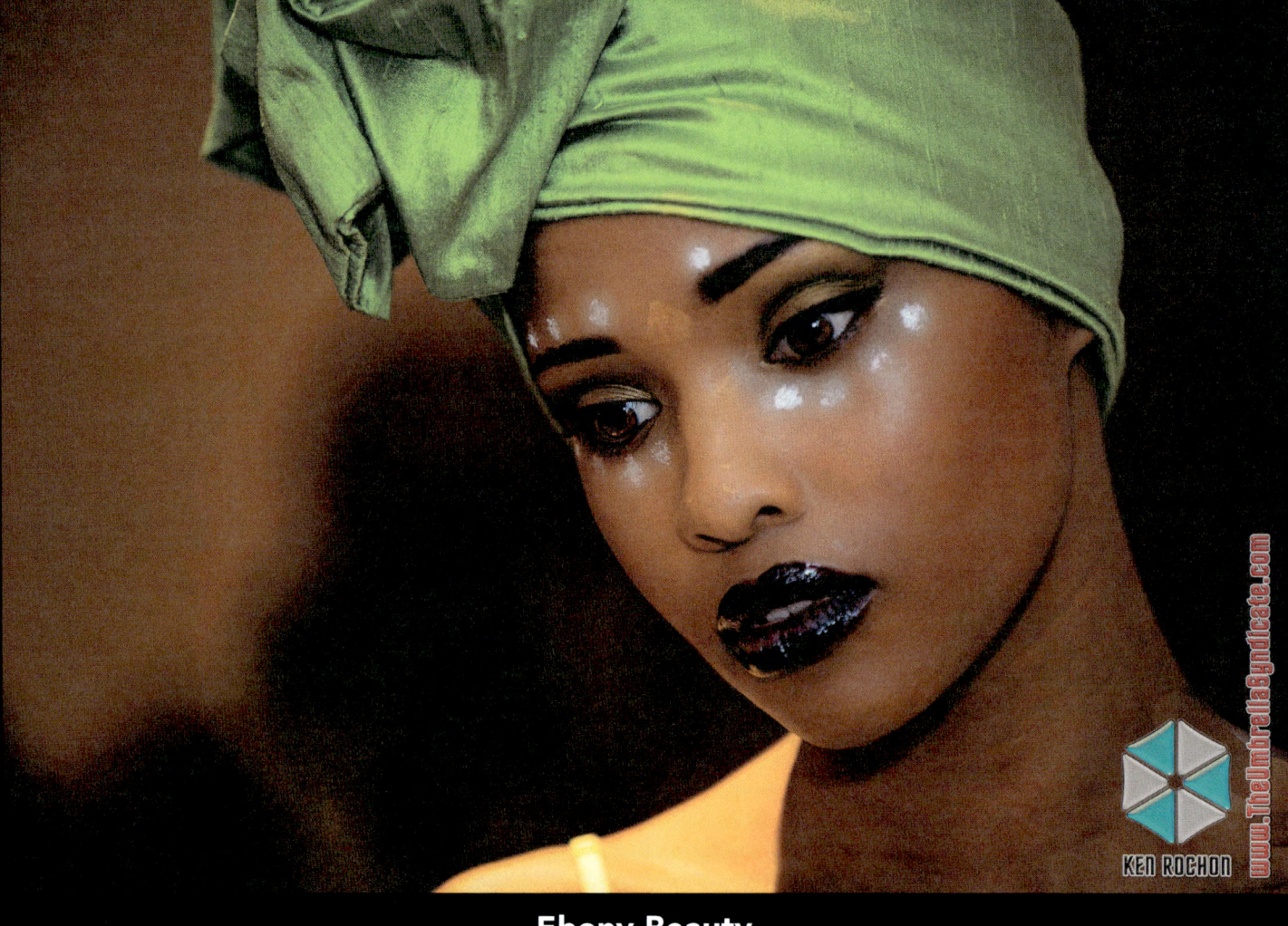

www.TheUmbrellaSyndicate.com

KEN ROCHON

Ebony Beauty

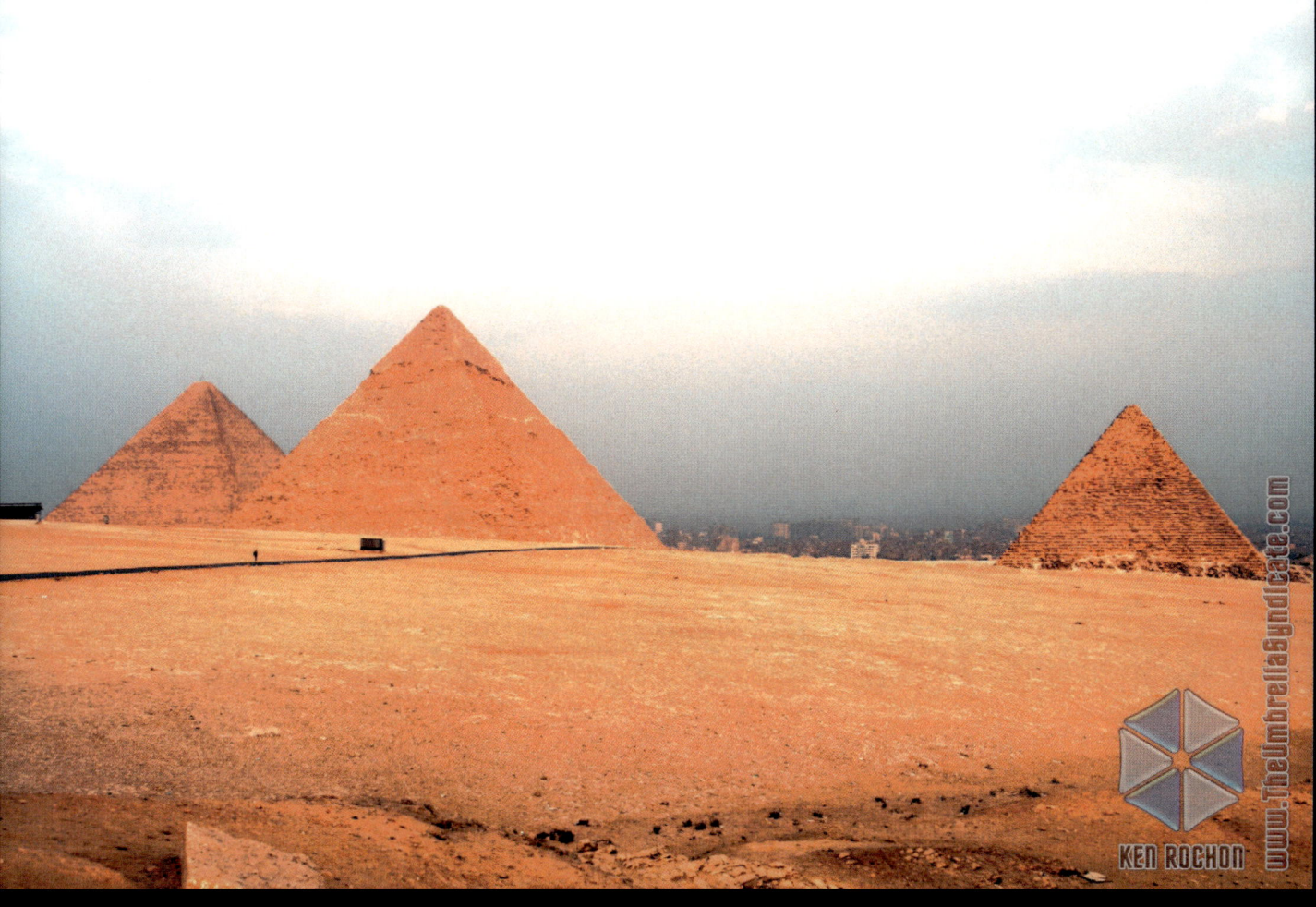

www.TheUmbrellaSyndicate.com

KEN ROCHON

Egypt Pyramids

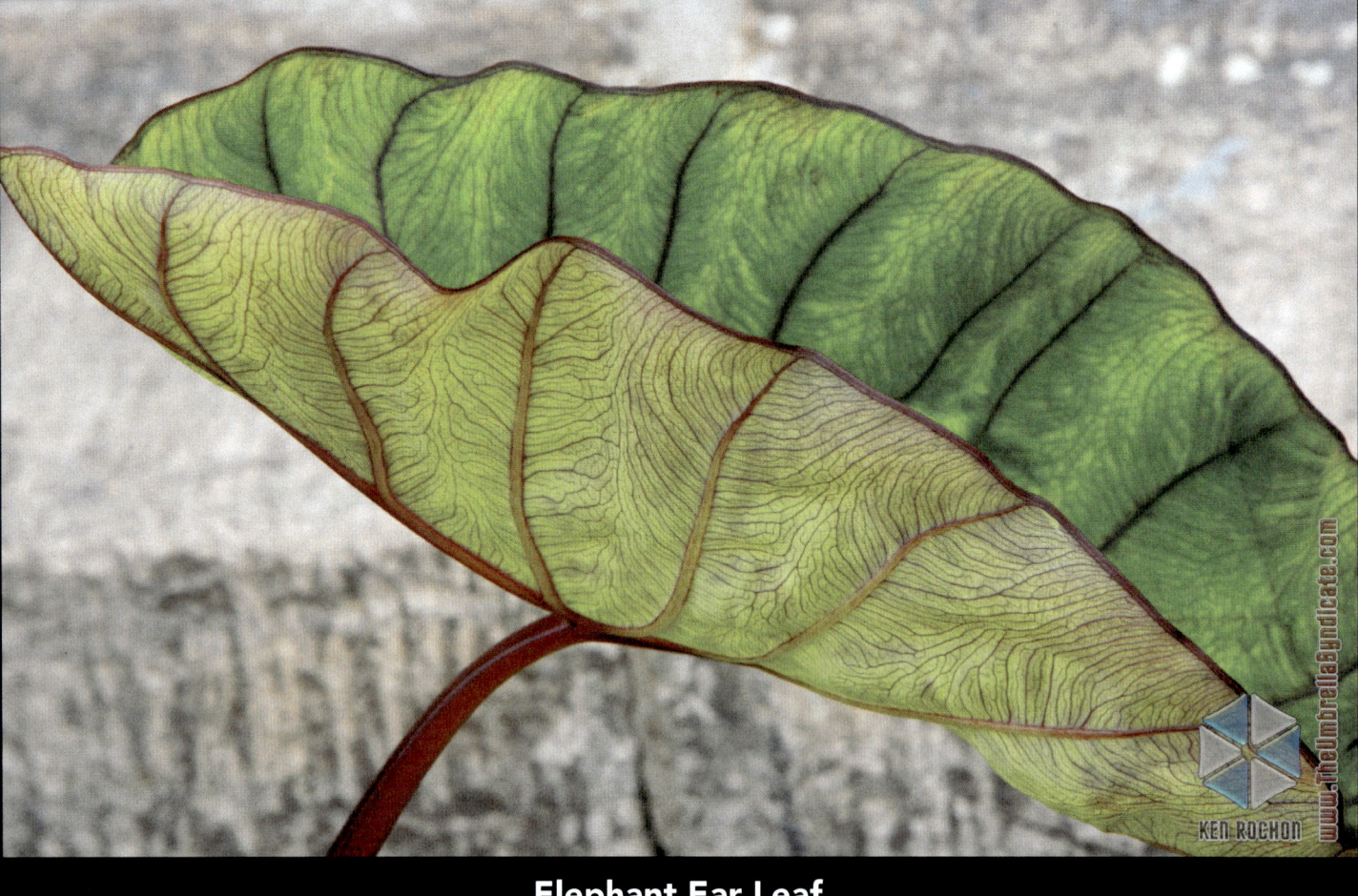

Elephant Ear Leaf

www.theumbrellasyndicate.com

KEN ROCHON

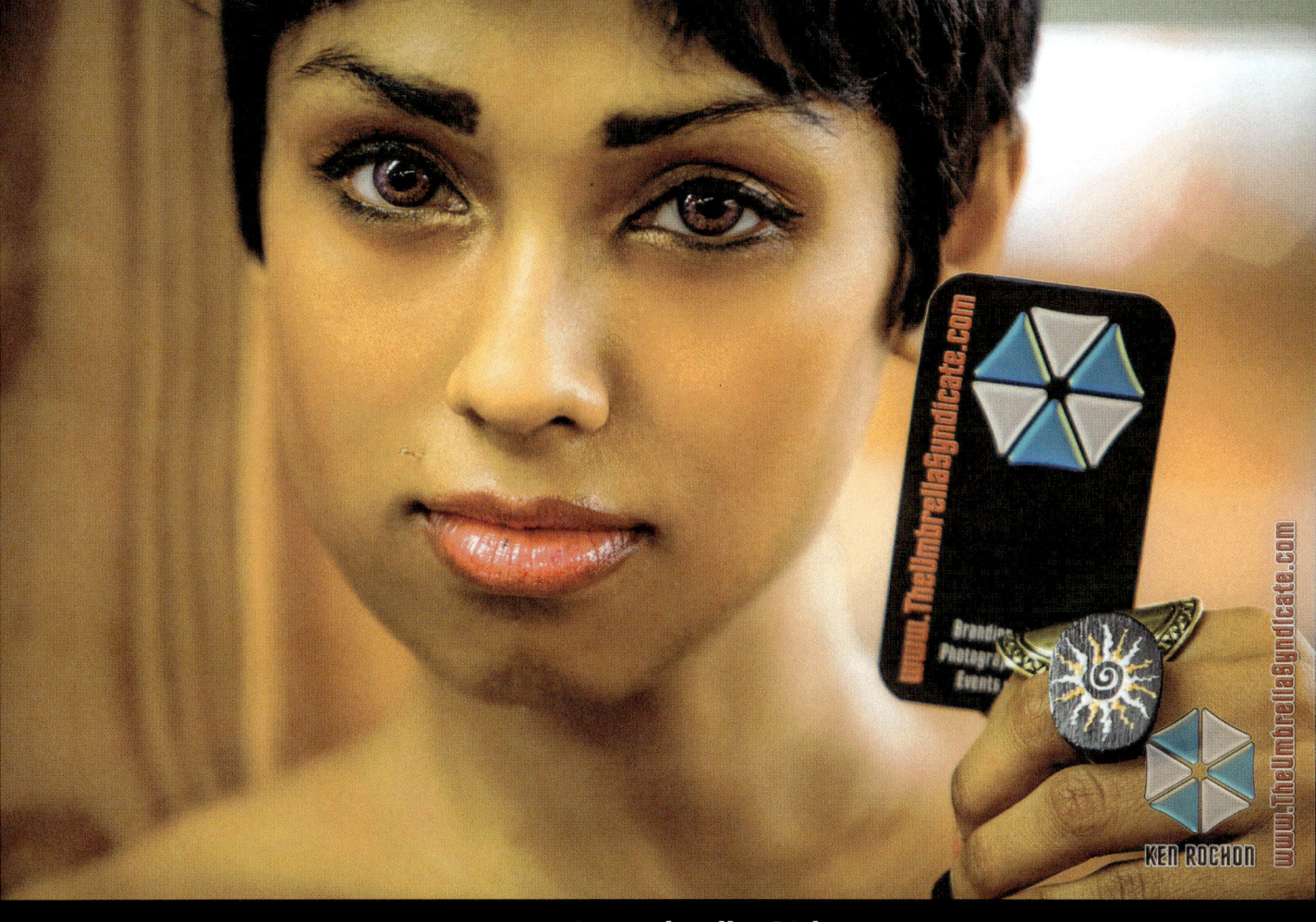

Exotic Umbrella Girl

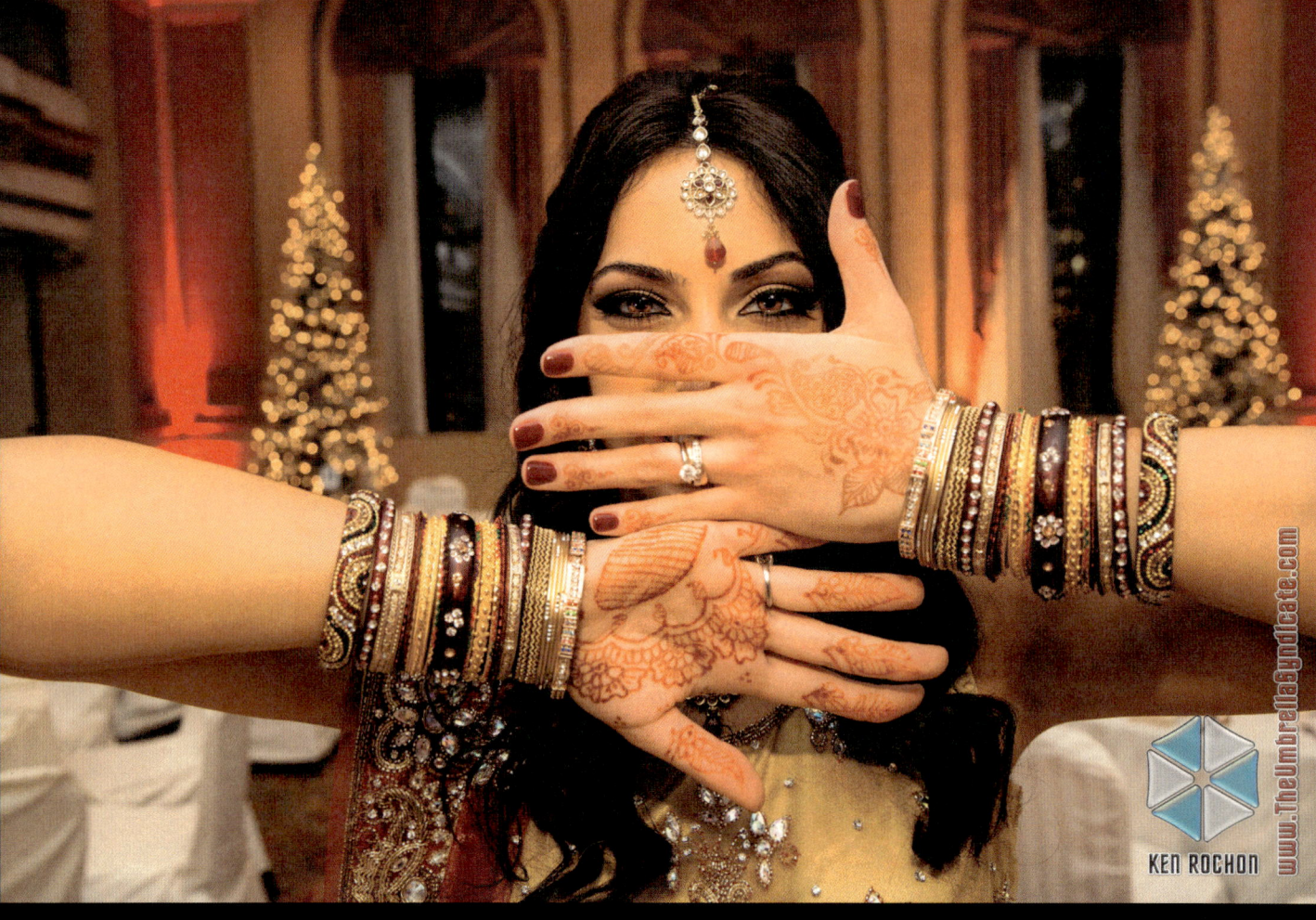

Exotic Eyes & Hands of Henna

www.TheUmbrellaSyndicate.com

KEN ROCHON

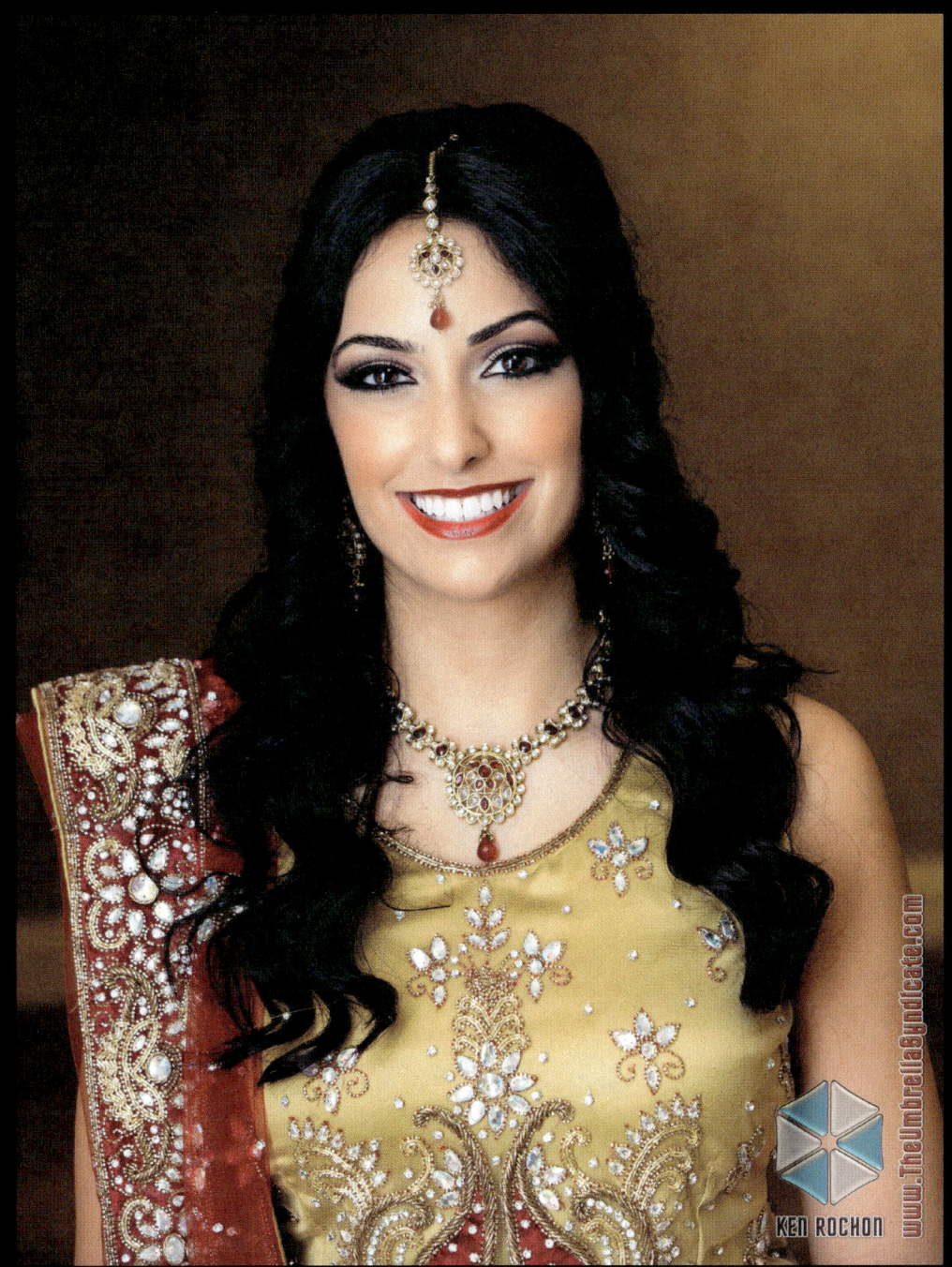

Exotic Indian Bride

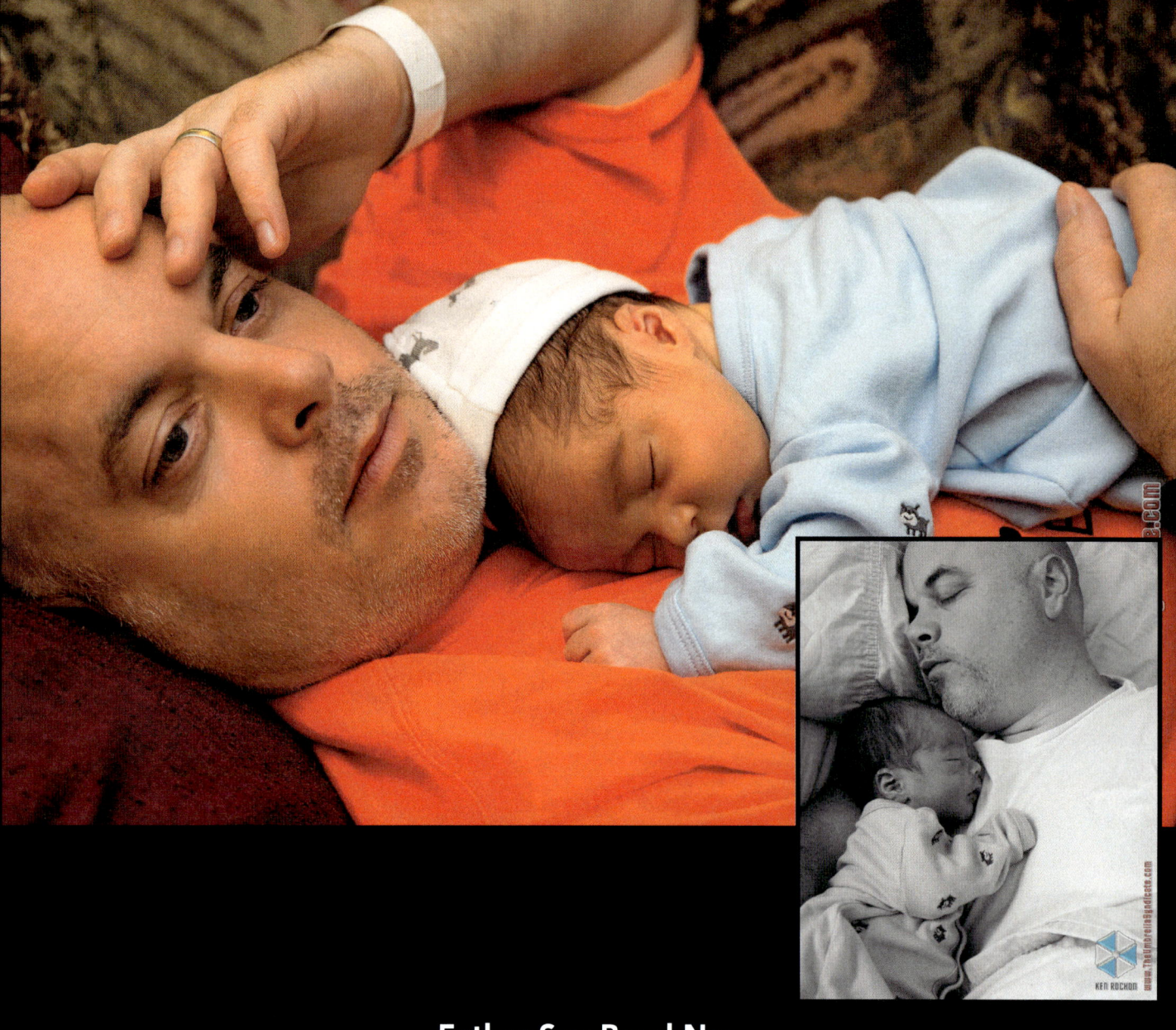

Father Son Bond Nap

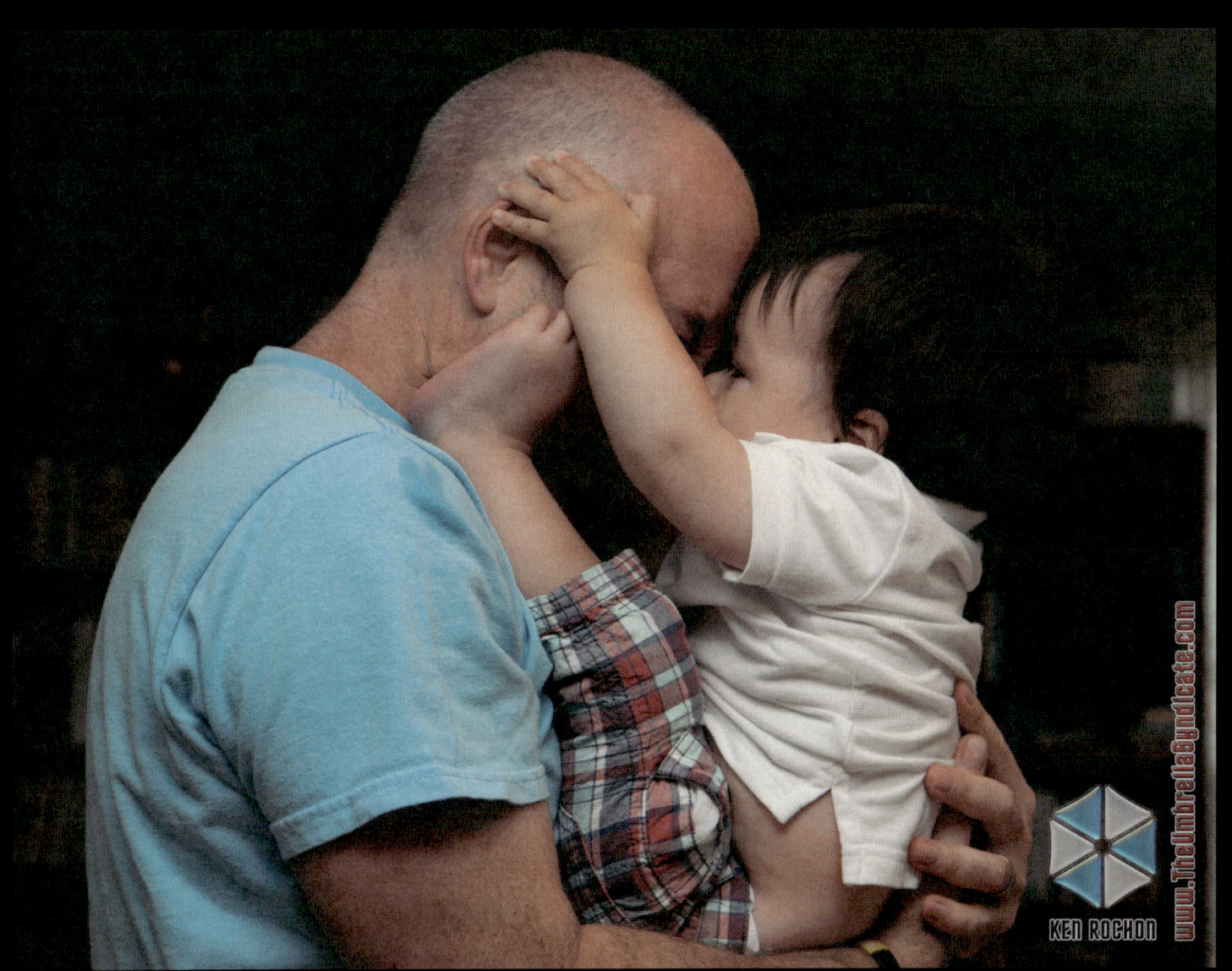

Father Son Bond Head 2 Head

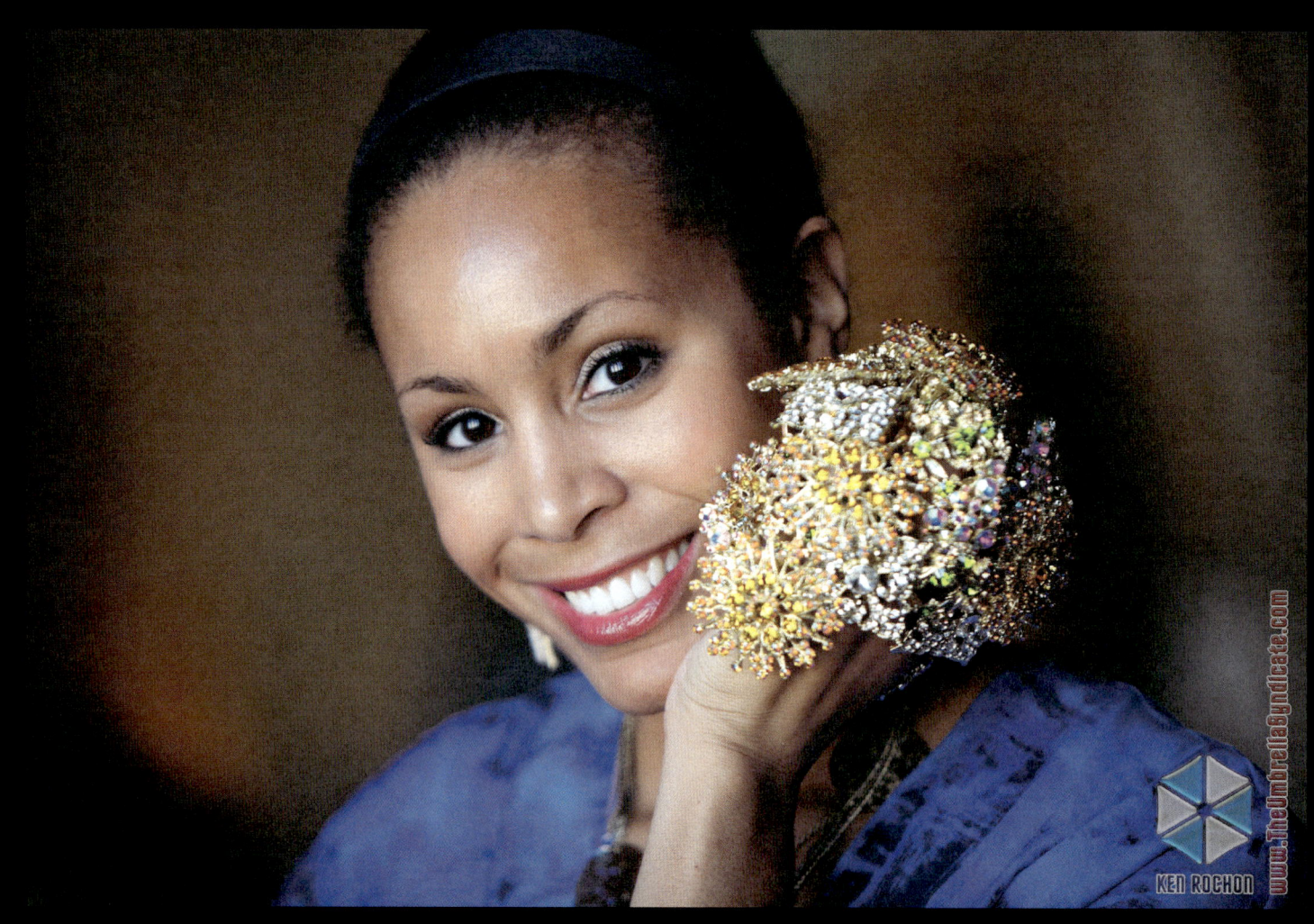

Flower Woman

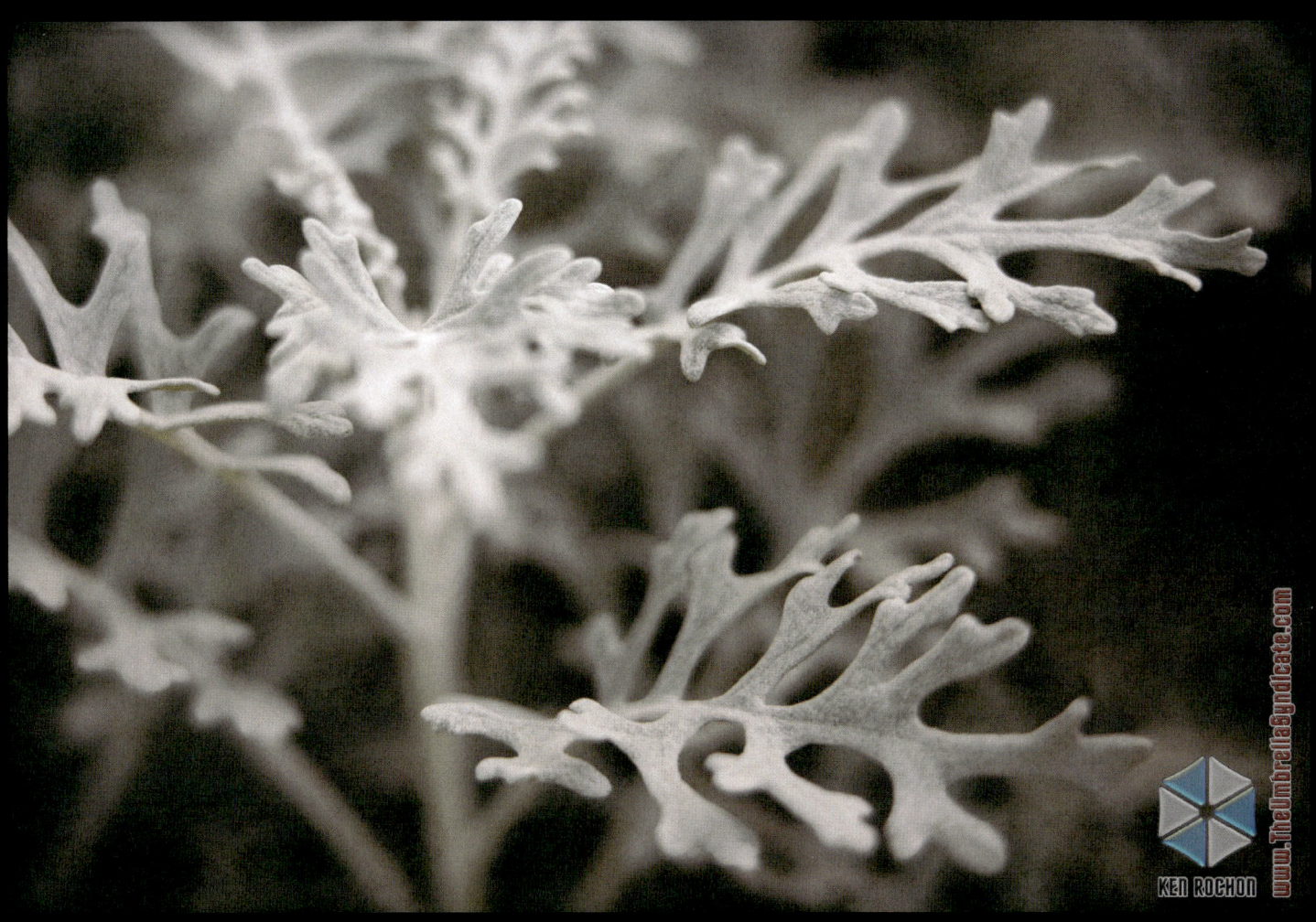

Frosted Leaves

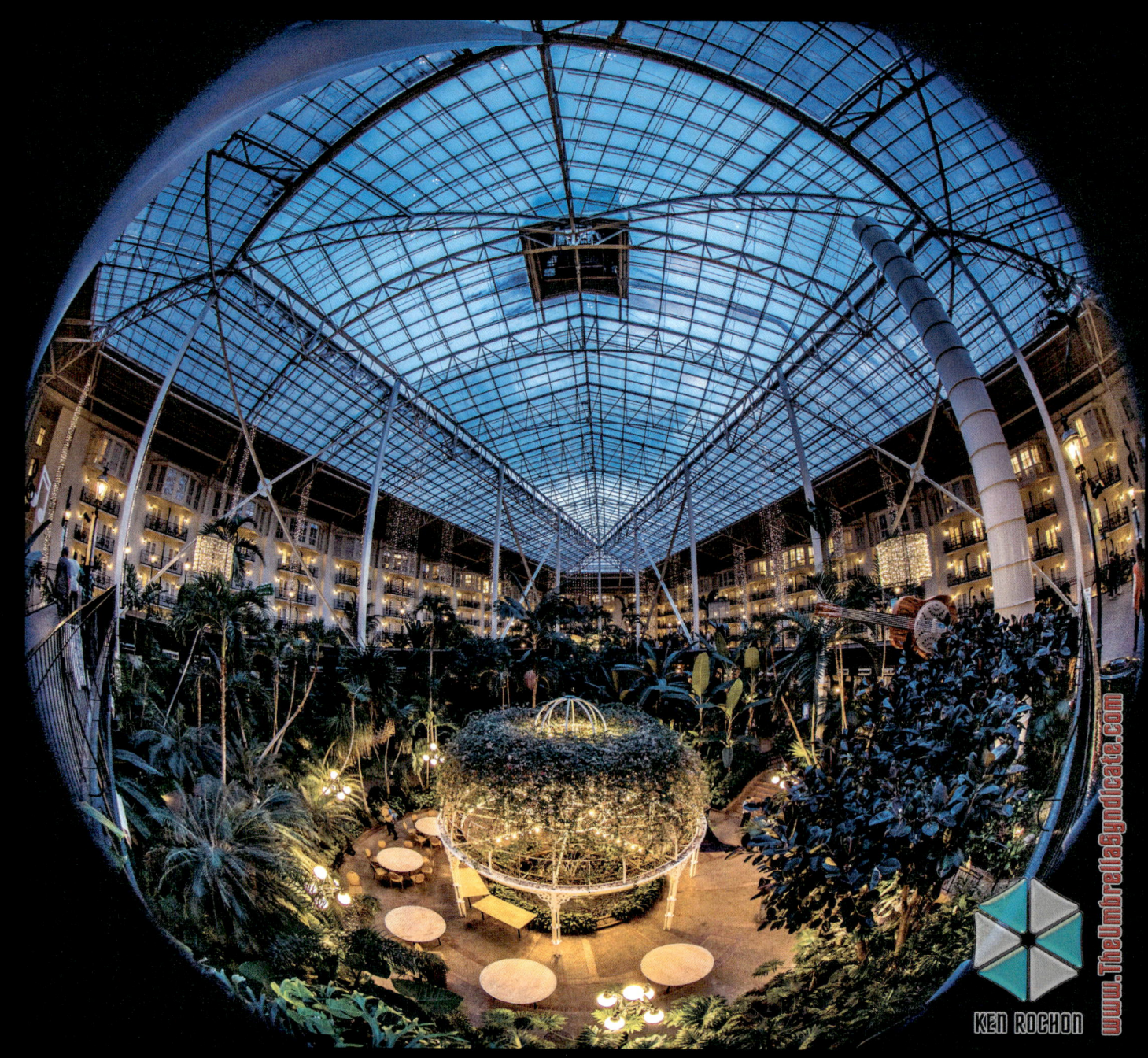

Gaylord Opryland Hotel

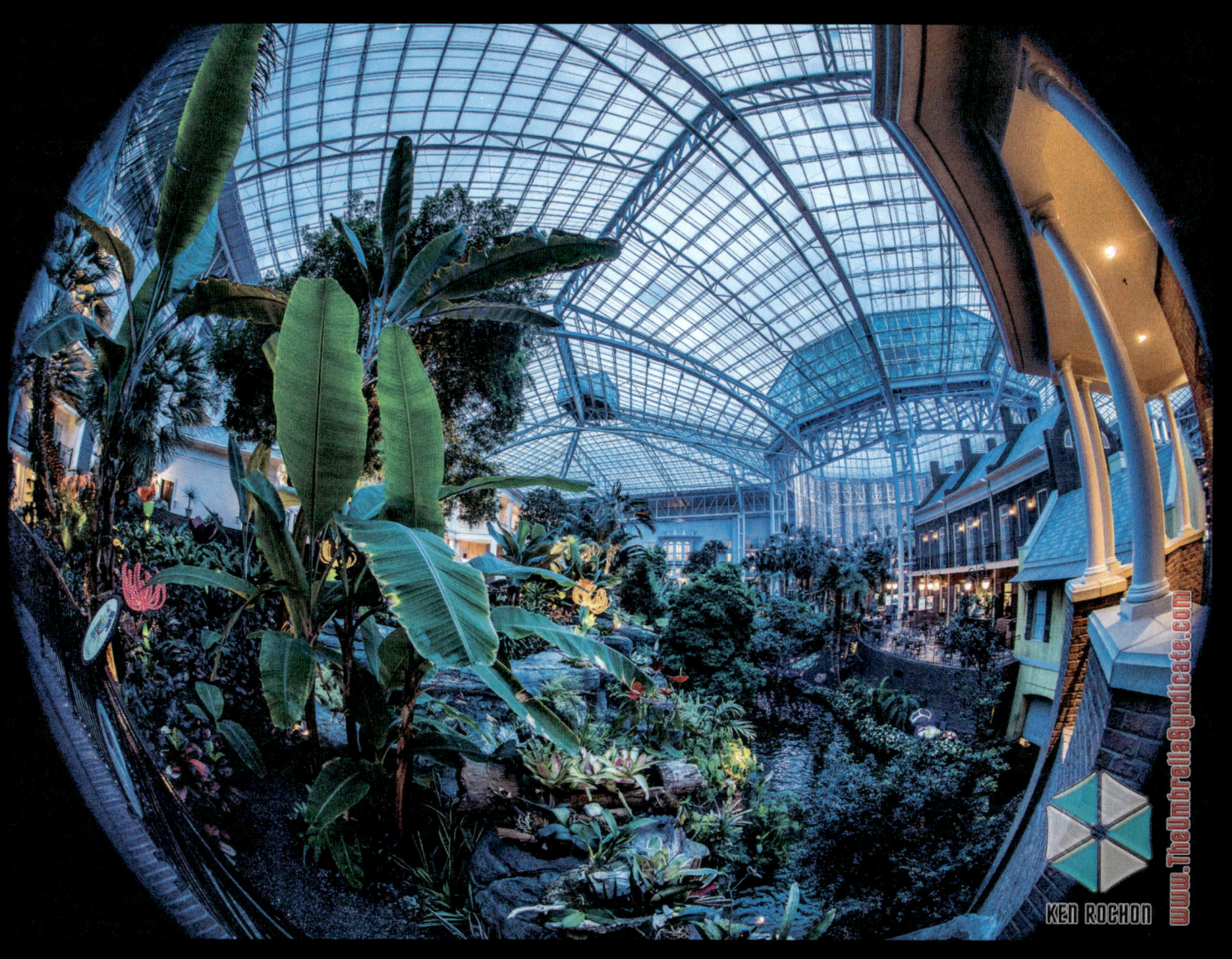

Gaylord Opryland Hotel

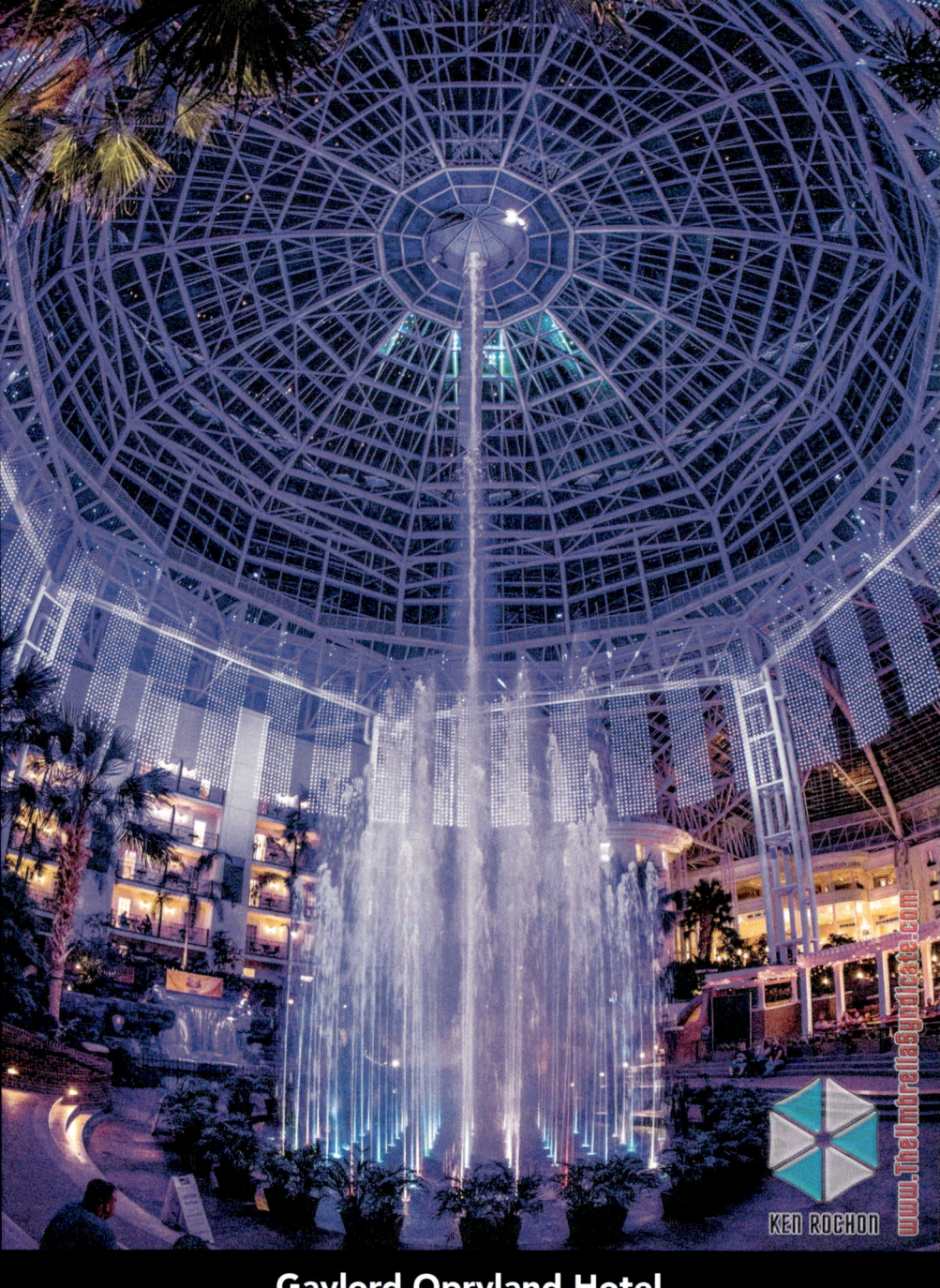

Gaylord Opryland Hotel

www.TheUmbrellaSyndicate.com

KEN ROCHON

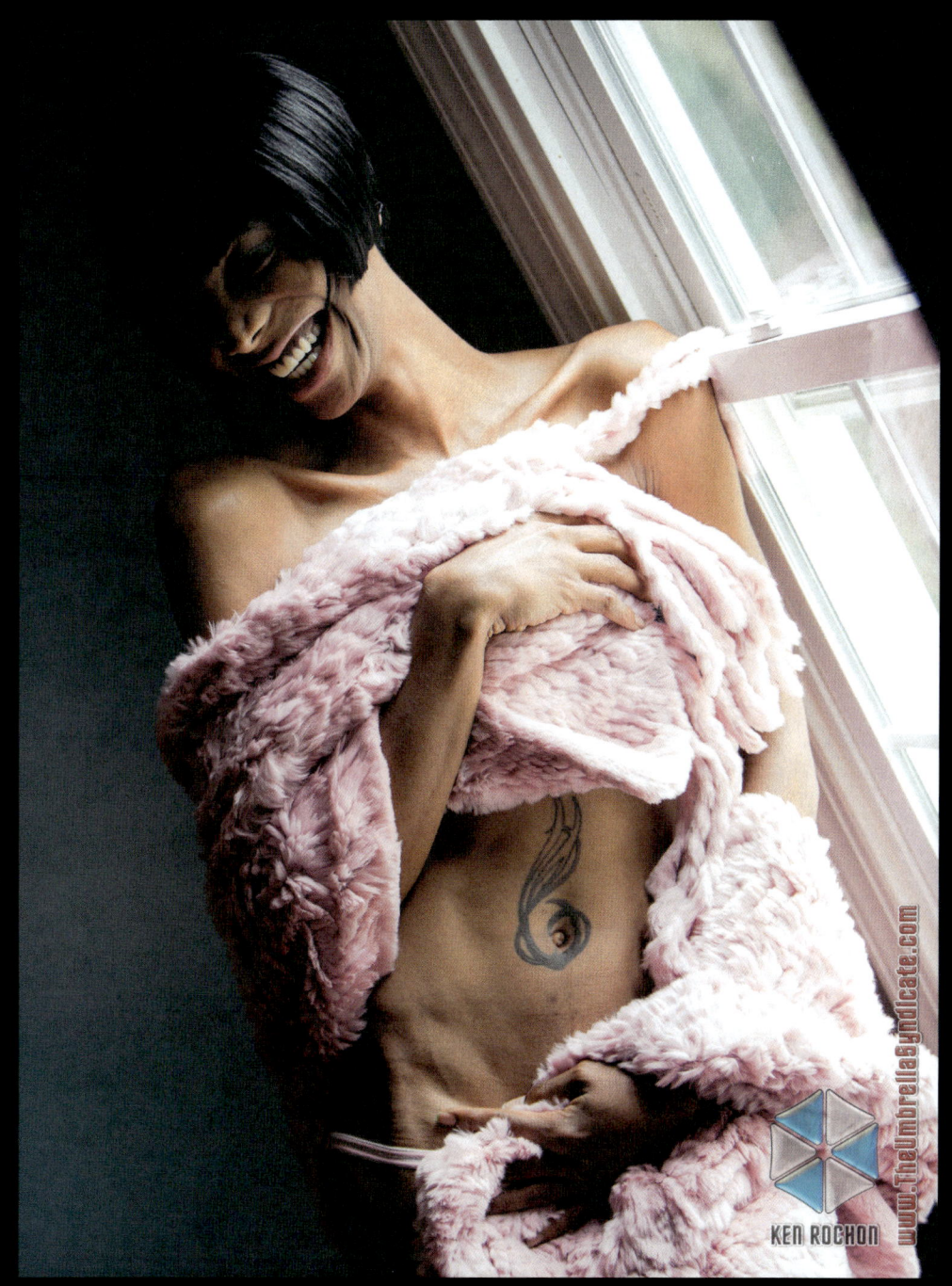

Goddess of Laughter & Love

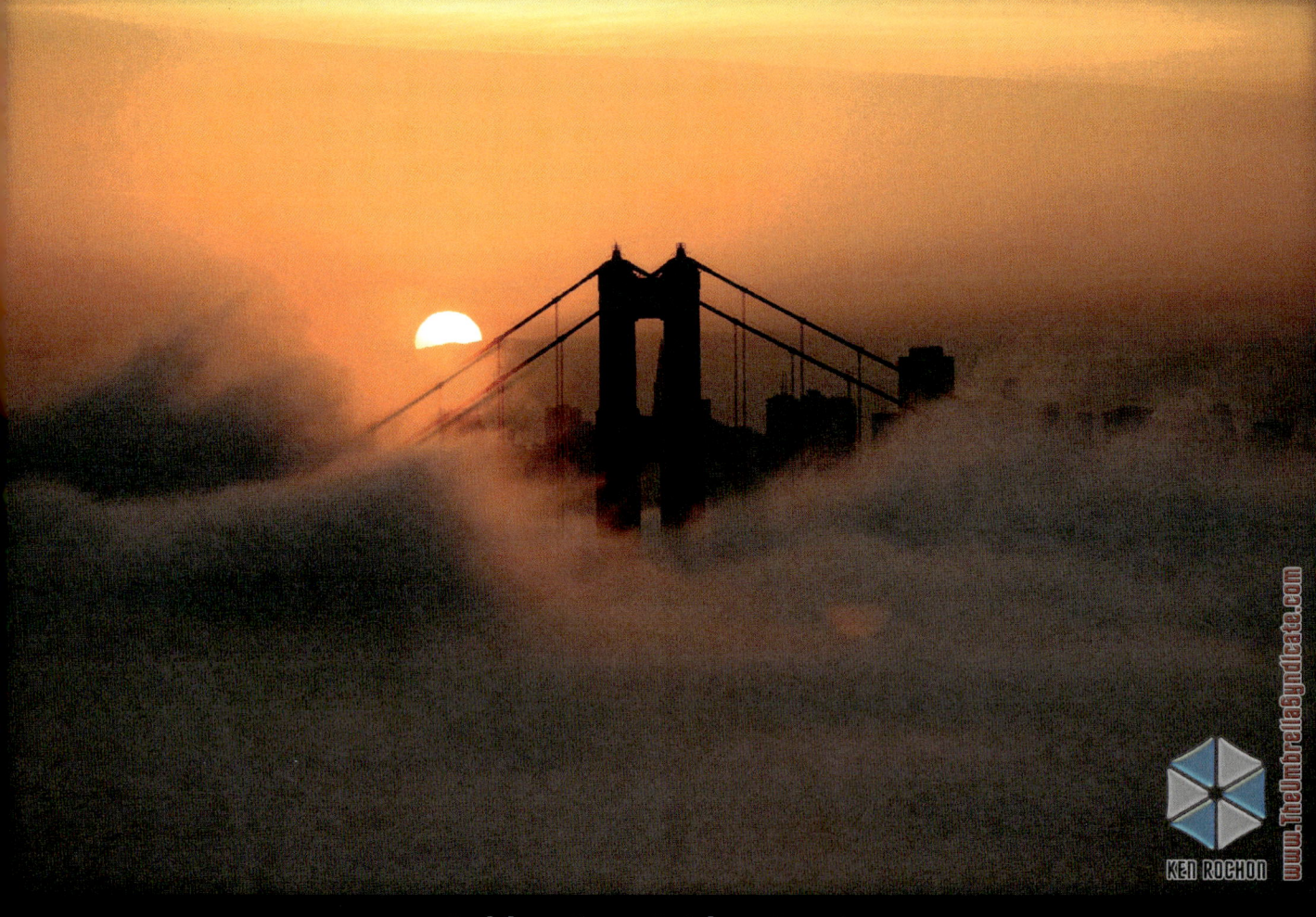

Golden Gate Bridge Sunrise

KEN ROCHON

www.TheUmbrellaSyndicate.com

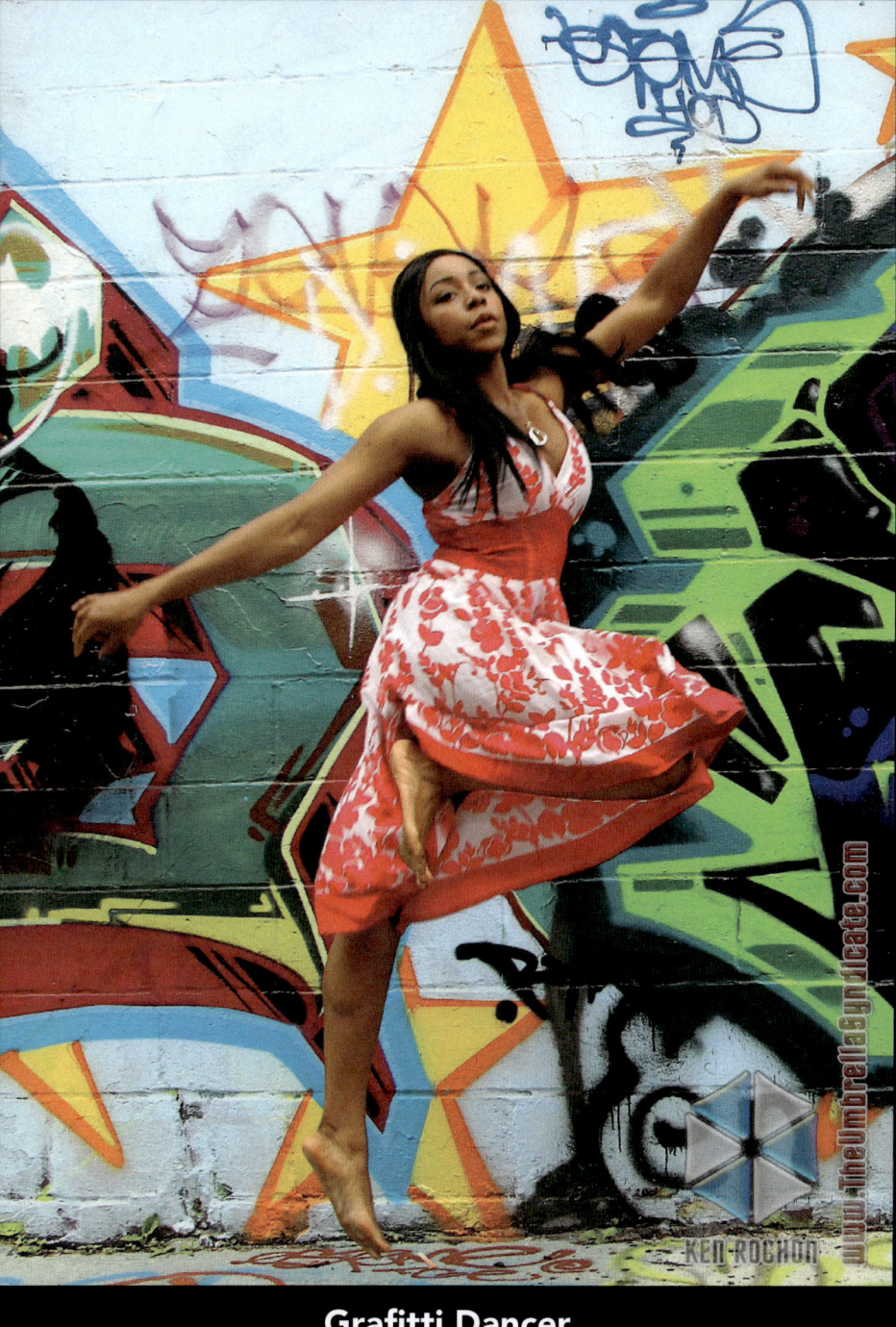

www.theUmbrellaSyndicate.com

KEN ROCHON

Grafitti Dancer

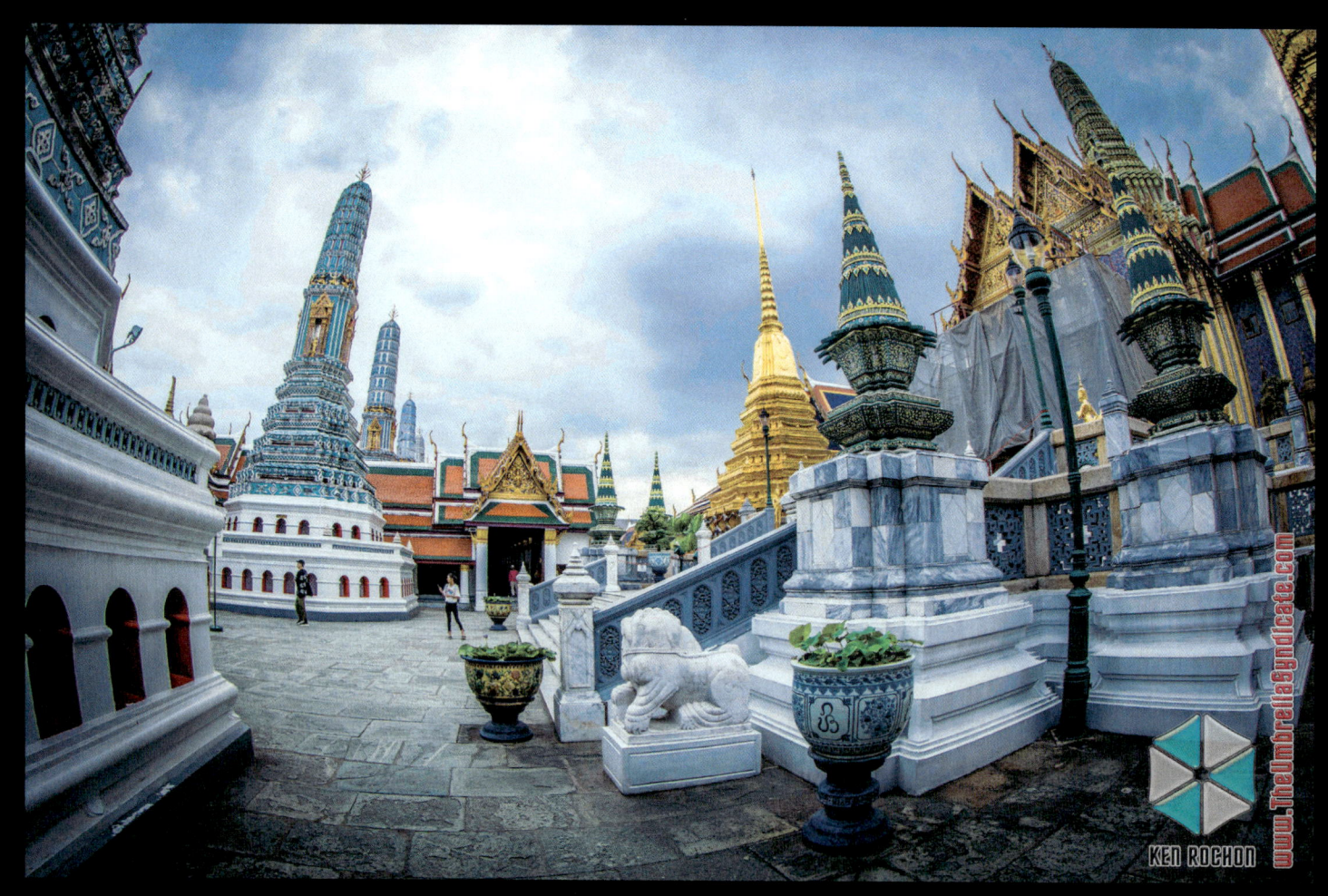

Grand Palace

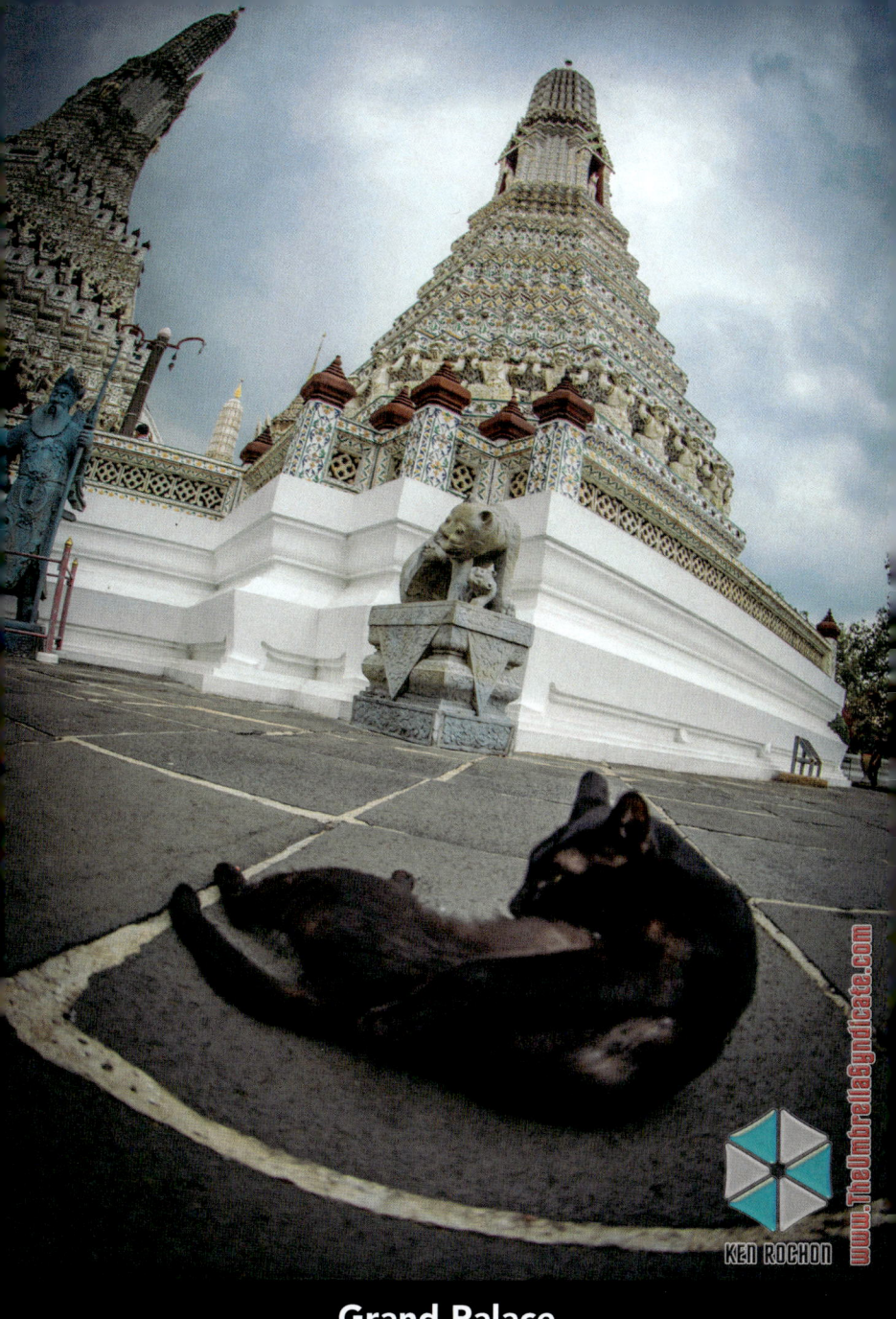

www.TheUmbrellaSyndicate.com

KEN ROCHON

Grand Palace

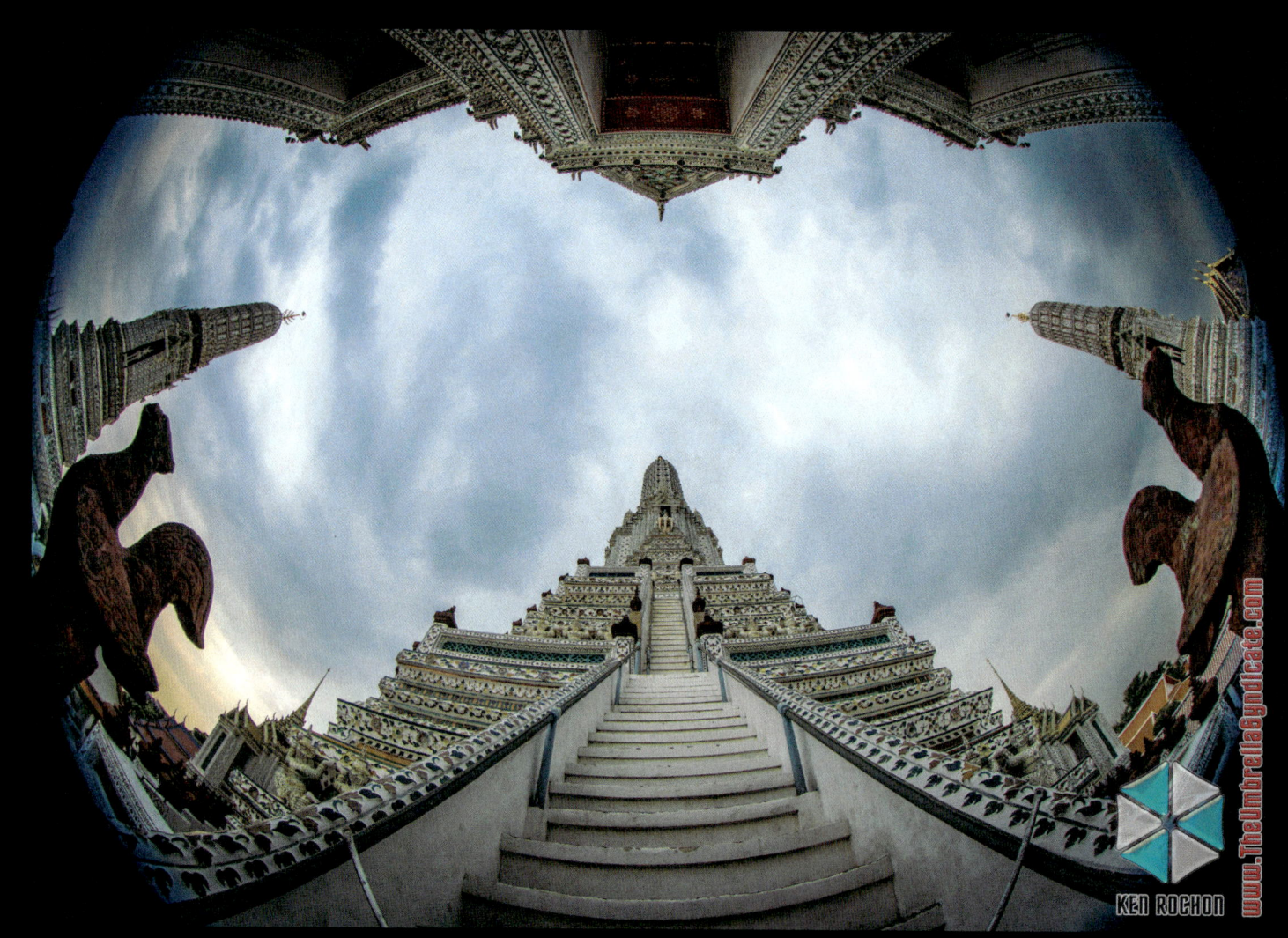

Grand Palace

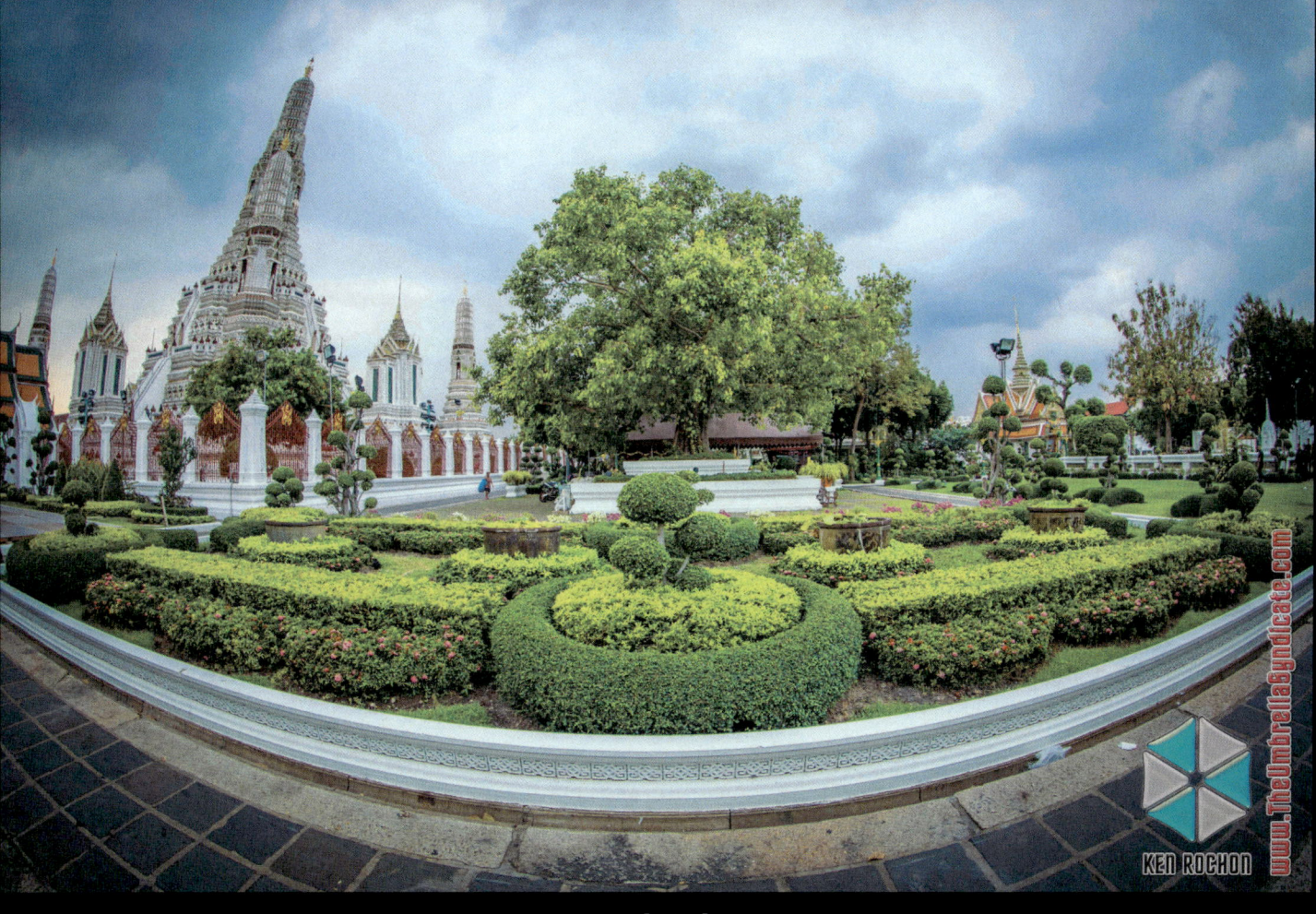

Grand Palace

www.TheUmbrellaSyndicate.com

KEN ROCHON

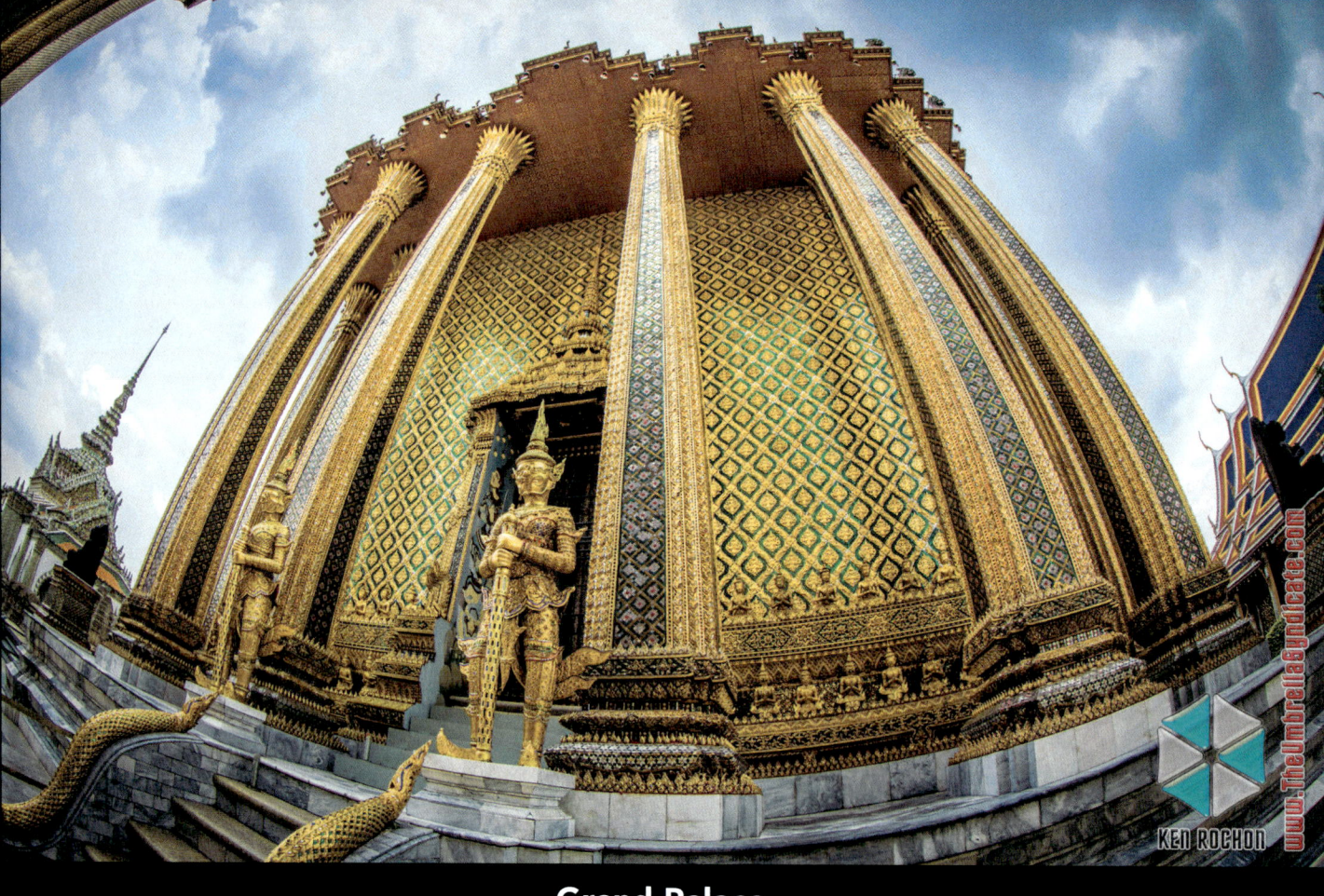

Grand Palace

www.TheUmbrellaSyndicate.com

KEN ROCHON

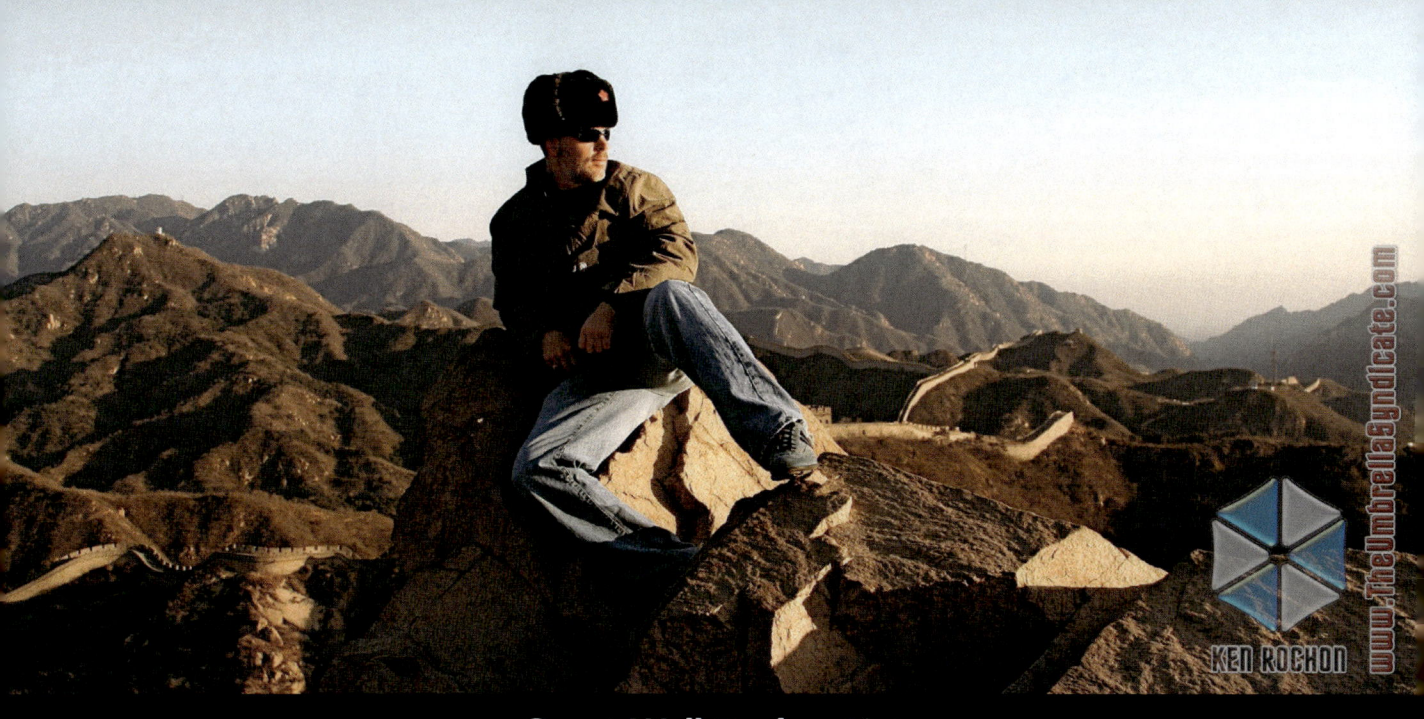

www.TheUmbrellaSyndicate.com

KEN ROCHON

Great Wall Bucket List

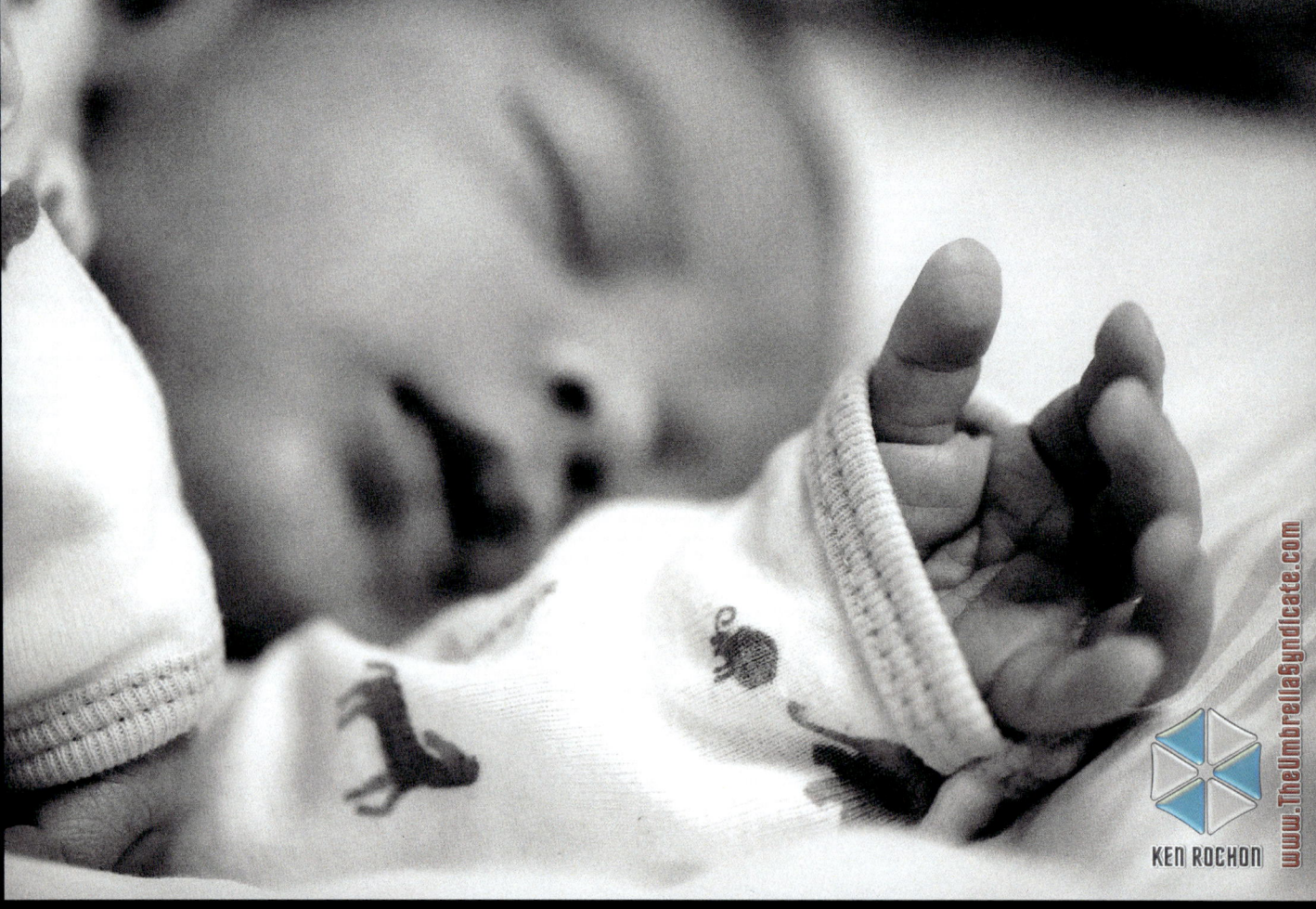

www.TheUmbrellaSyndicate.com

KEN ROCHON

Hand at Peace

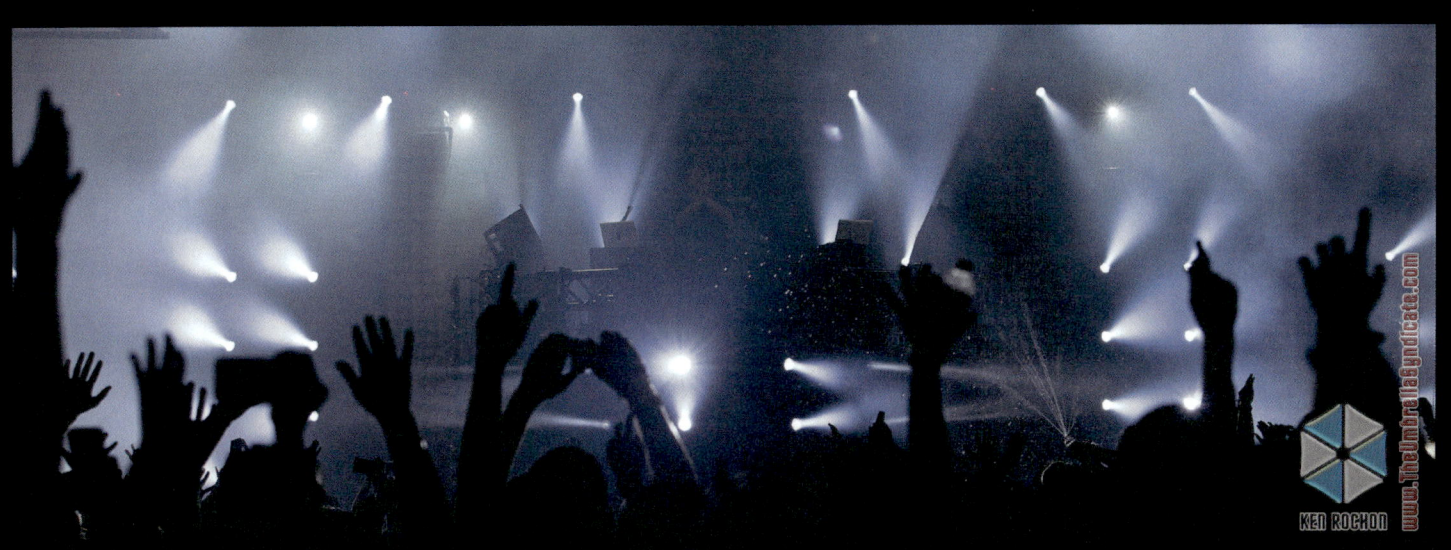

Hands Up Light Storm

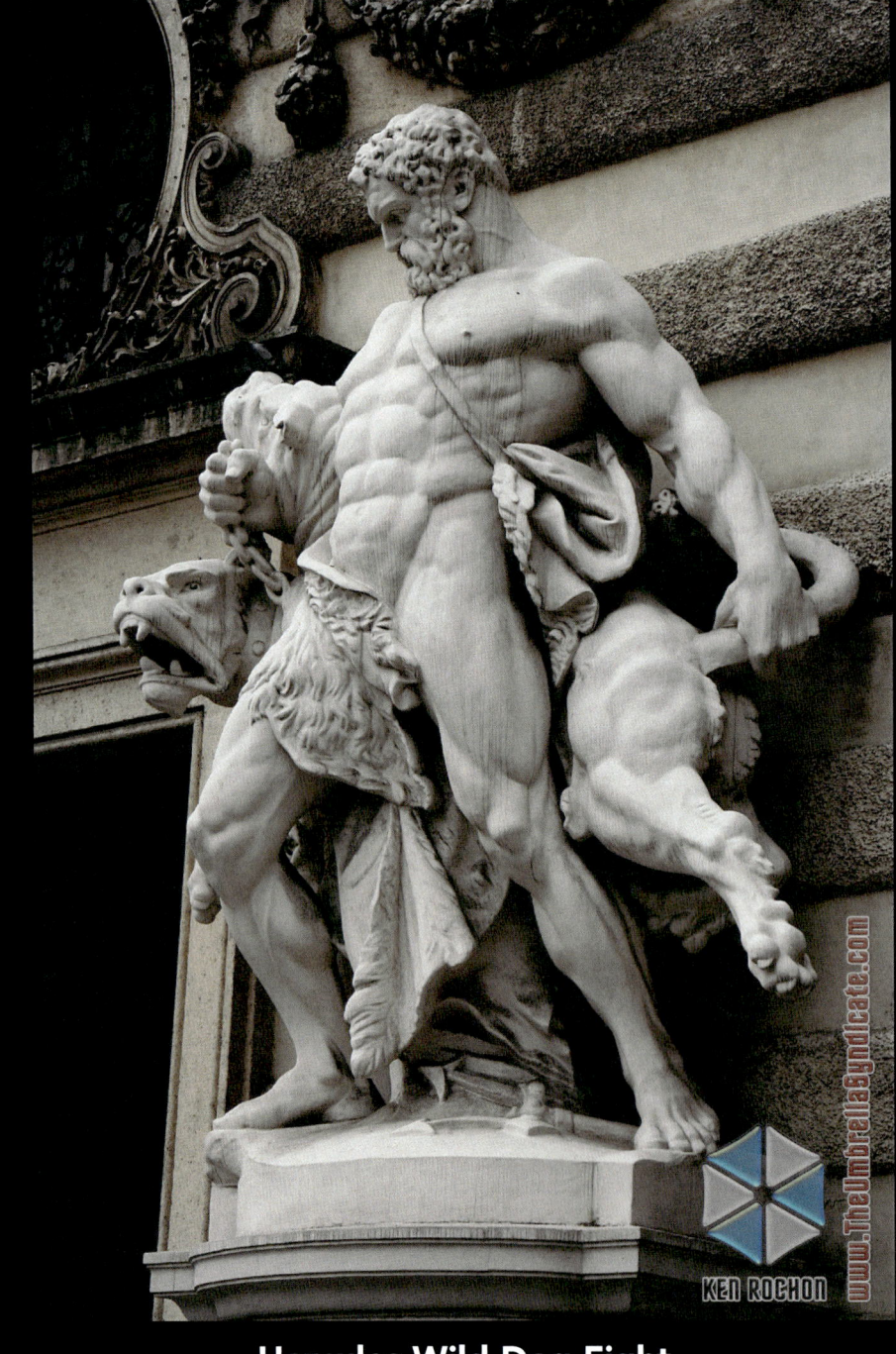

www.TheUmbrellaSyndicate.com

KEN ROCHON

Hercules Wild Dog Fight

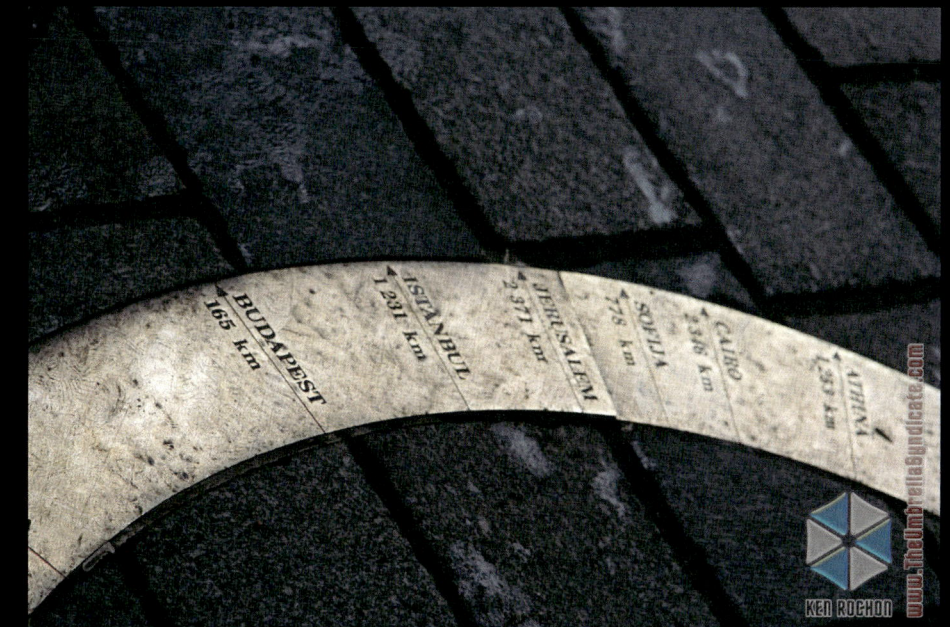

How Far to Istanbul

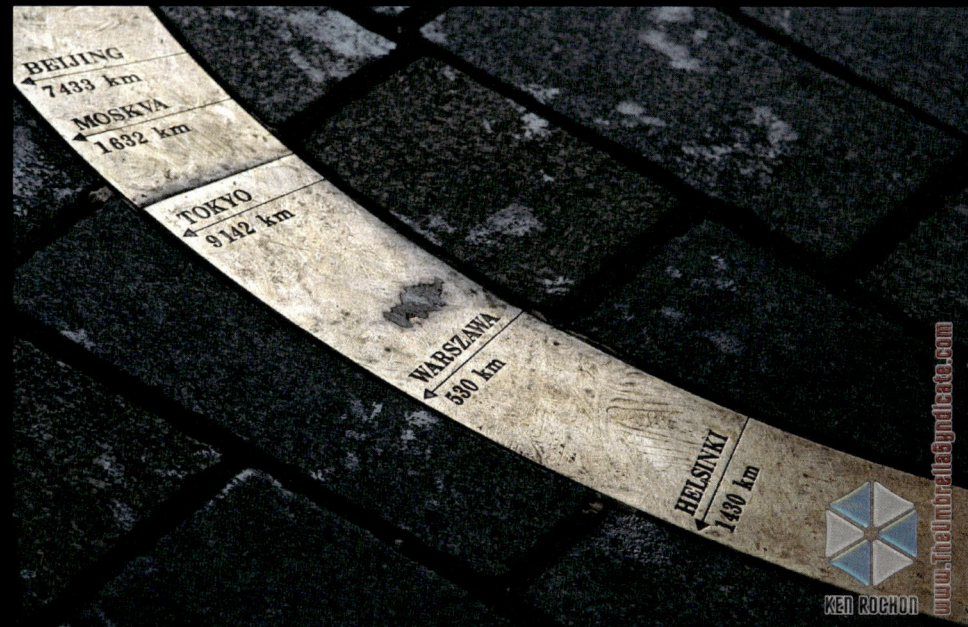

Let's Go 2 Tokyo

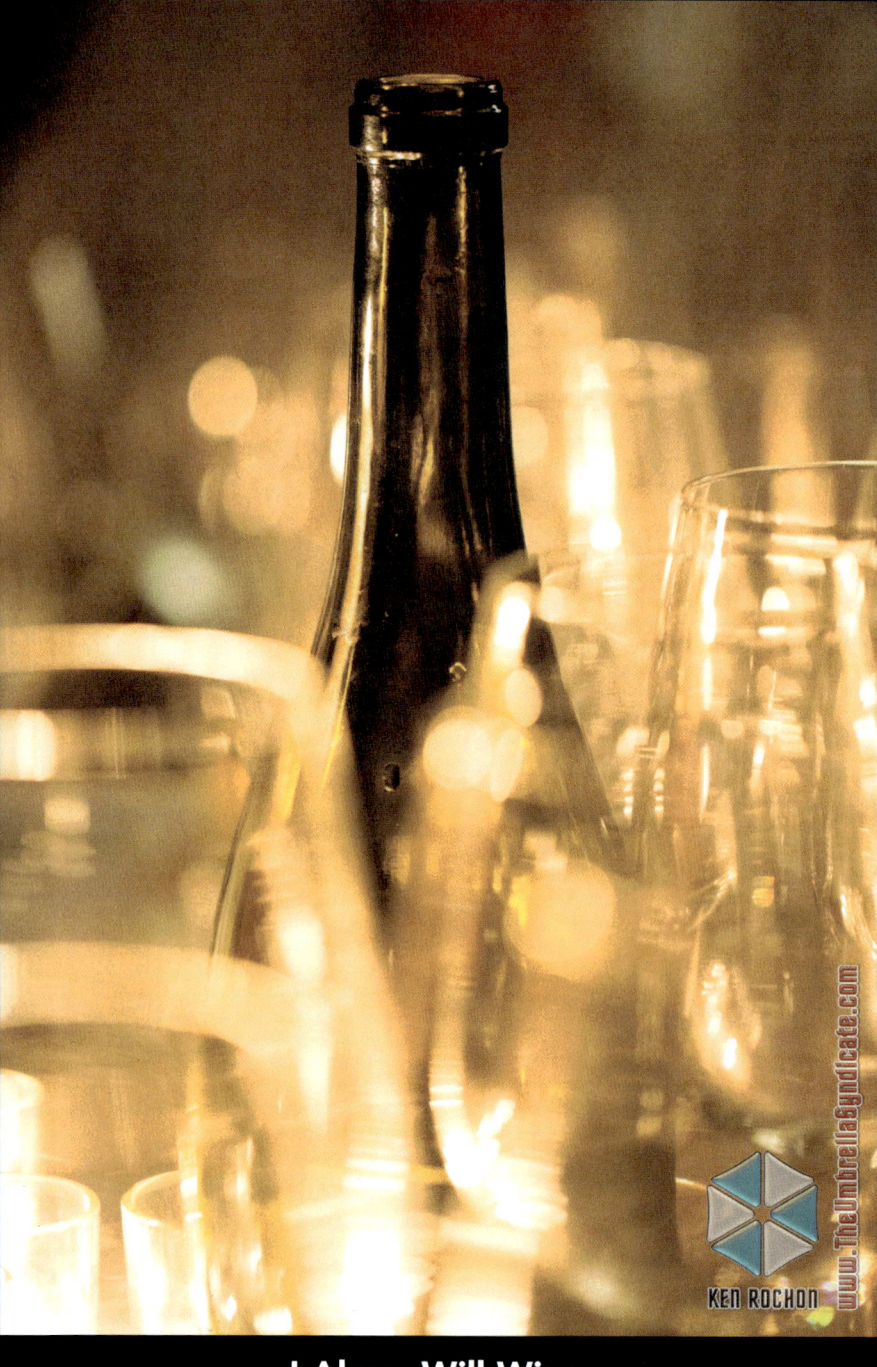

I Alone Will Wine

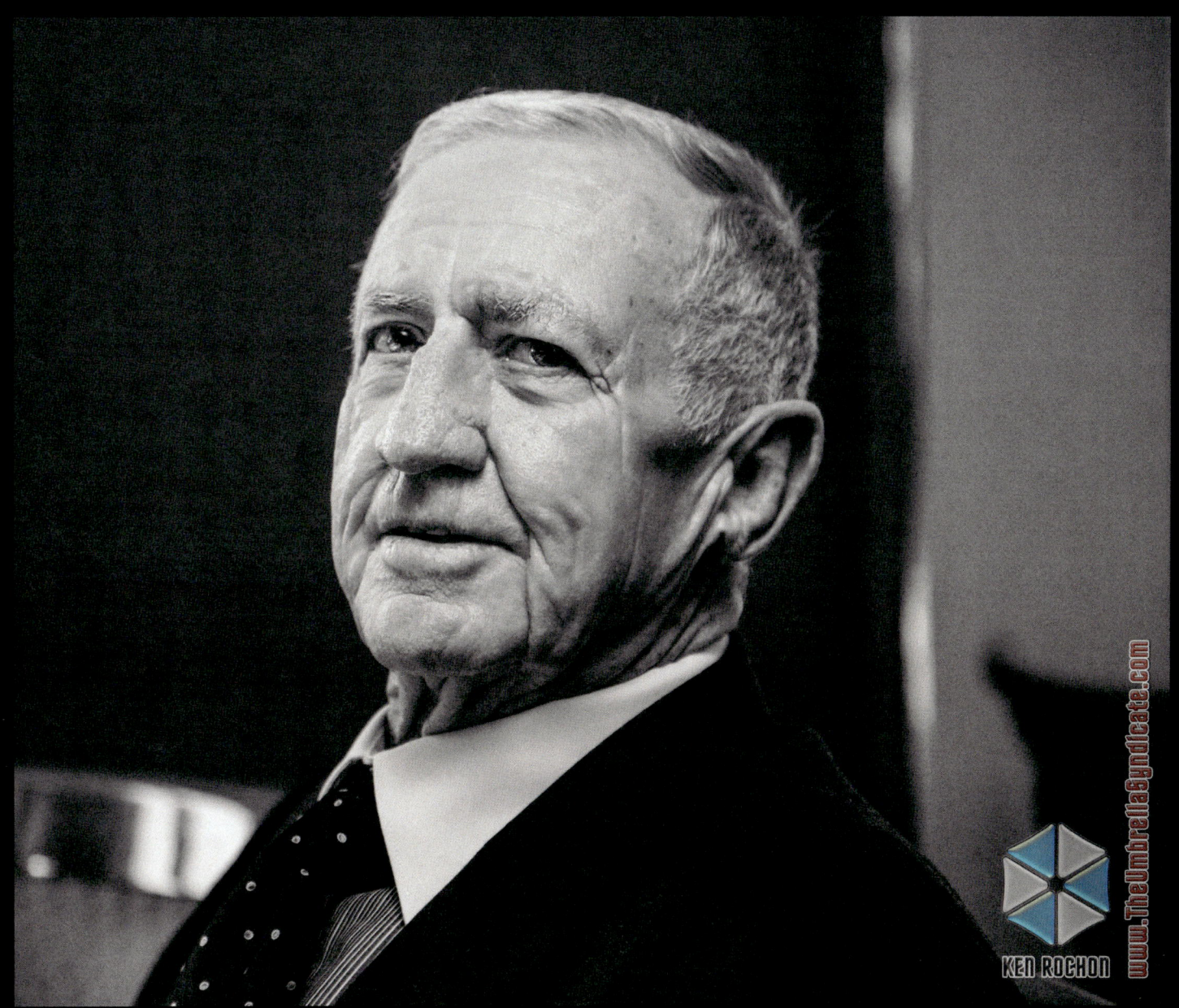

I Have Seen So Much

KEN ROCHON

www.TheUmbrellaSyndicate.com

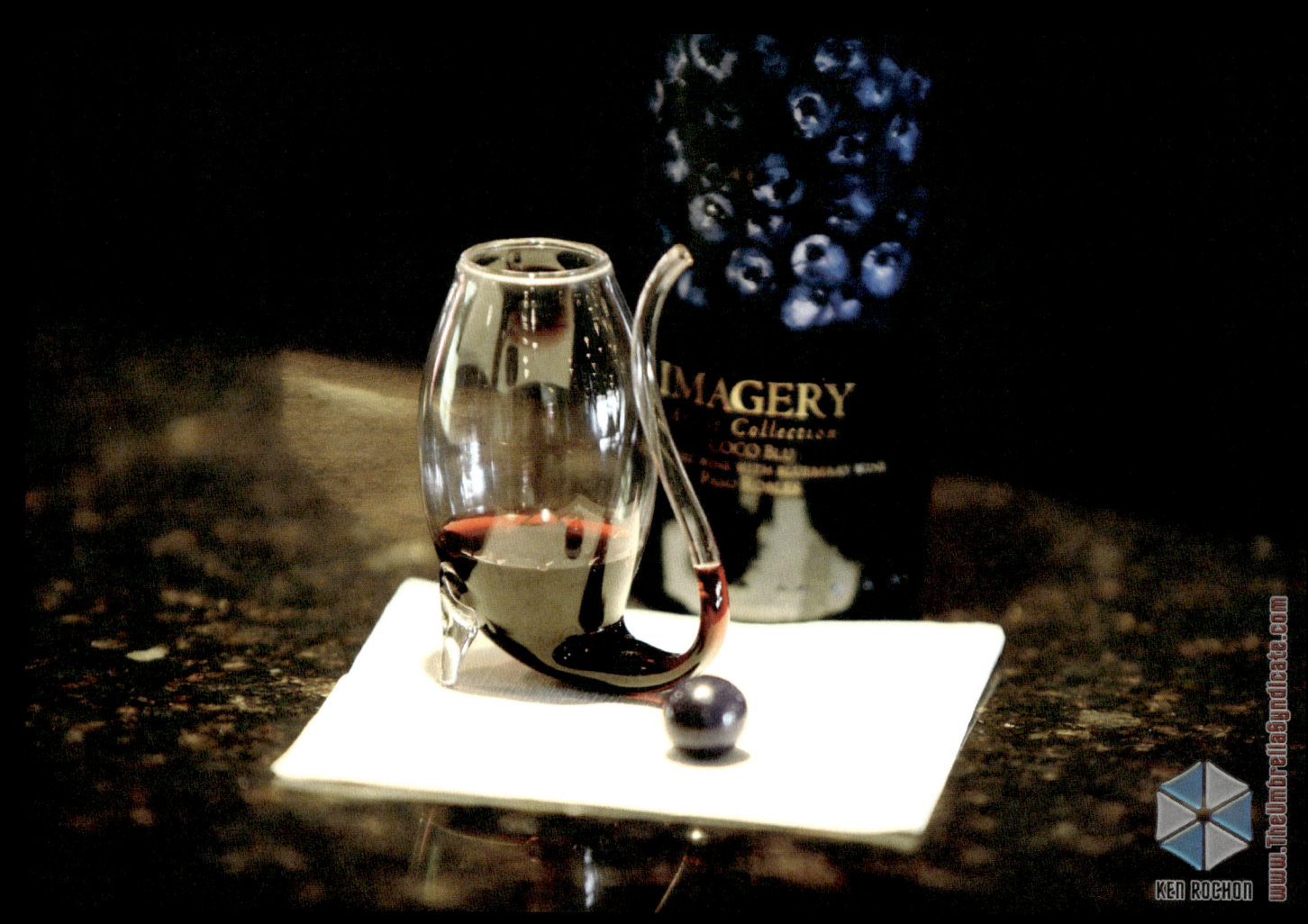

Imagery Fine Wine

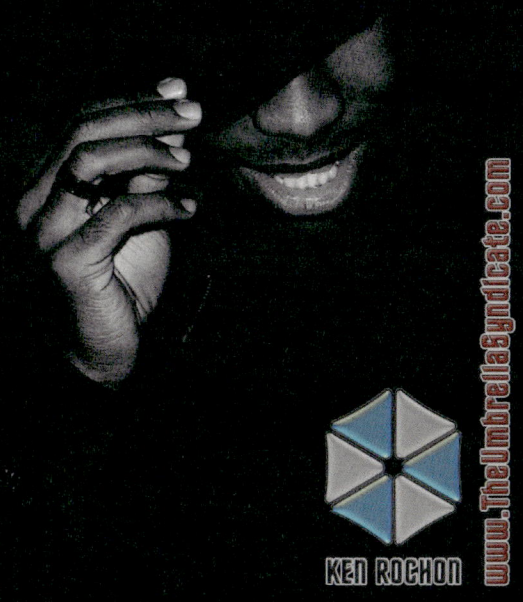

I Tip My Hat

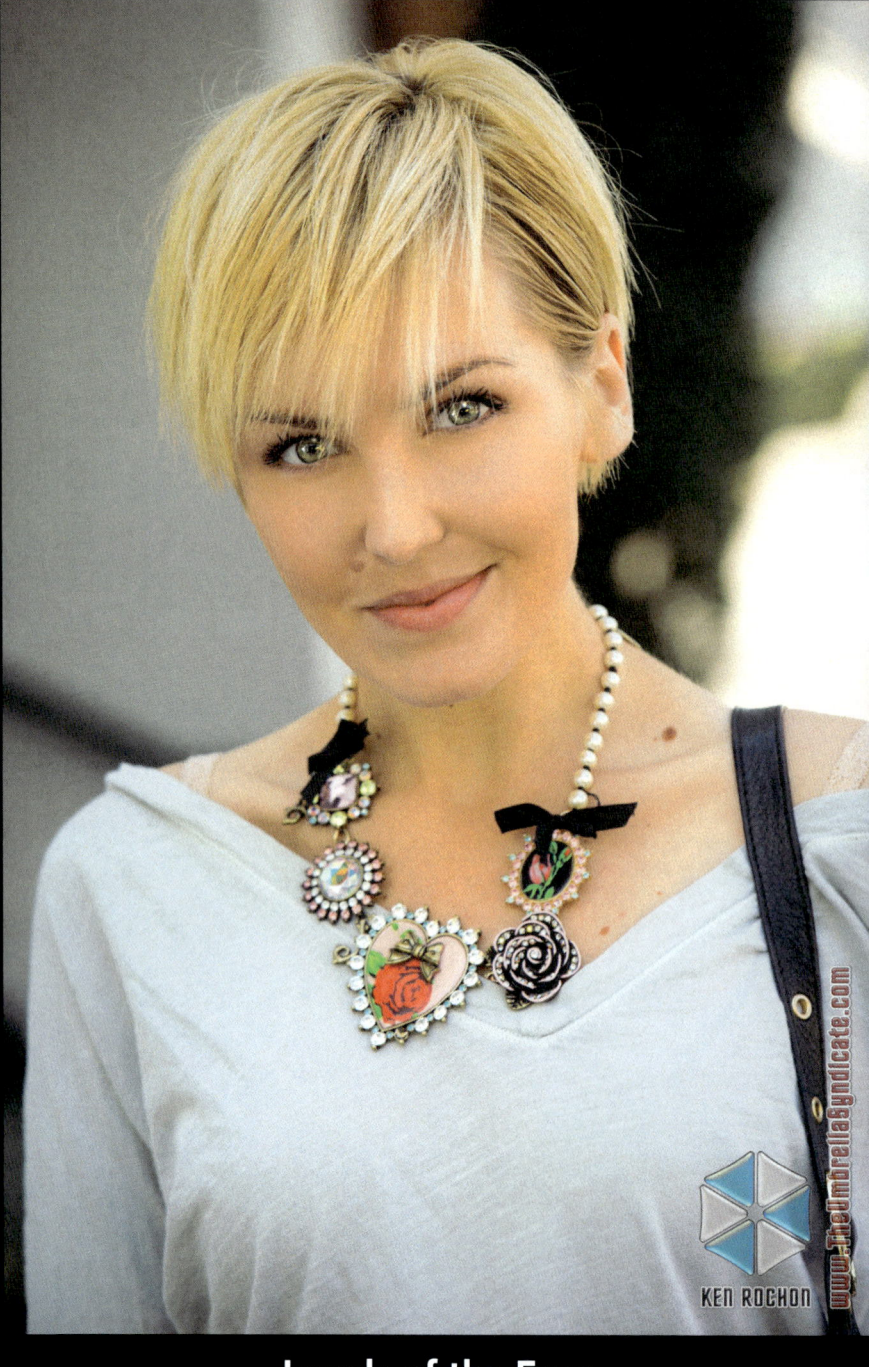

Jewels of the Eyes

KEN ROCHON www.theumbrellasyndicate.com

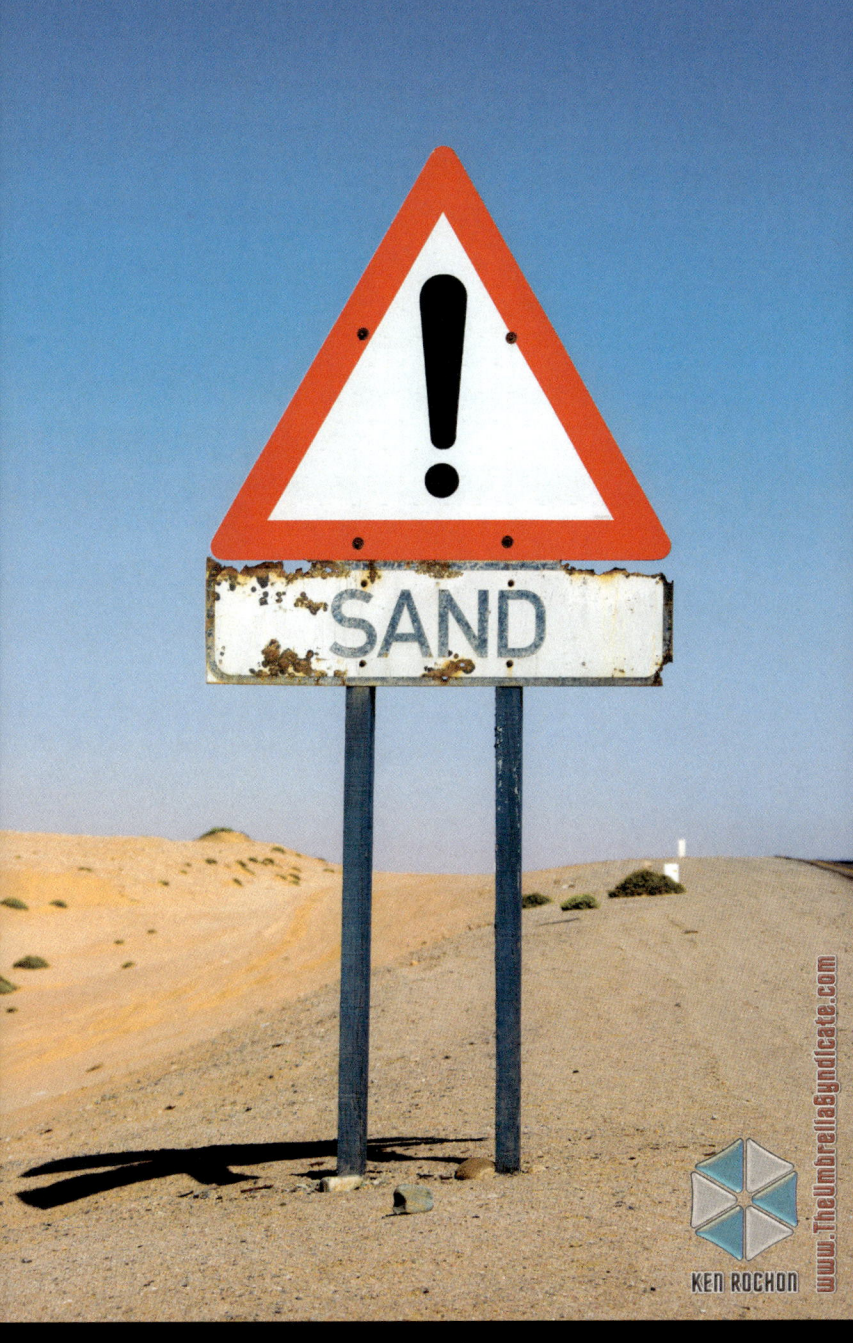

www.TheUmbrellaSyndicate.com

KEN ROCHON

Sand

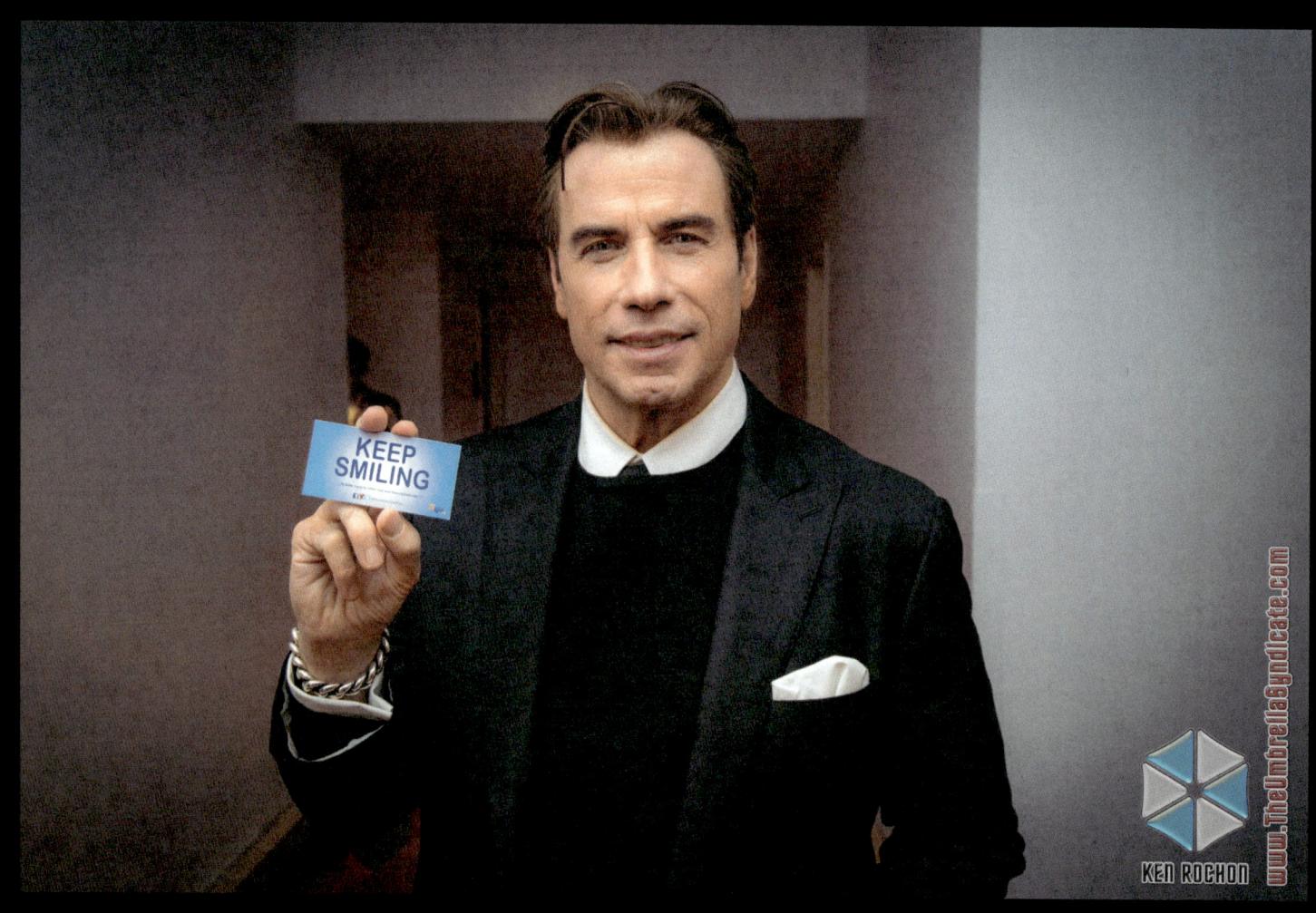

John Travolta

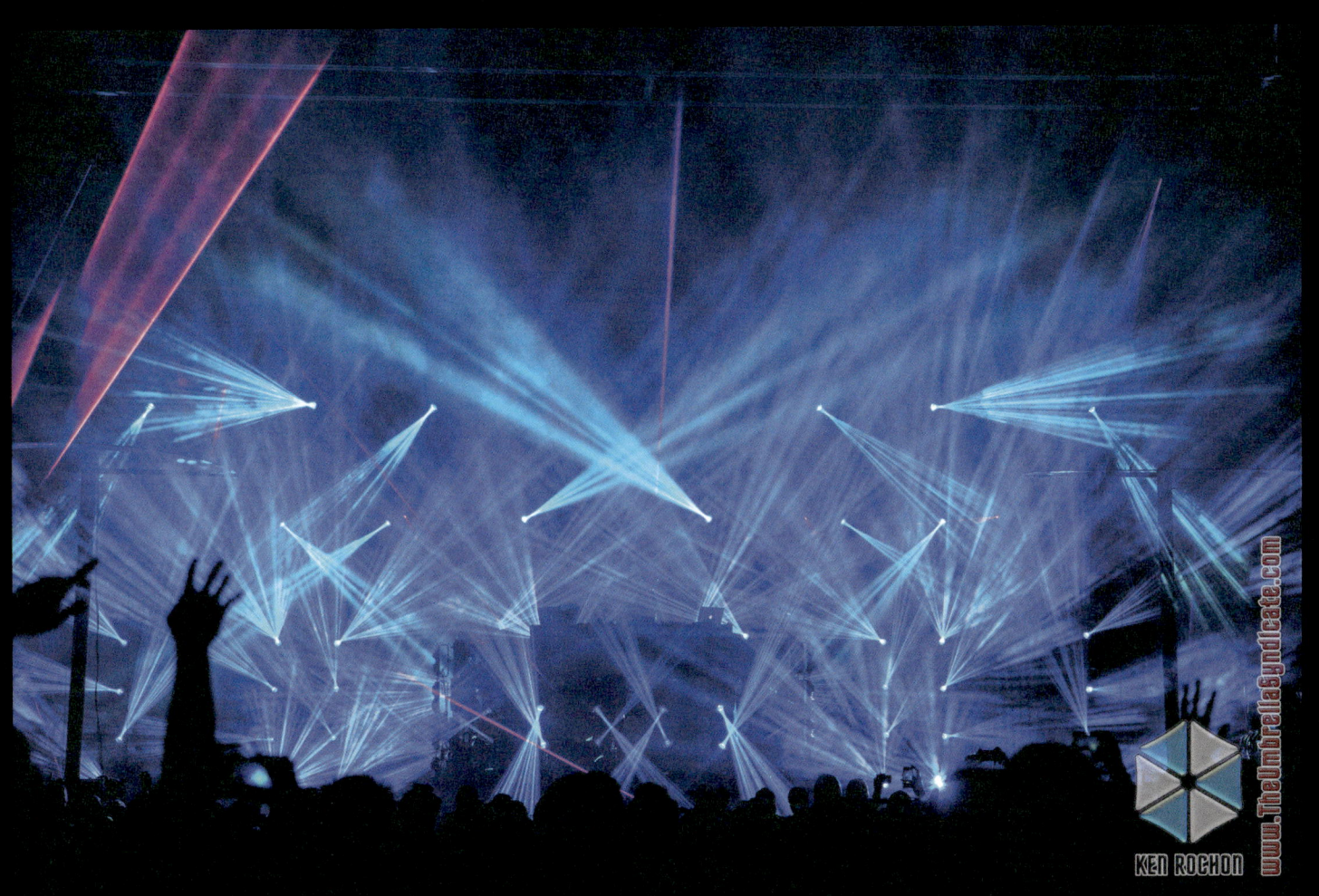

Lightshow Storm

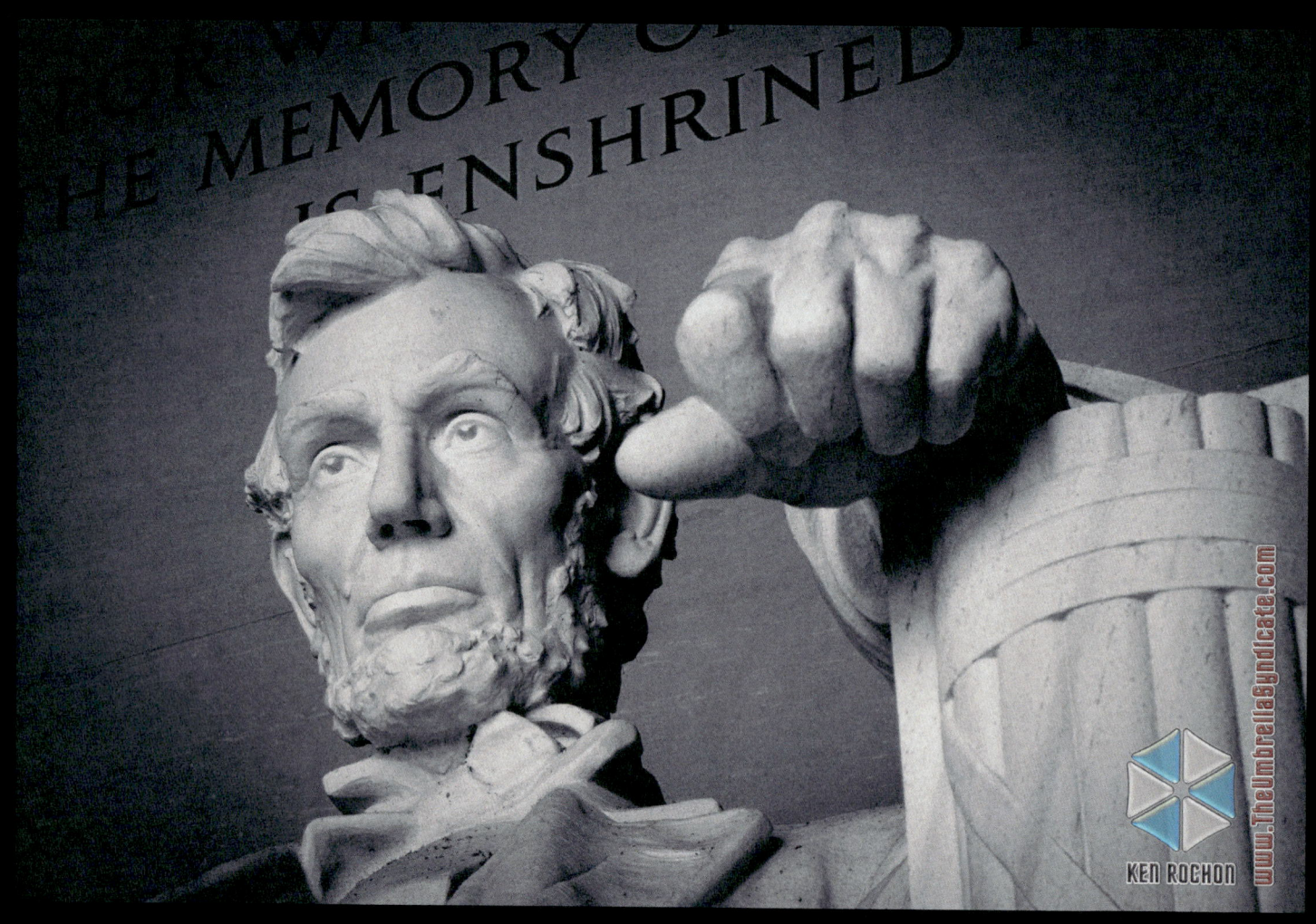

Lincoln Enshrined

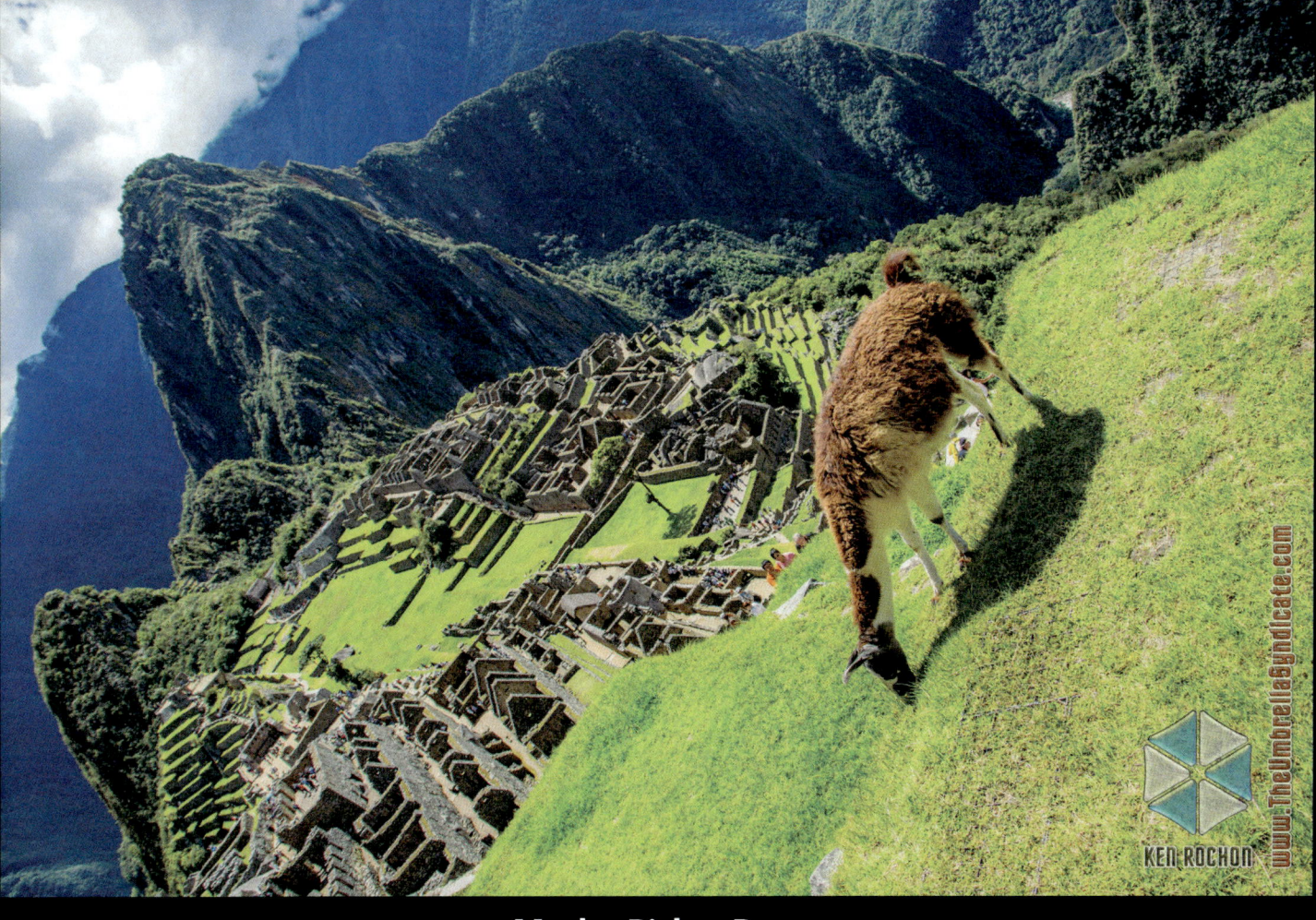

Machu Pichu, Peru

www.TheUmbrellaSyndicate.com

KEN ROCHON

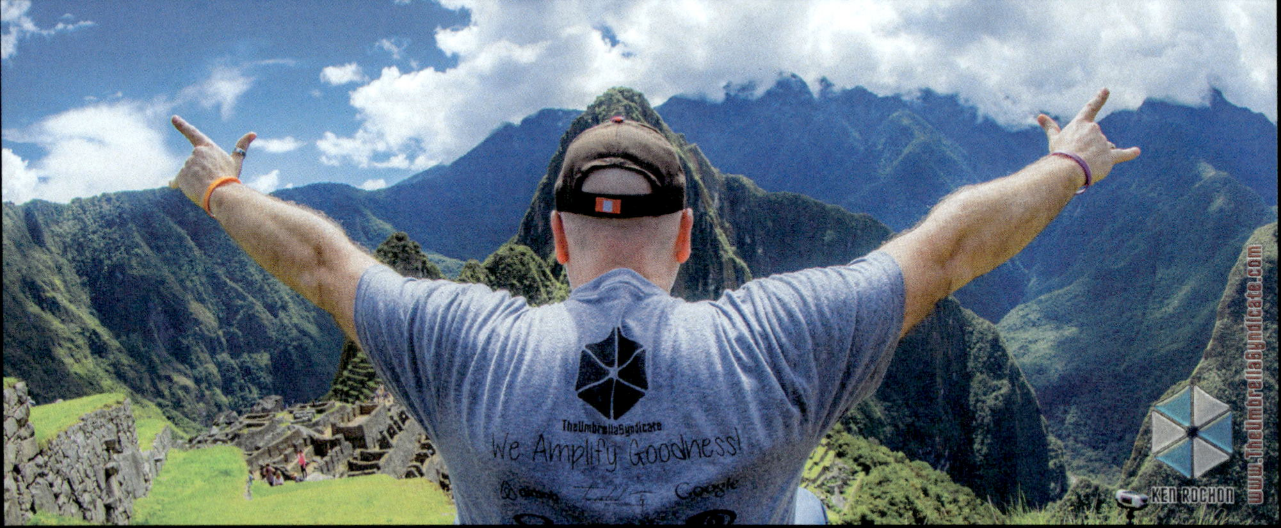

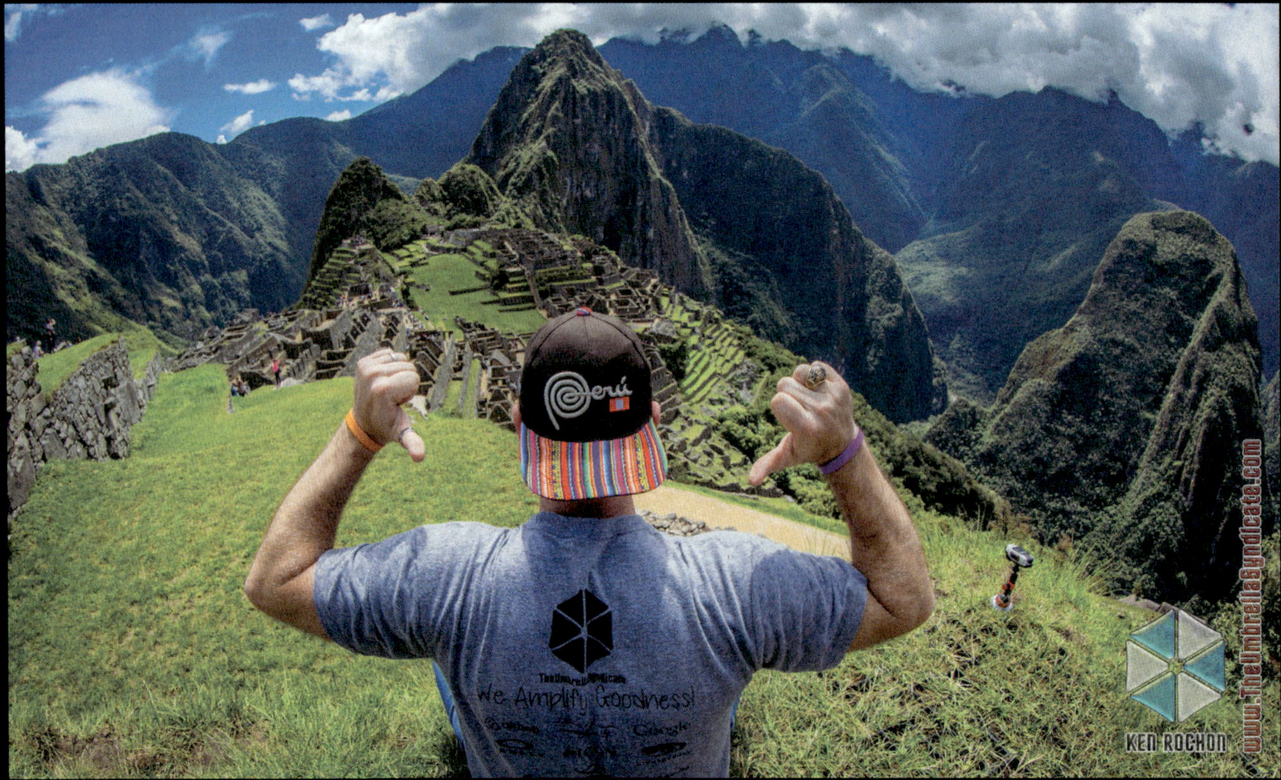

Machu Pichu, Peru

www.theumbrellasyndicate.com

KEN ROCHON

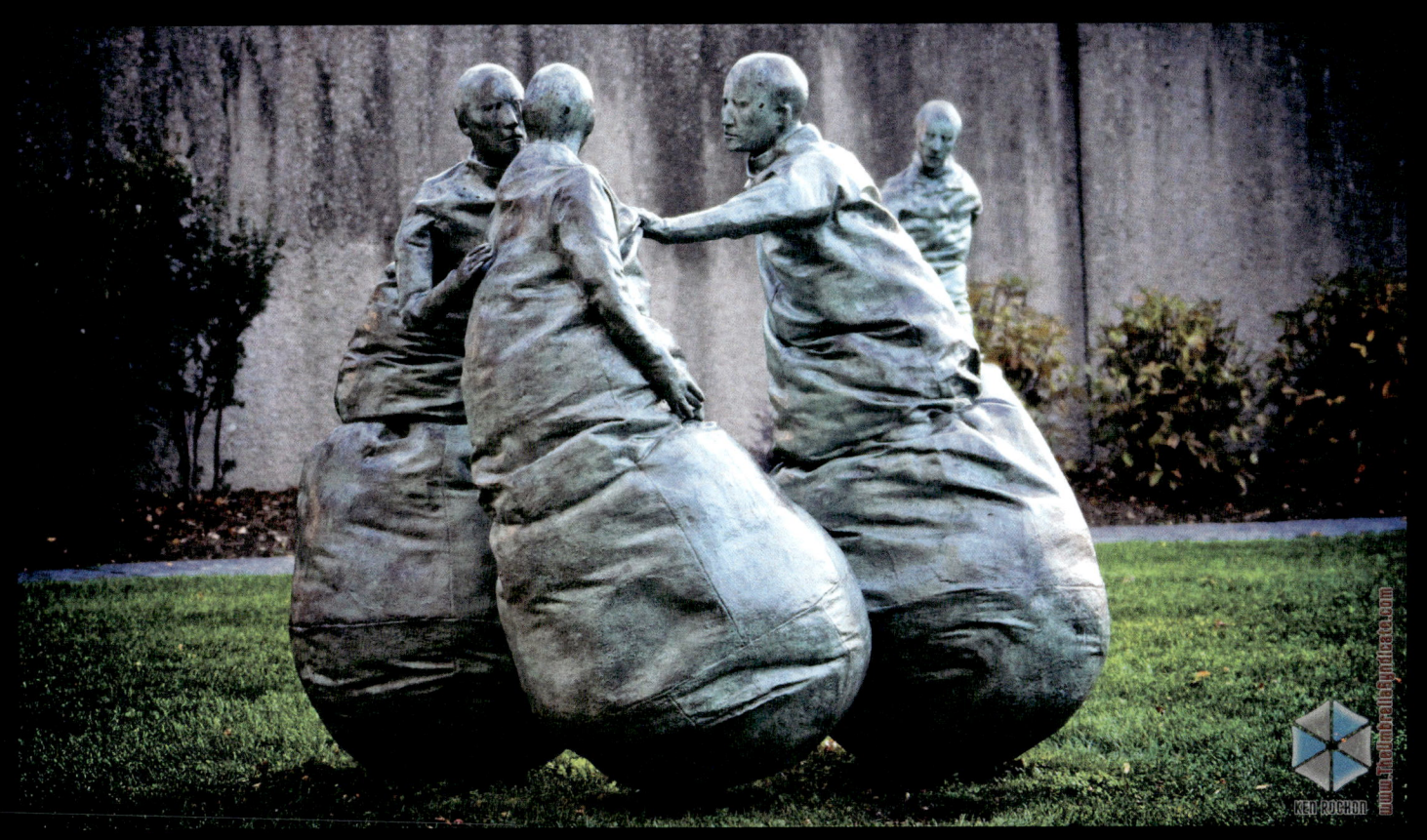

Meeting of the Bobble People

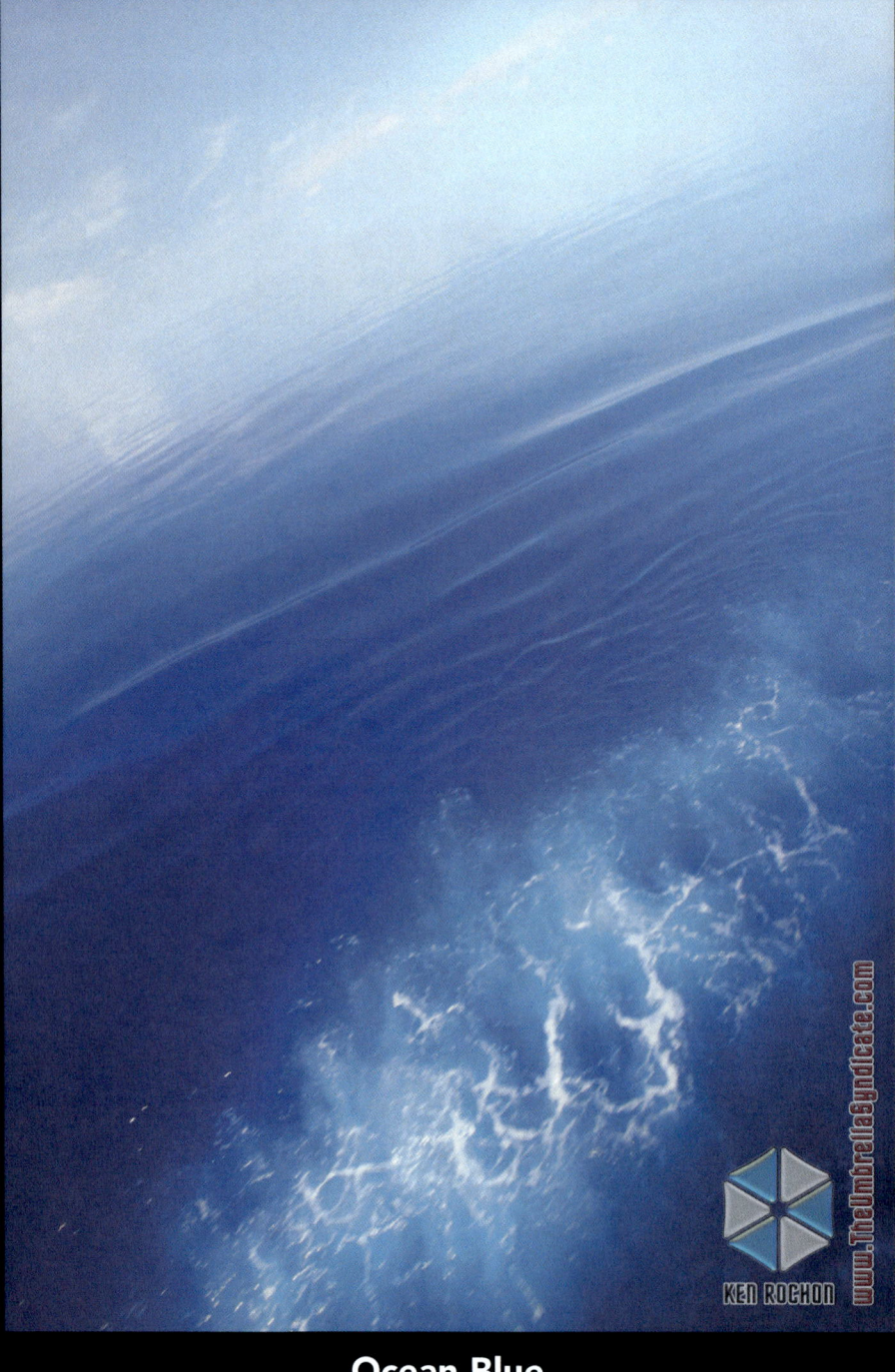

www.TheUmbrellaSyndicate.com

KEN ROCHON

Ocean Blue

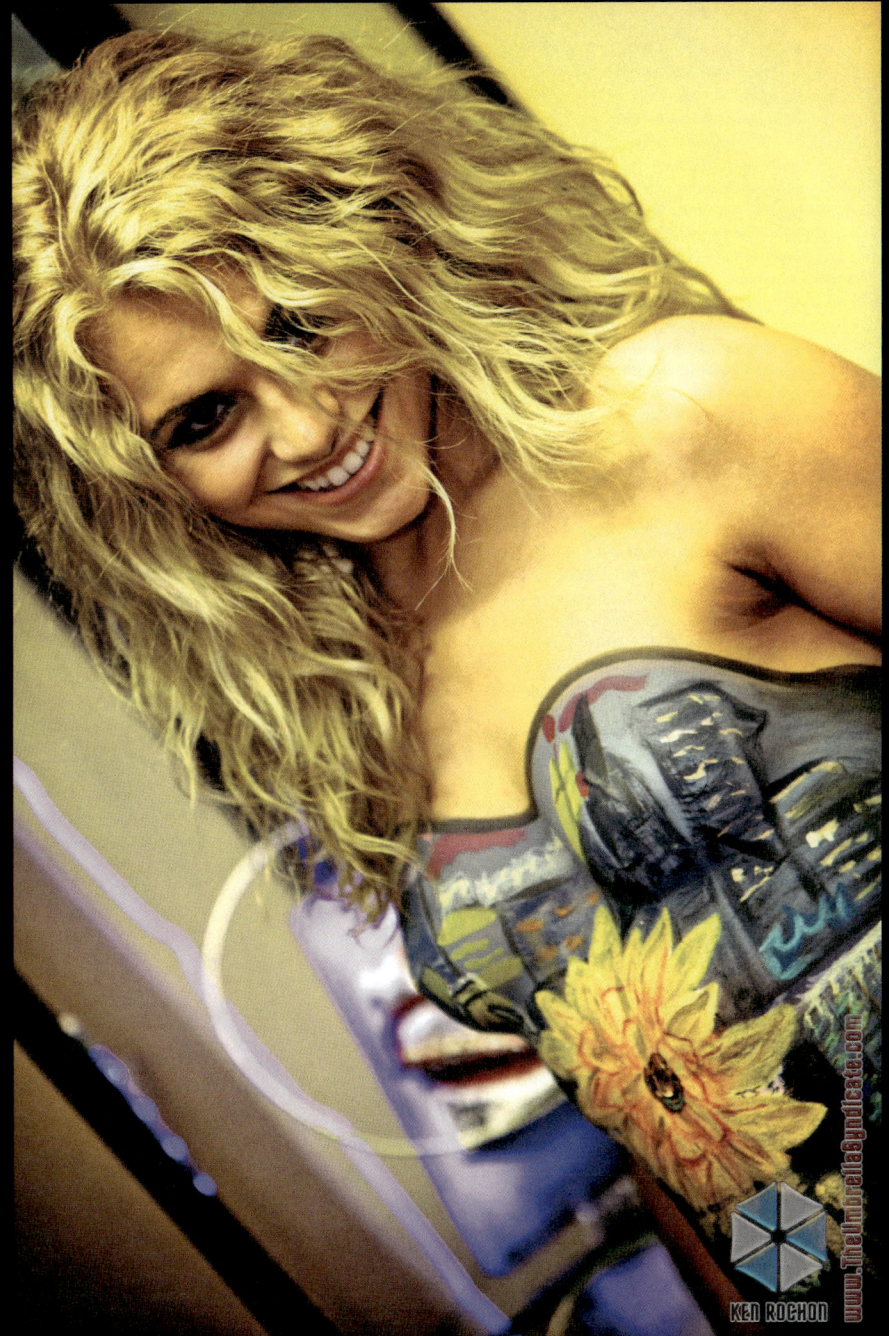

Painted Bombshell

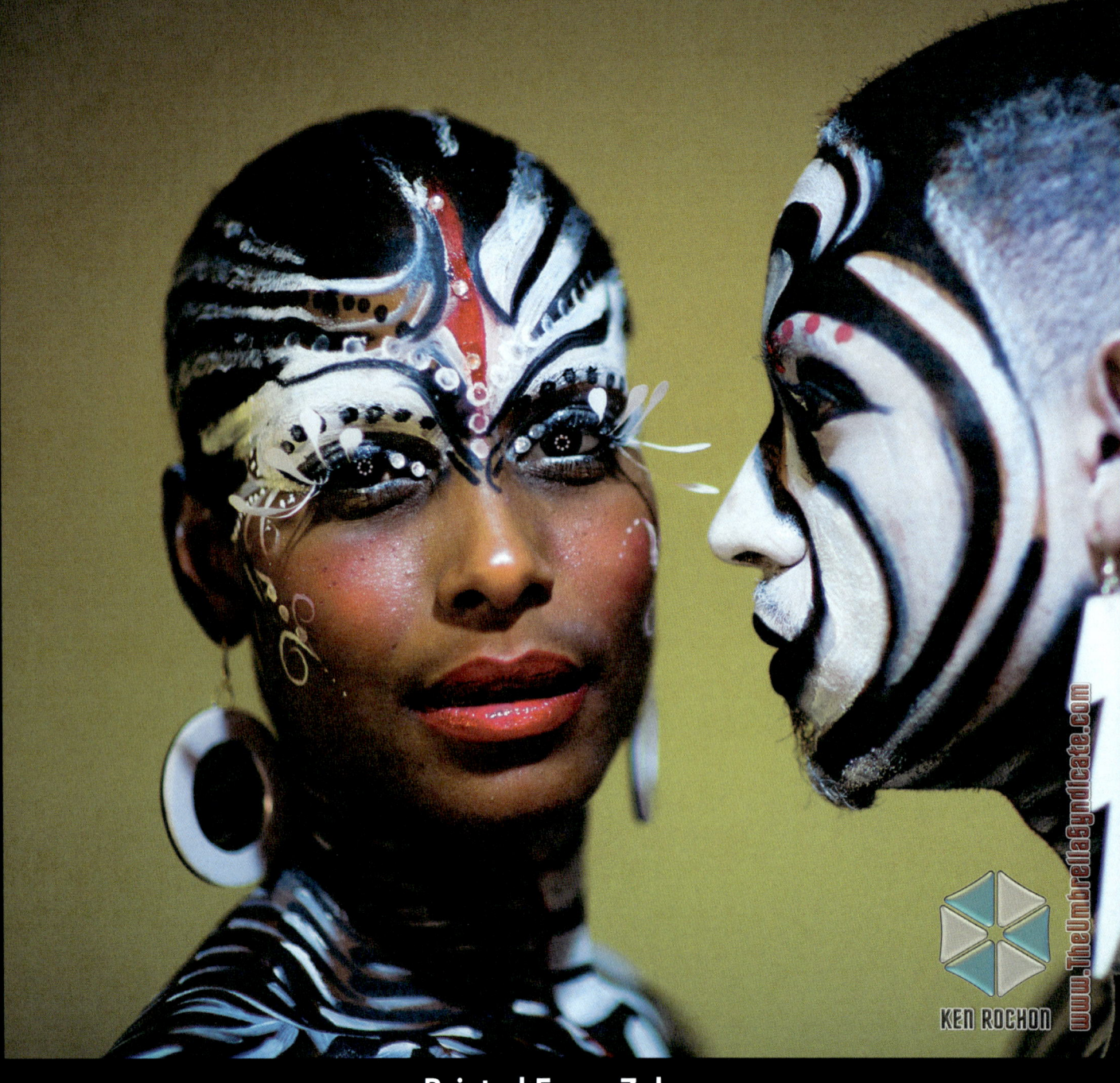

KEN ROCHON www.TheUmbrellaSyndicate.com

Painted Faces Zebra

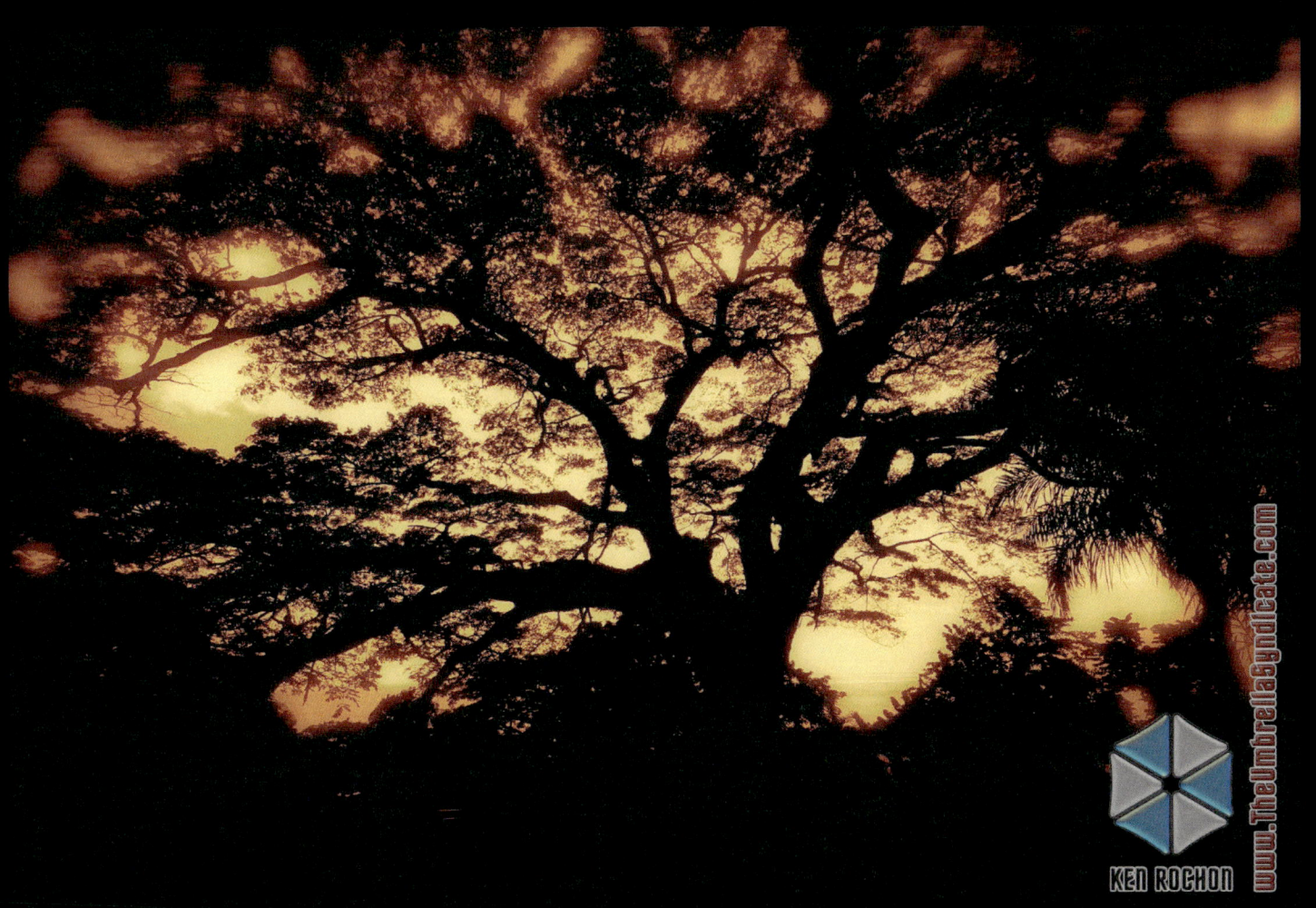

St. Kitts Tree on Fire

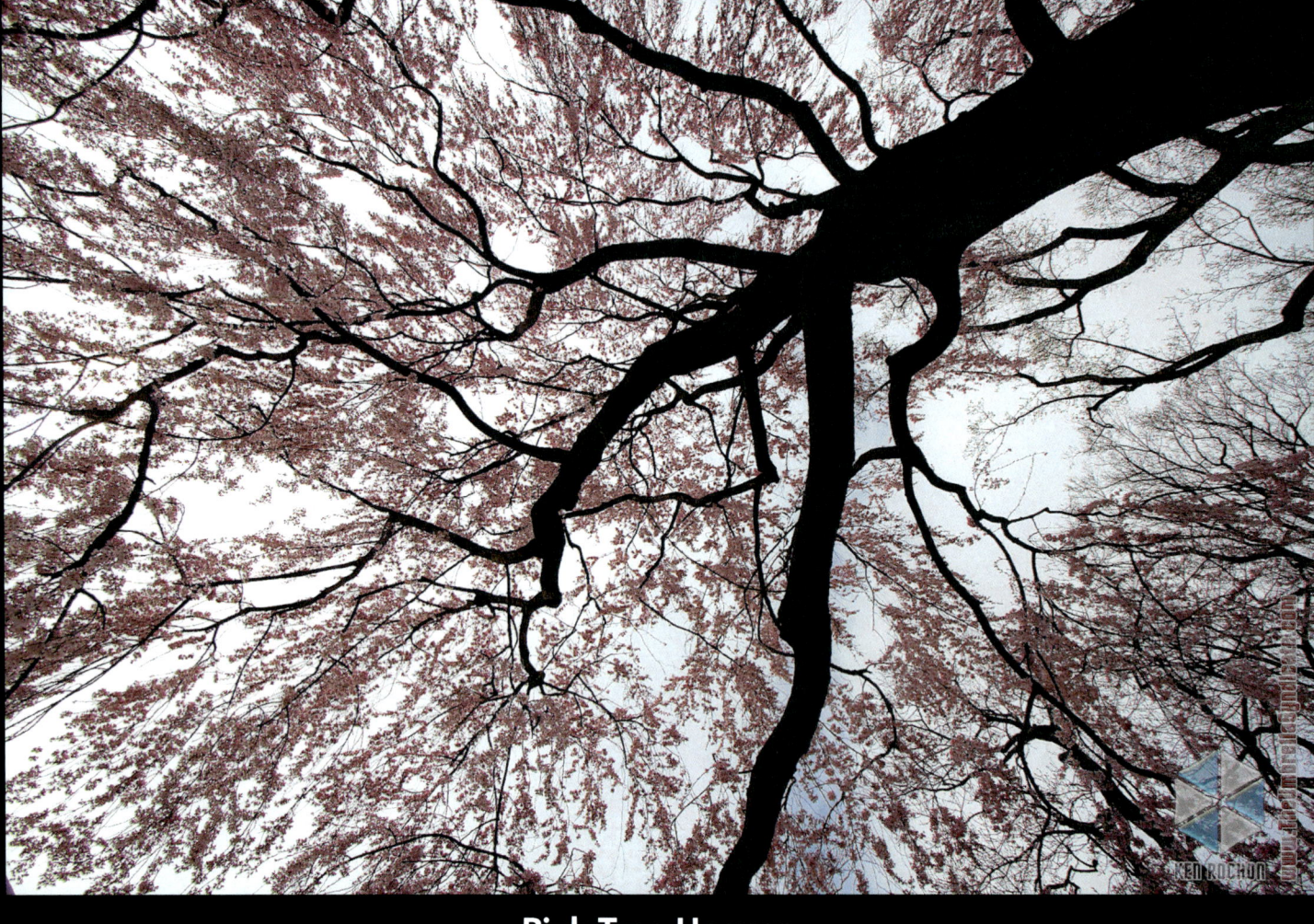

Pink Tree Heaven

KENROCHON

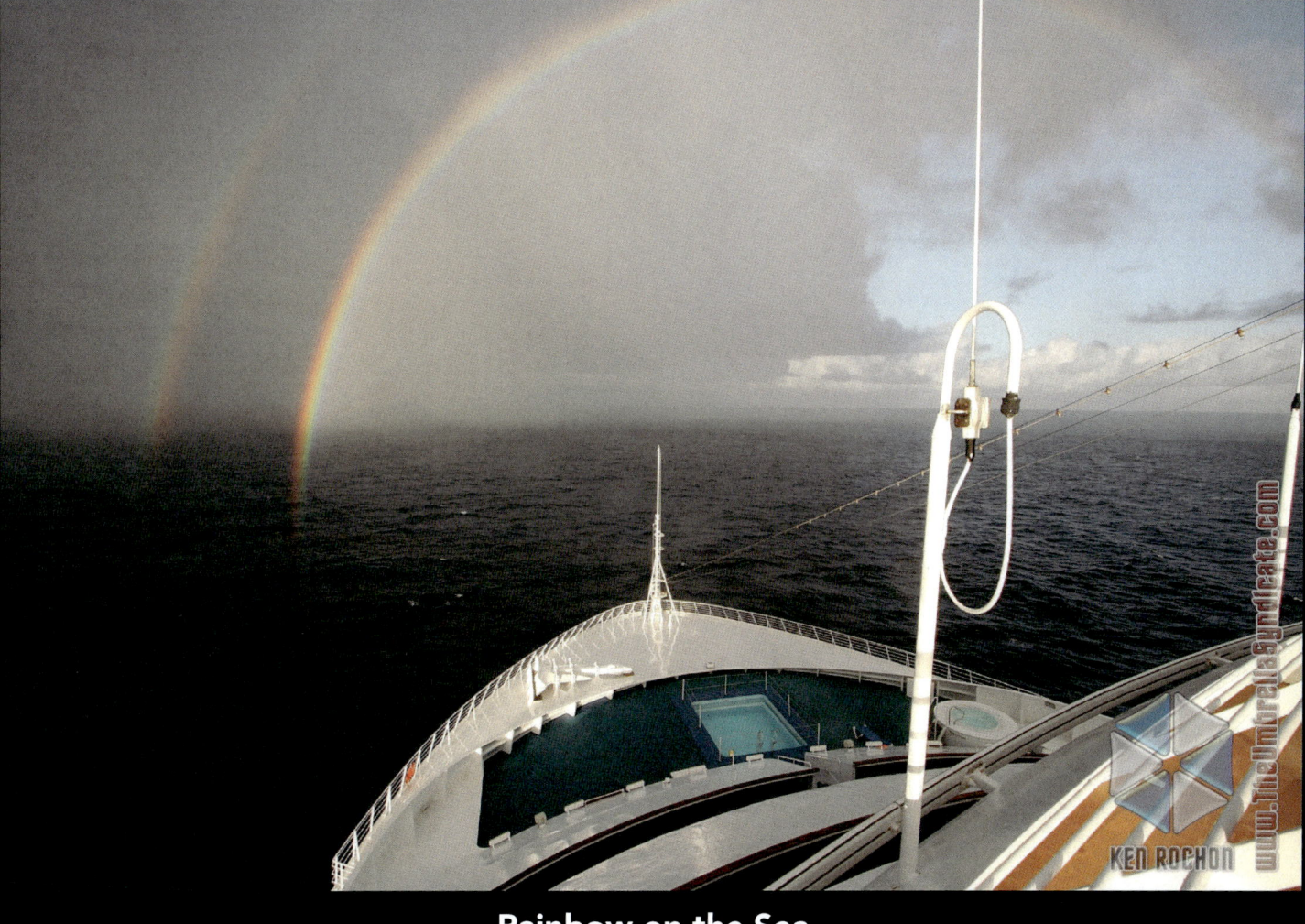

Rowinbow on the Sea

www.TheUmbrellaSyndicate.com

KEN ROCHON

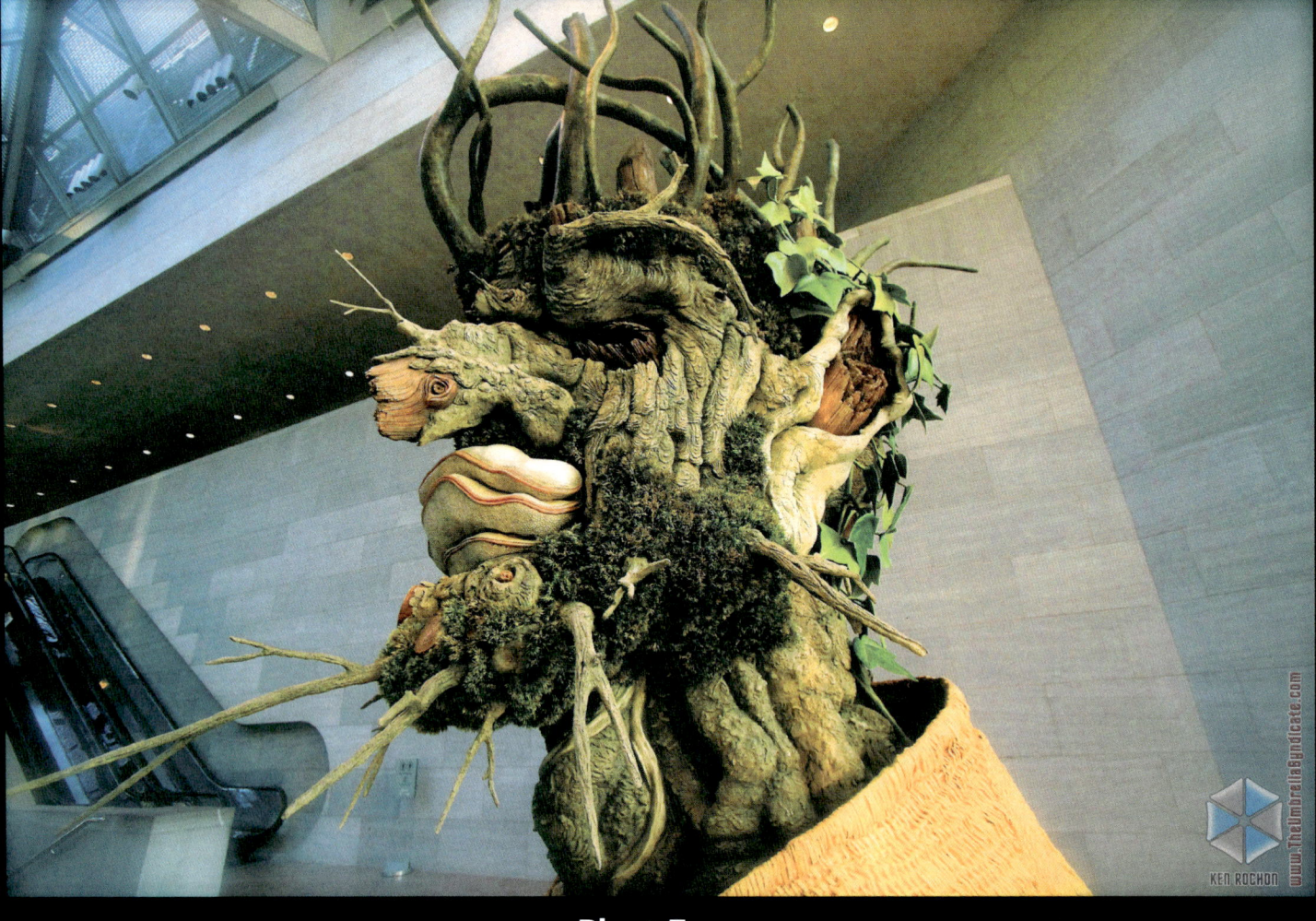

Plant Face

KEN ROCHON

www.TheUmbrellaSyndicate.com

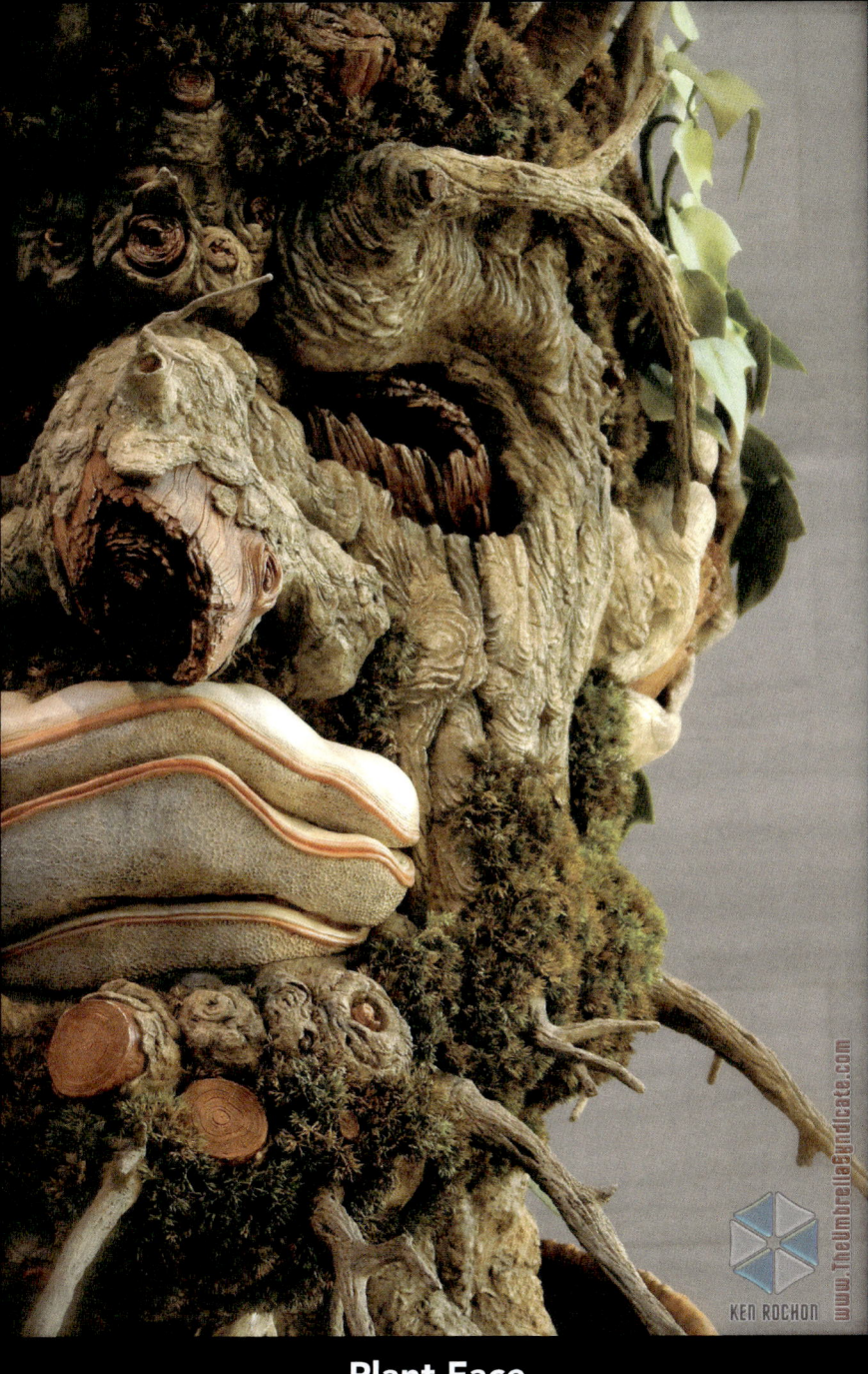

www.TheUmbrellaSyndicate.com

KEN ROCHON

Plant Face

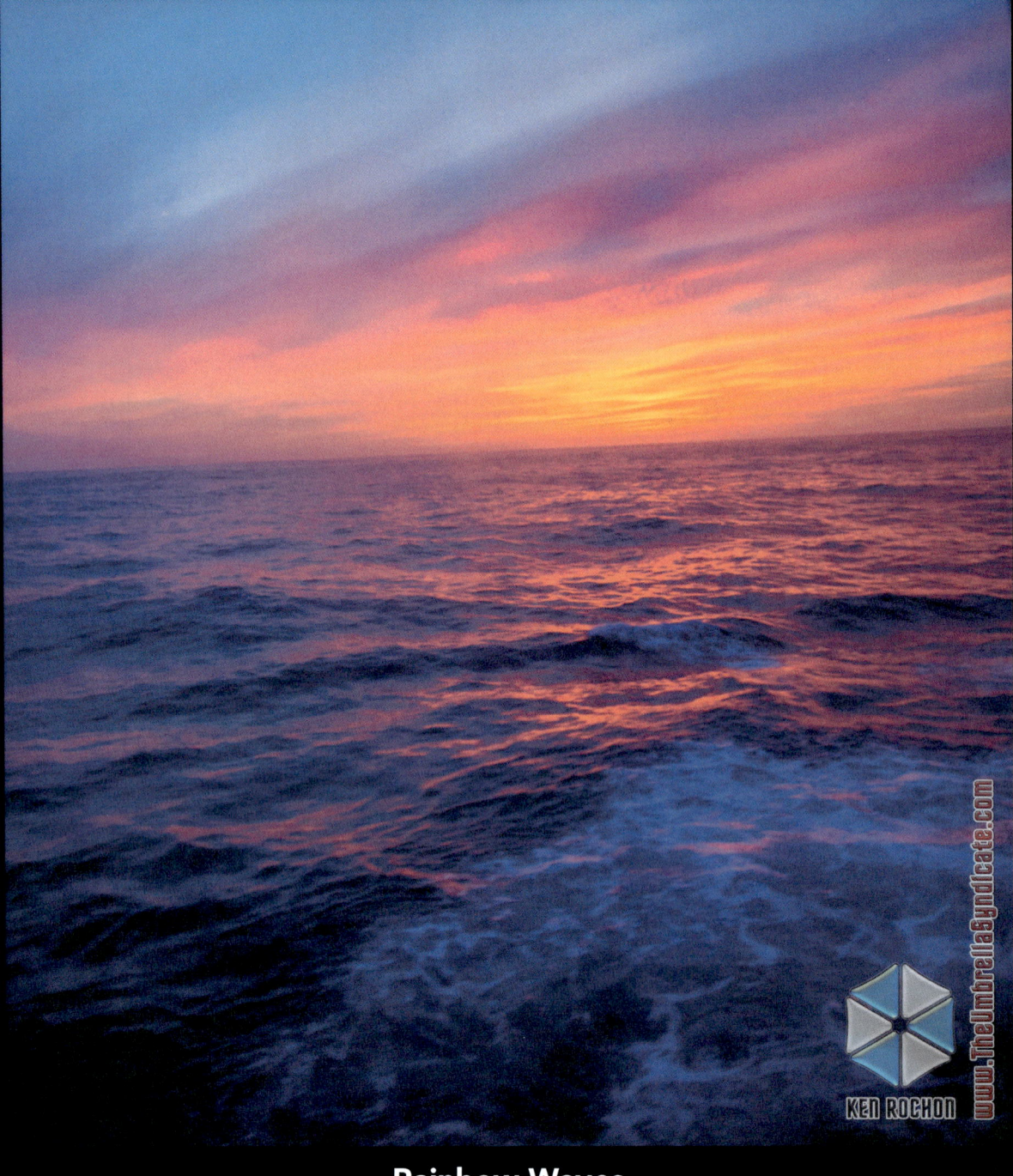

KEN ROCHON

www.TheUmbrellaSyndicate.com

Rainbow Waves

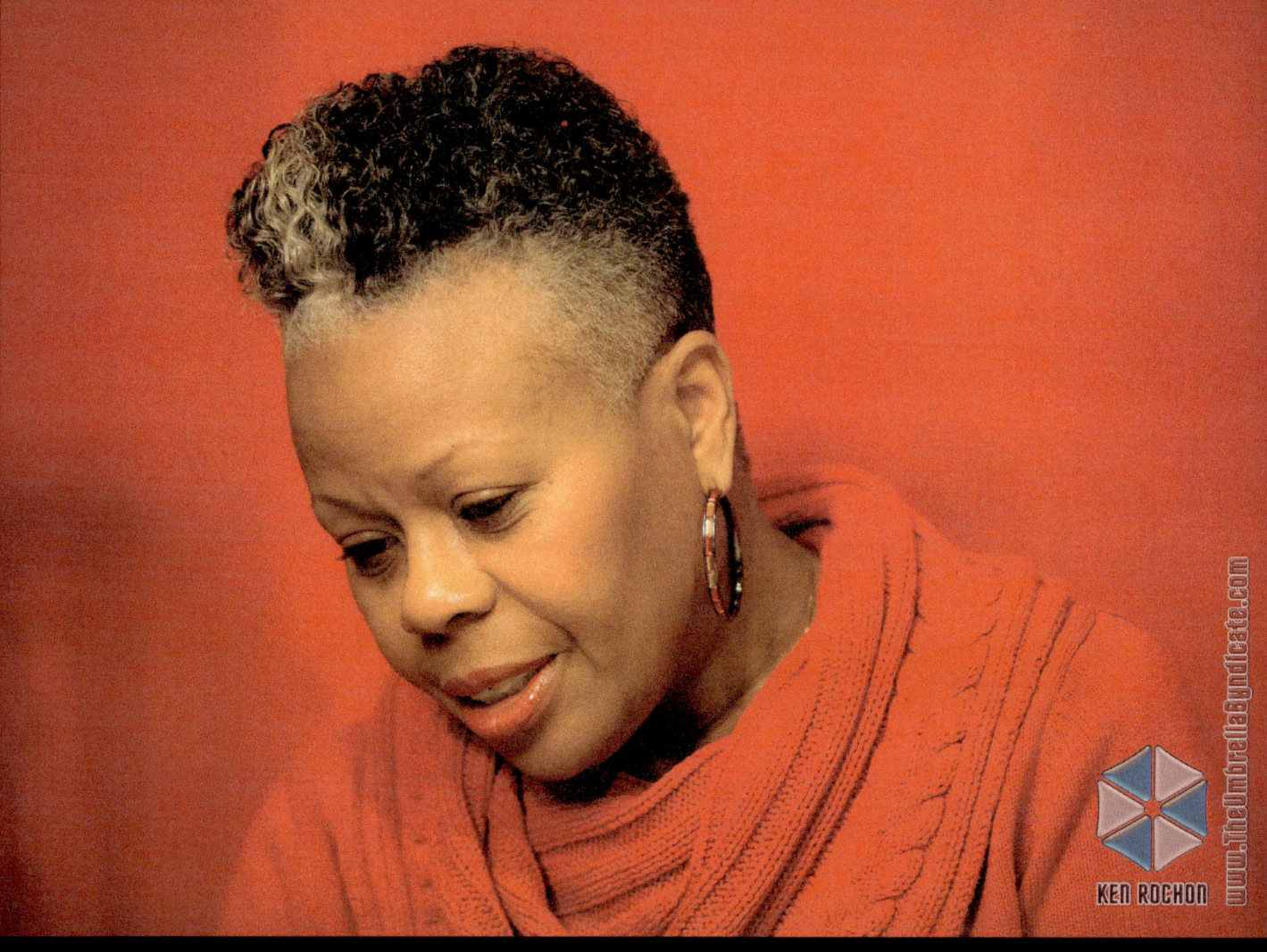

Red Passion & Peace

KEN ROCHON

www.TheUmbrellaSyndicate.com

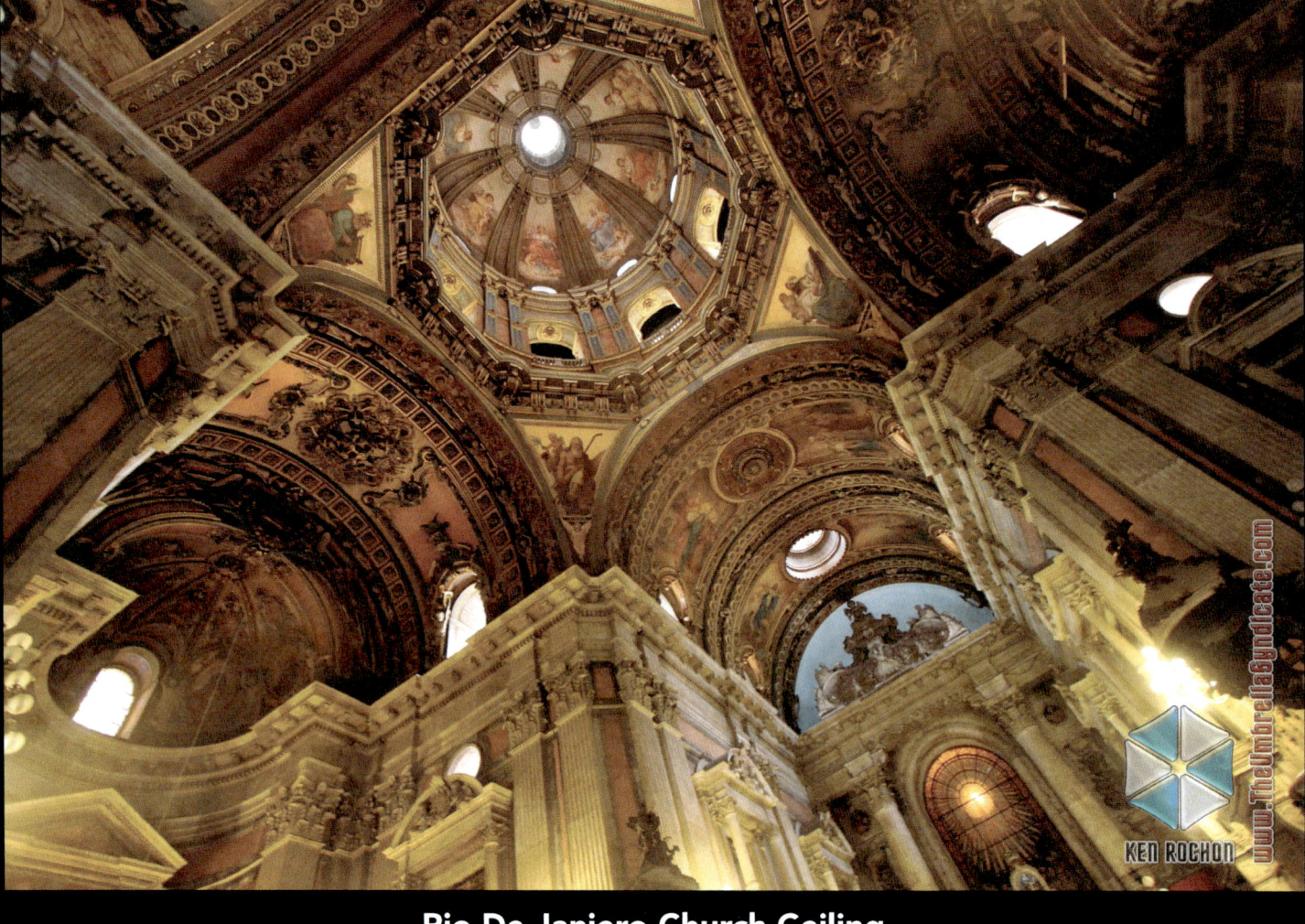

KEN ROCHON

www.TheUmbrellaSyndicate.com

Rio De Janiero Church Ceiling

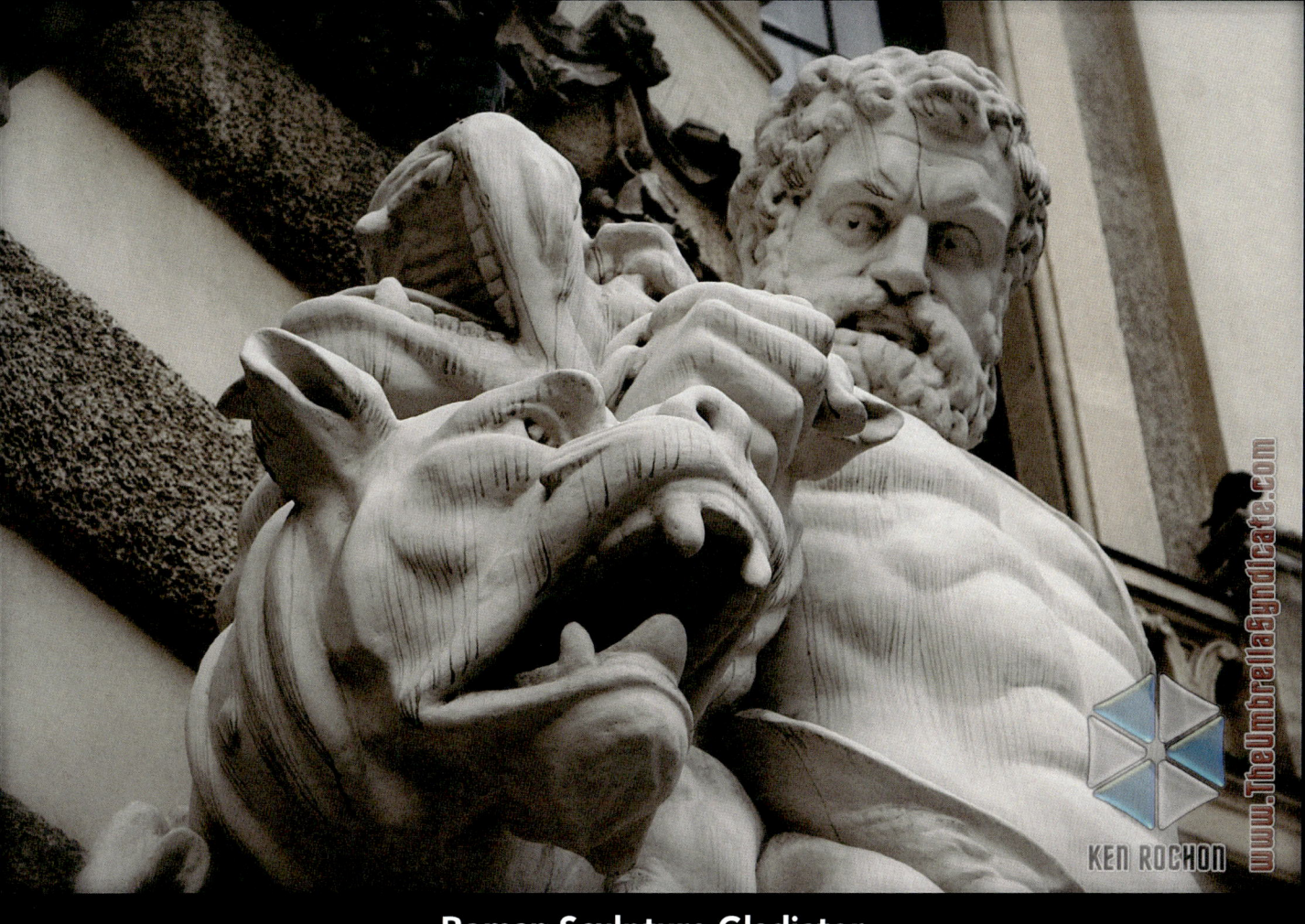

Roman Sculpture Gladiator

www.TheUmbrellaSyndicate.com

KEN ROCHON

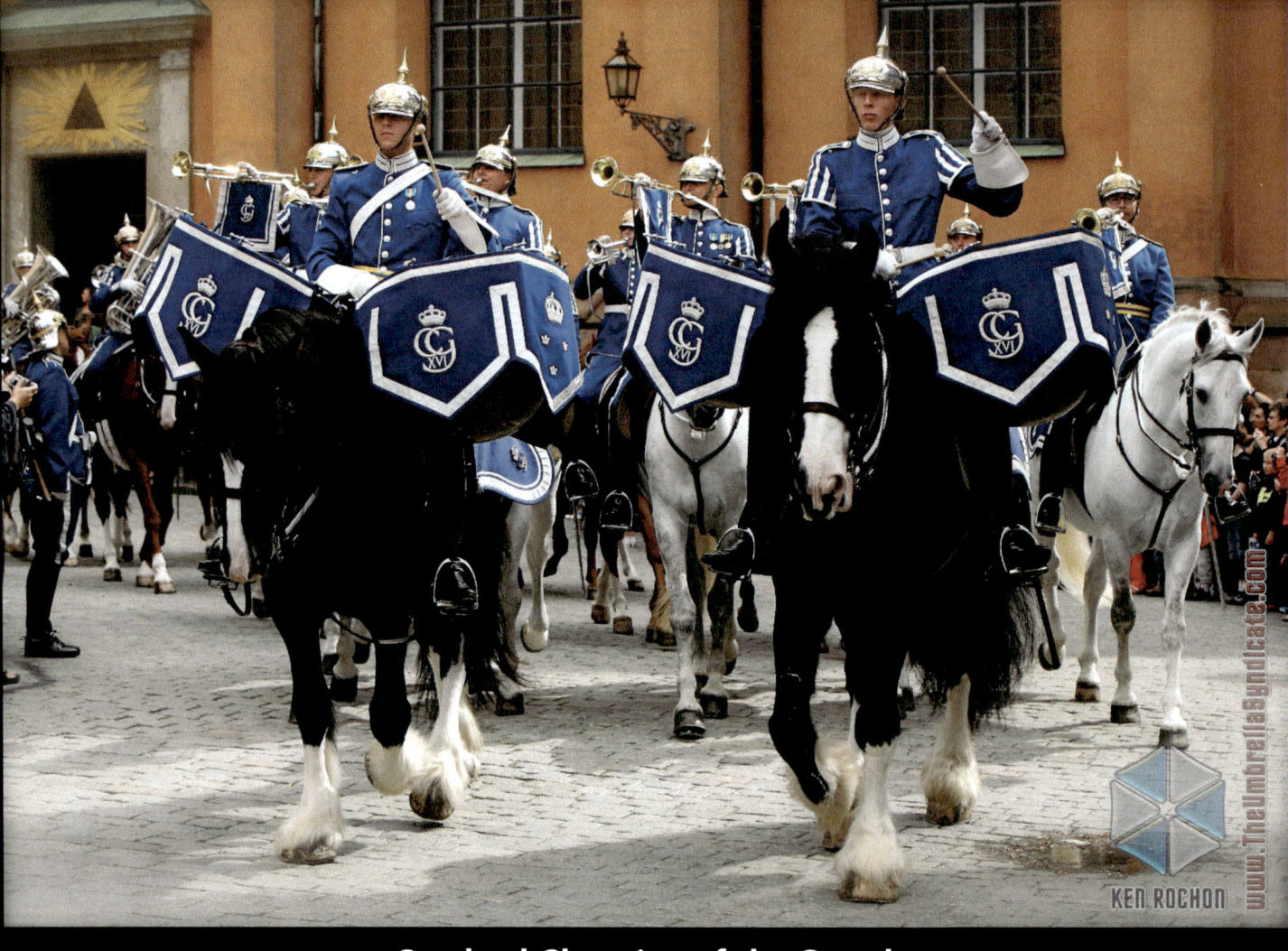

Scotland Changing of the Guard

www.TheUmbrellaSyndicate.com

KEN ROCHON

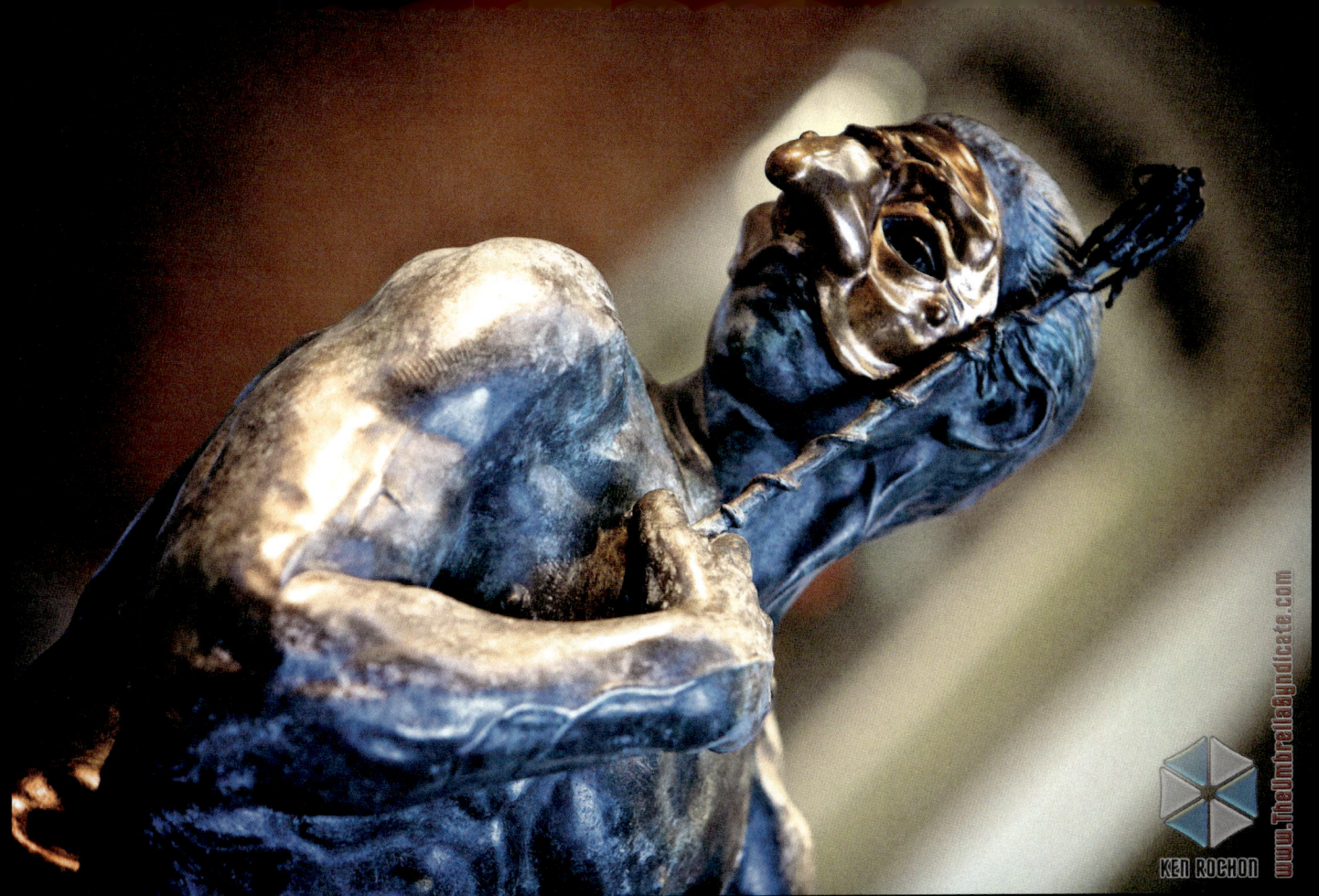

Sculpture Masked Warrior

www.TheUmbrellaSyndicate.com

KEN ROCHON

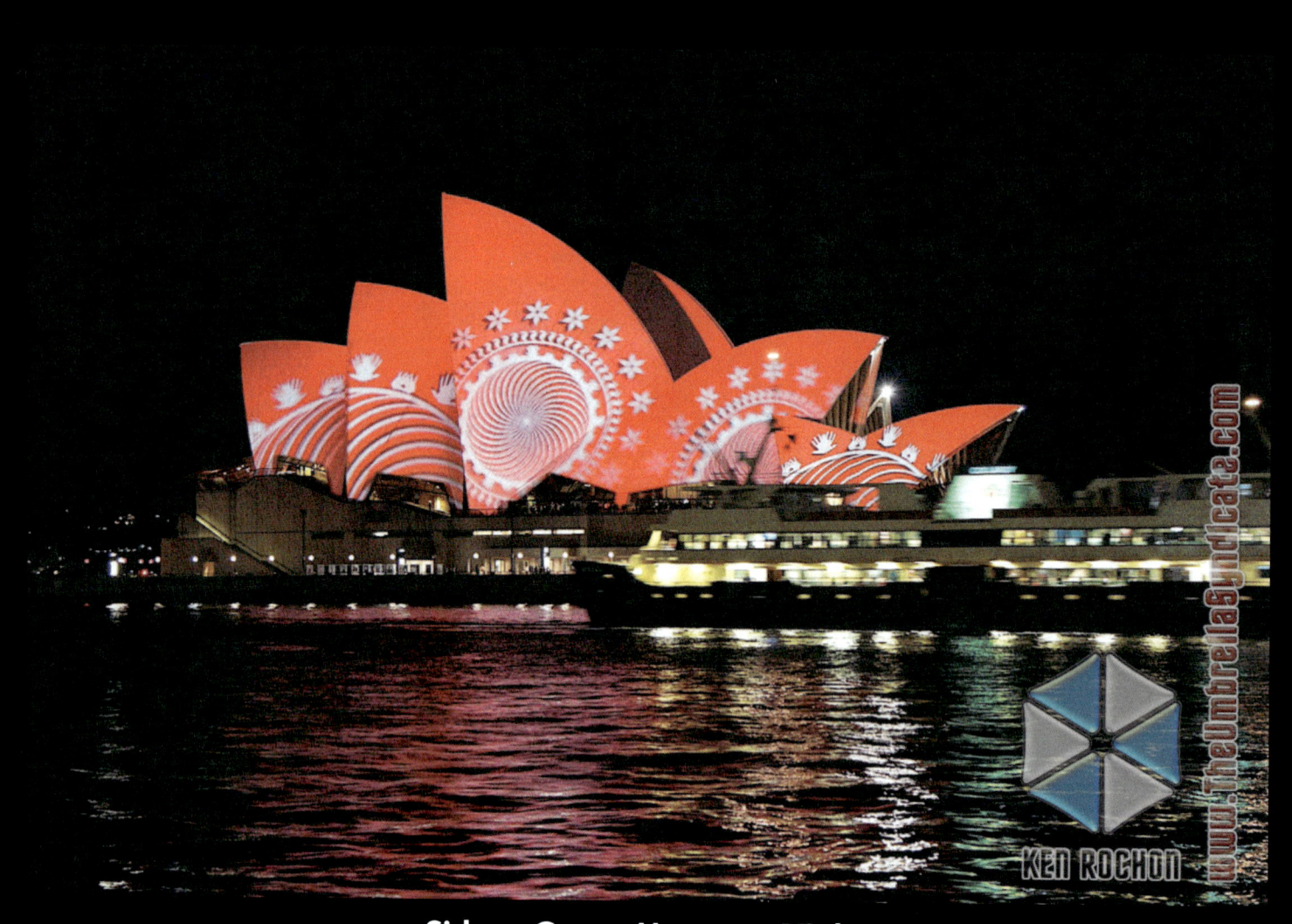

Sidney Opera House at Night

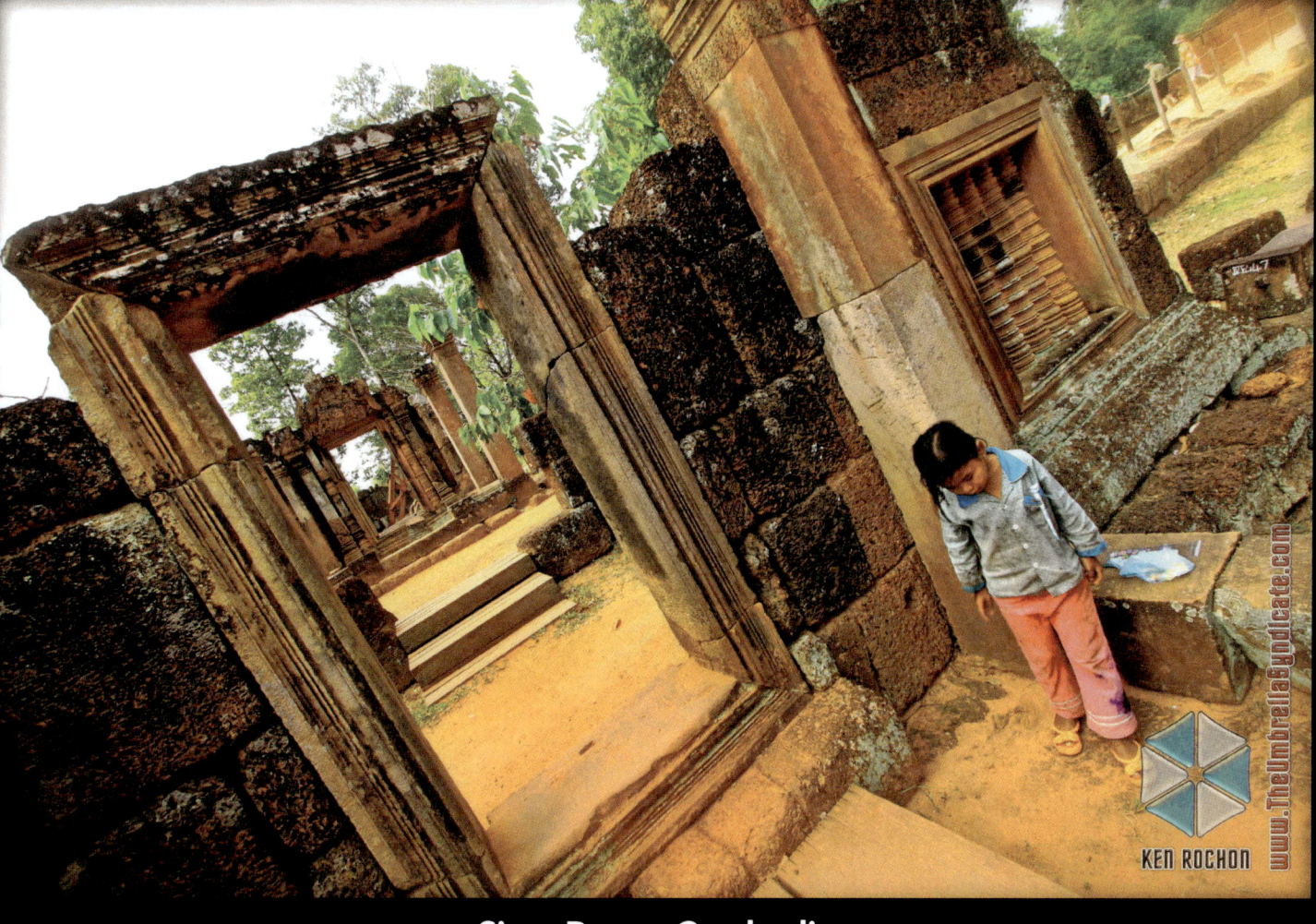

Siem Reap, Cambodia

KEN ROCHON

www.TheUmbrellaSyndicate.com

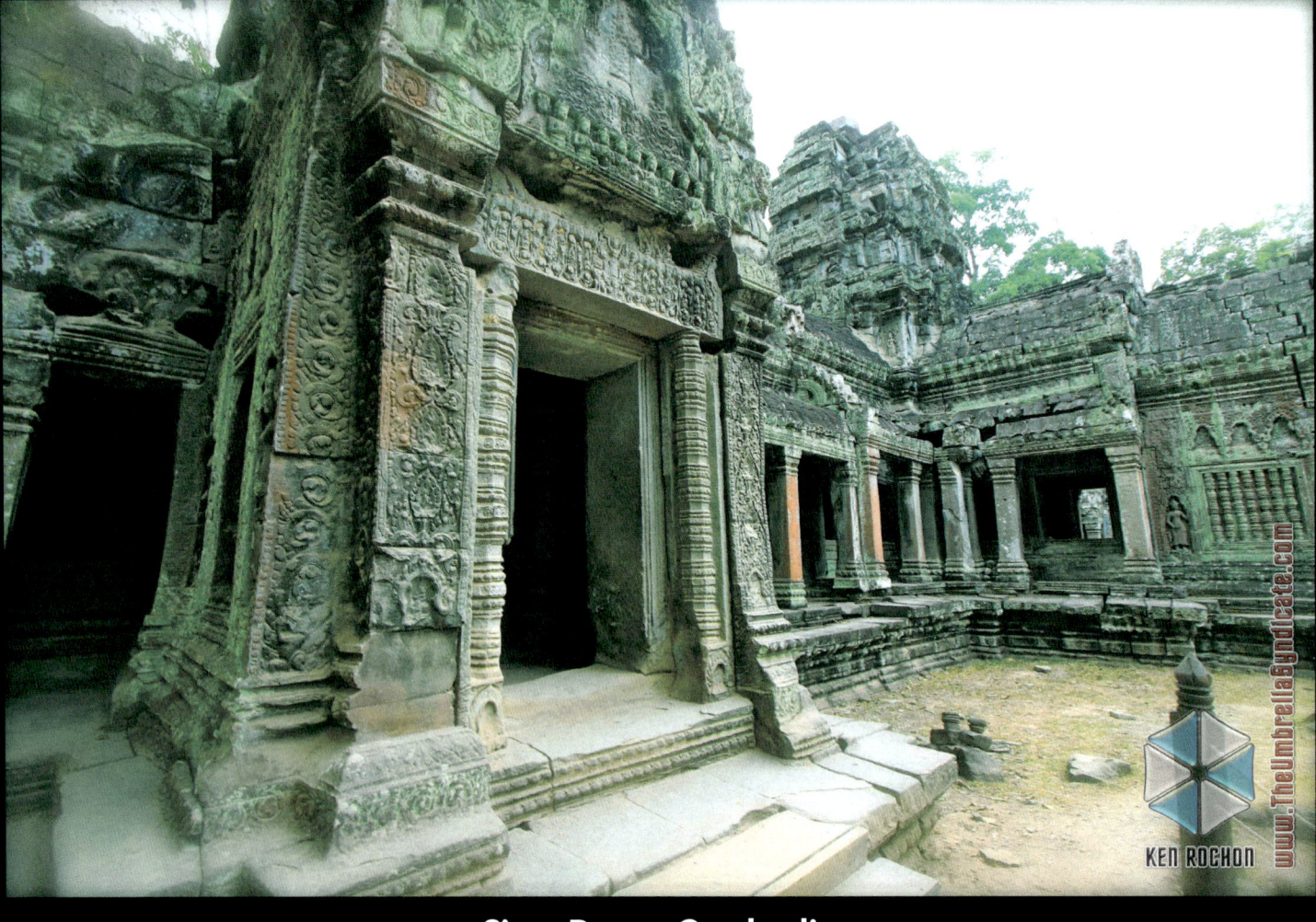

Siem Reap, Cambodia

KEN ROCHON www.TheUmbrellaSyndicate.com

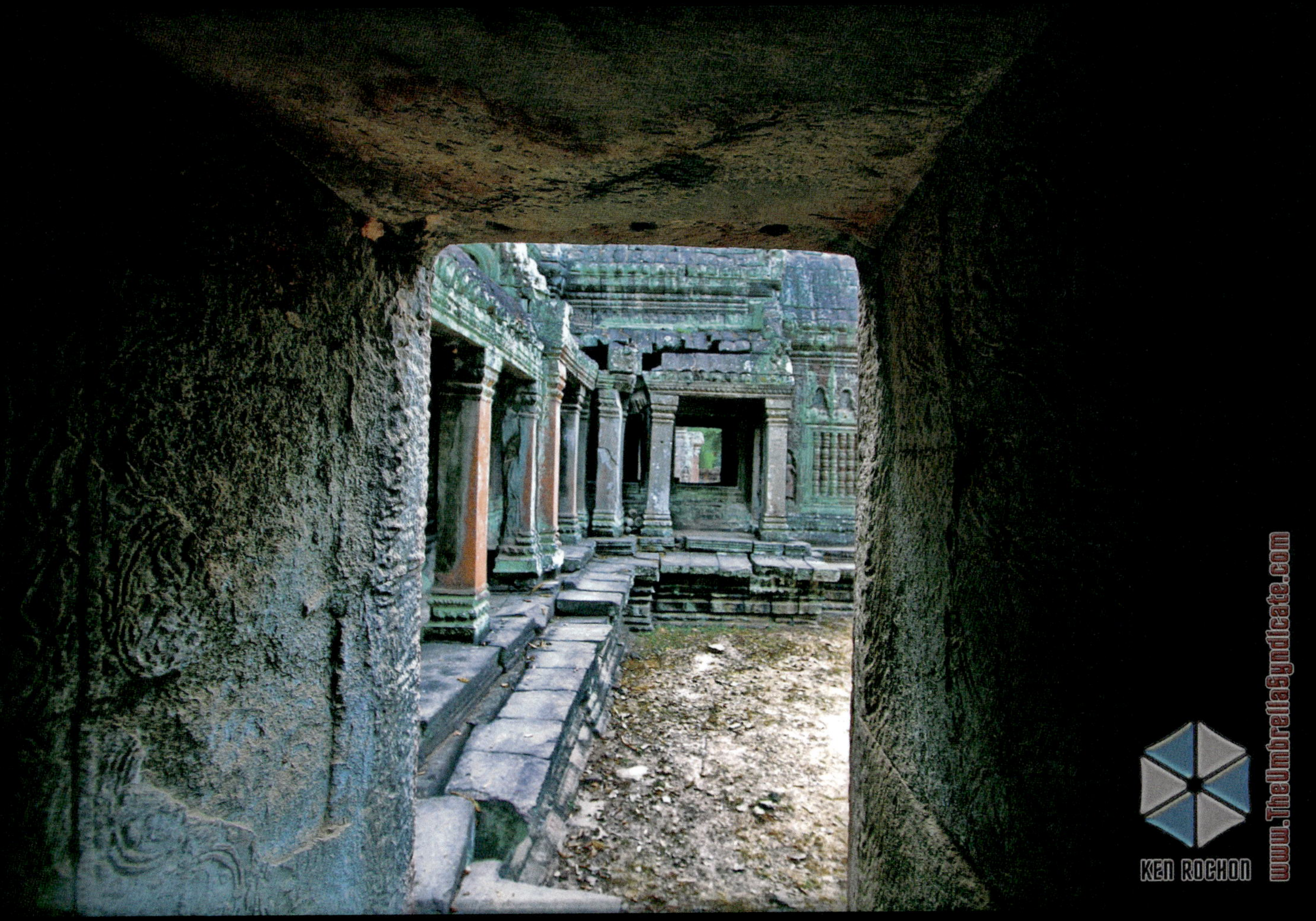

Siem Reap, Cambodia

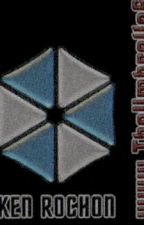

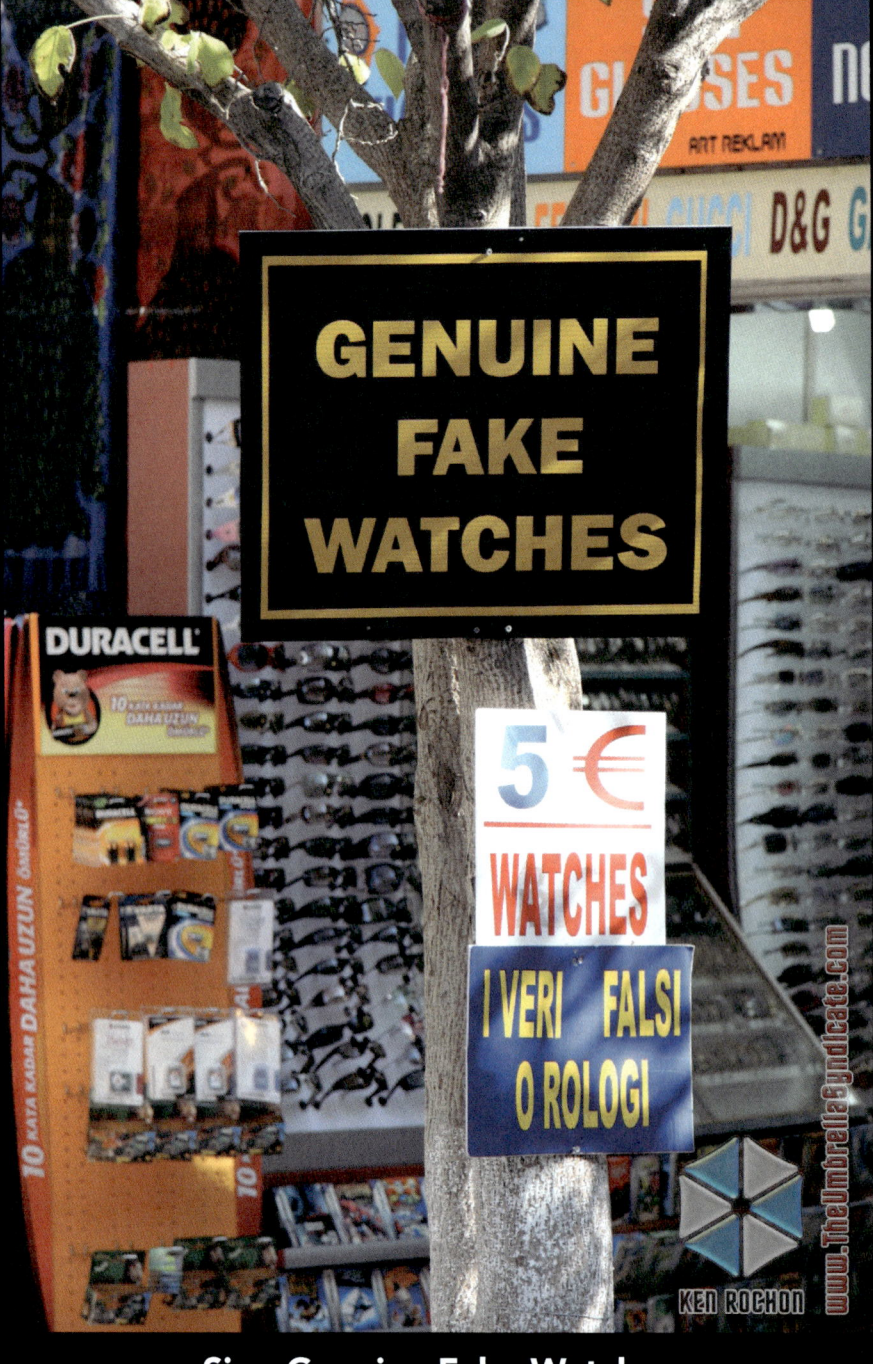

Sign Genuine Fake Watches

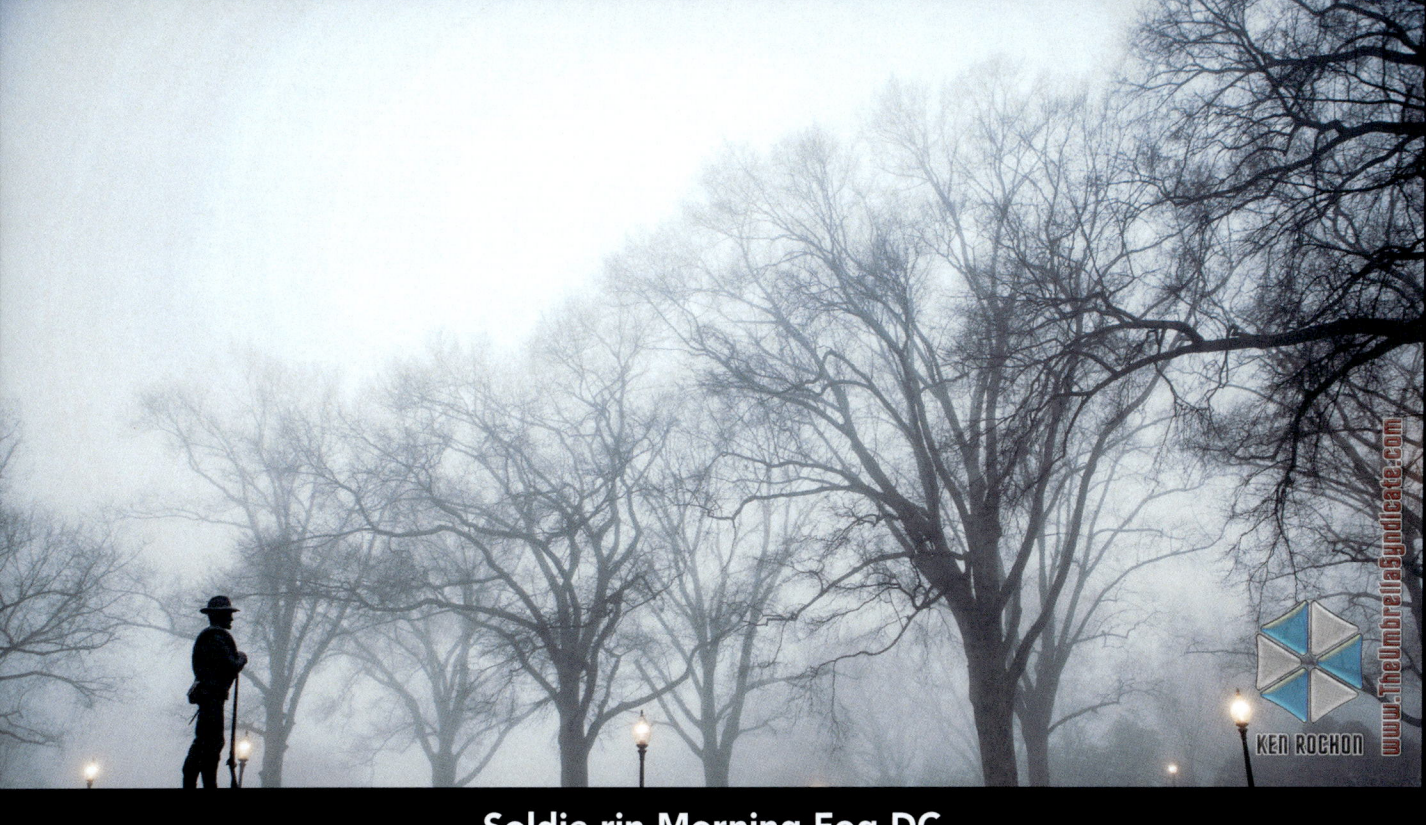

Soldie rin Morning Fog DC

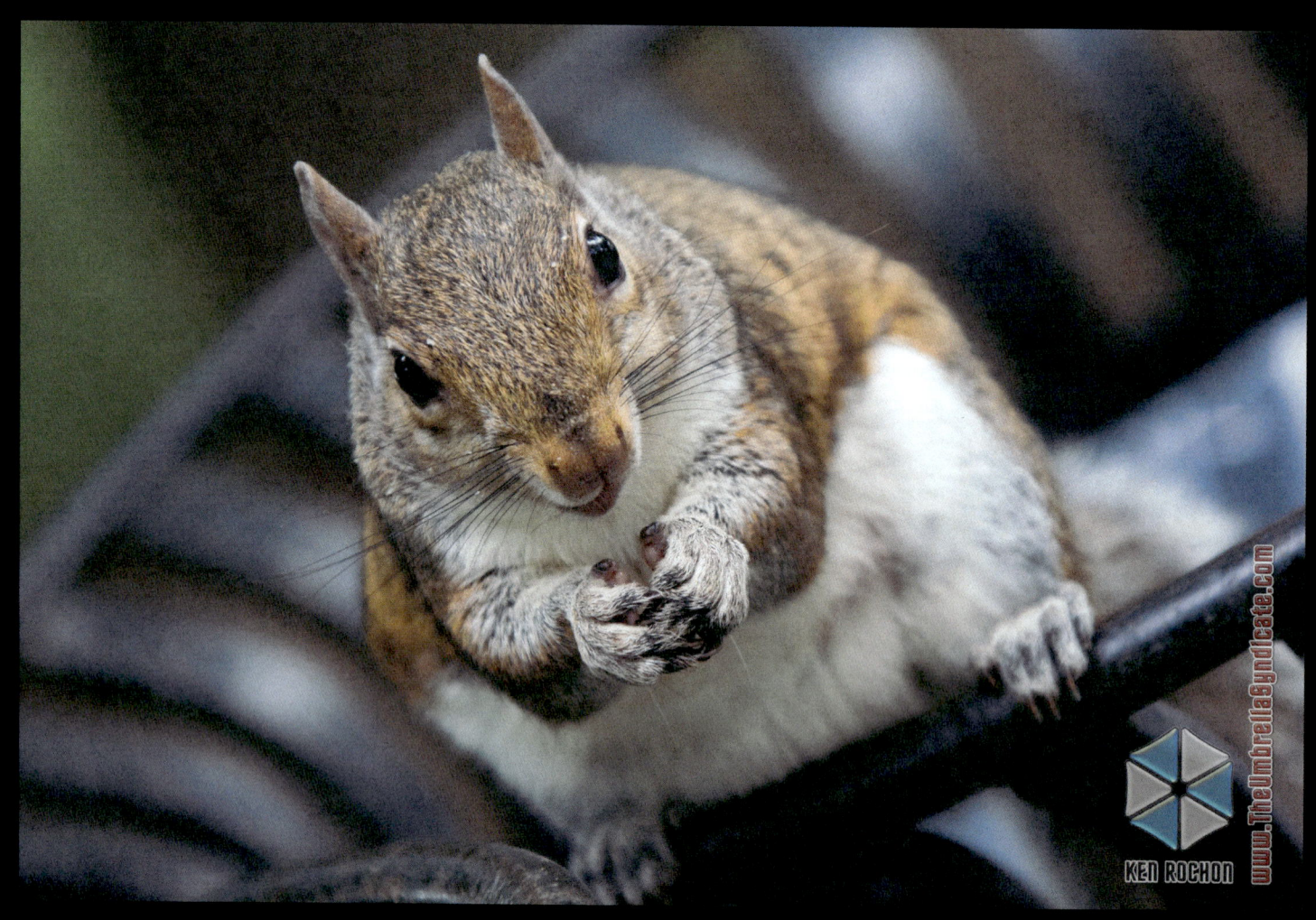

Squirrel Break

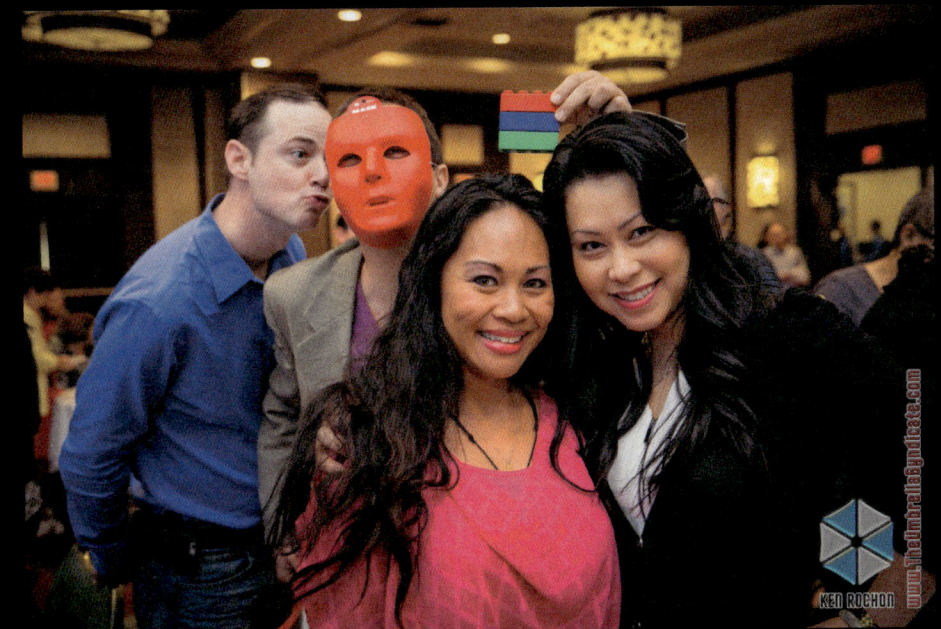

Photobomb

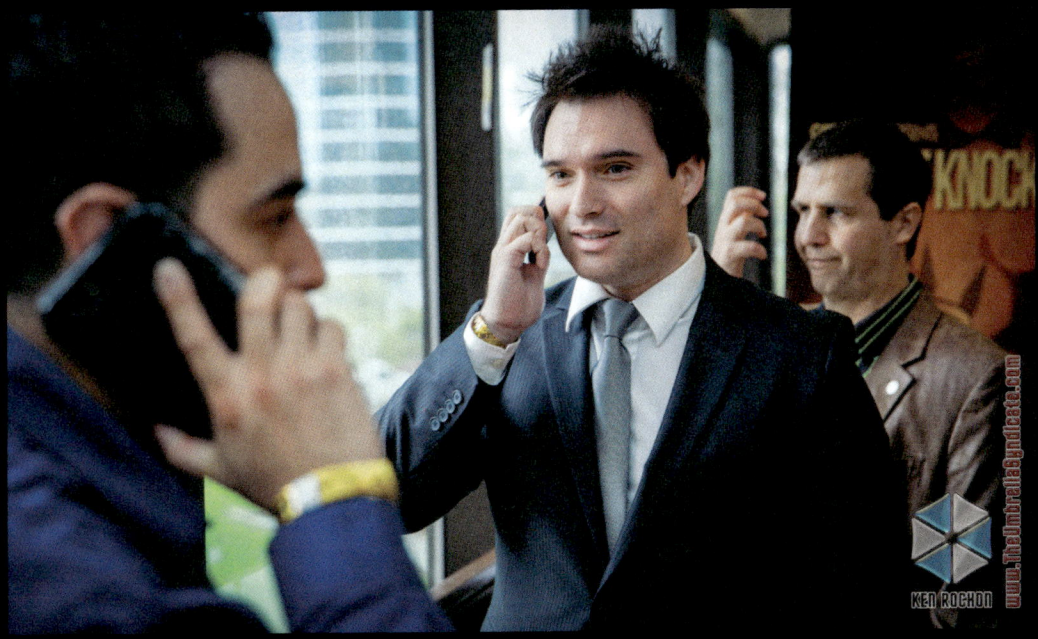

Triple Phone Photobomb

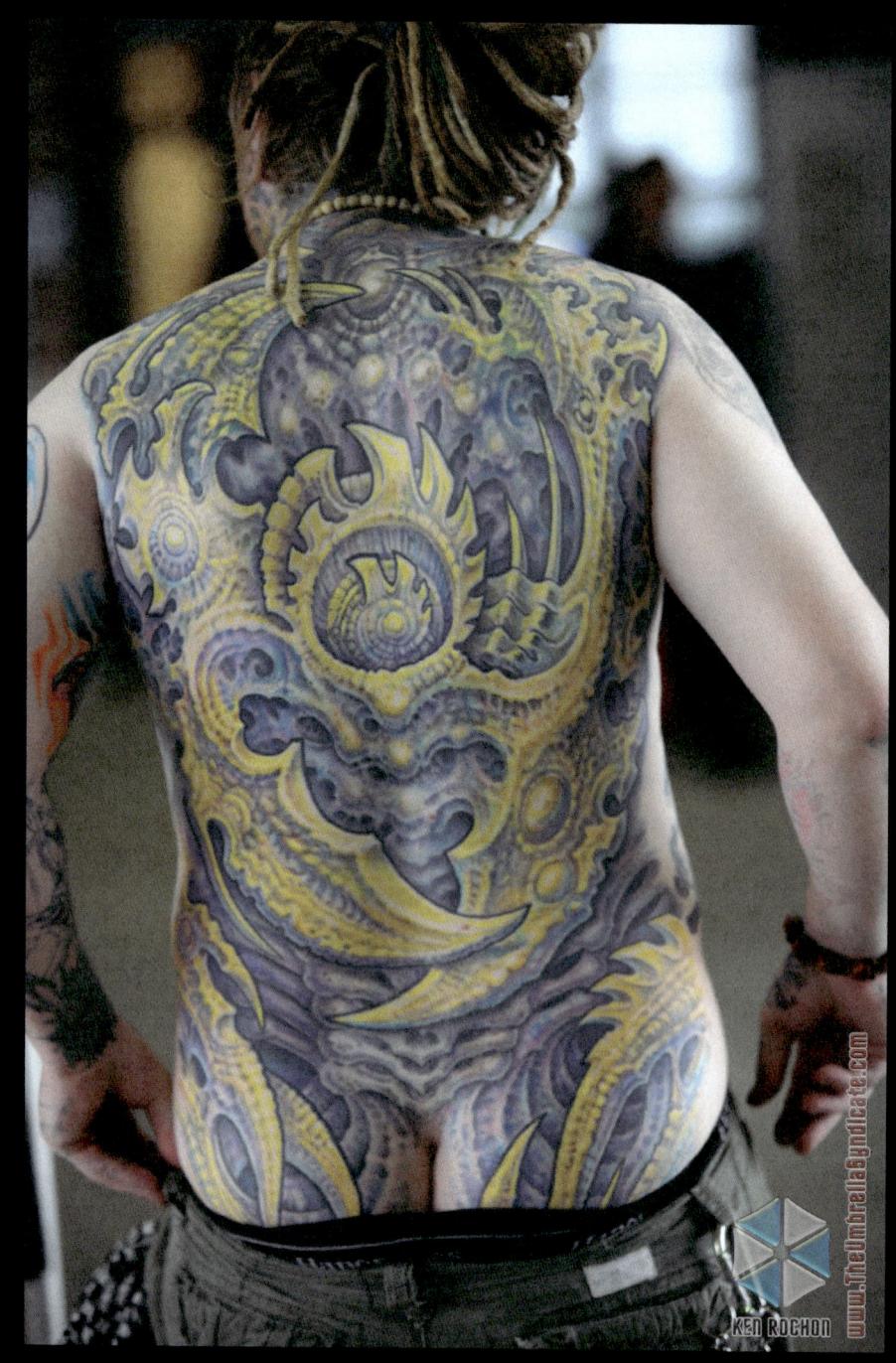

Tattoo My Ass

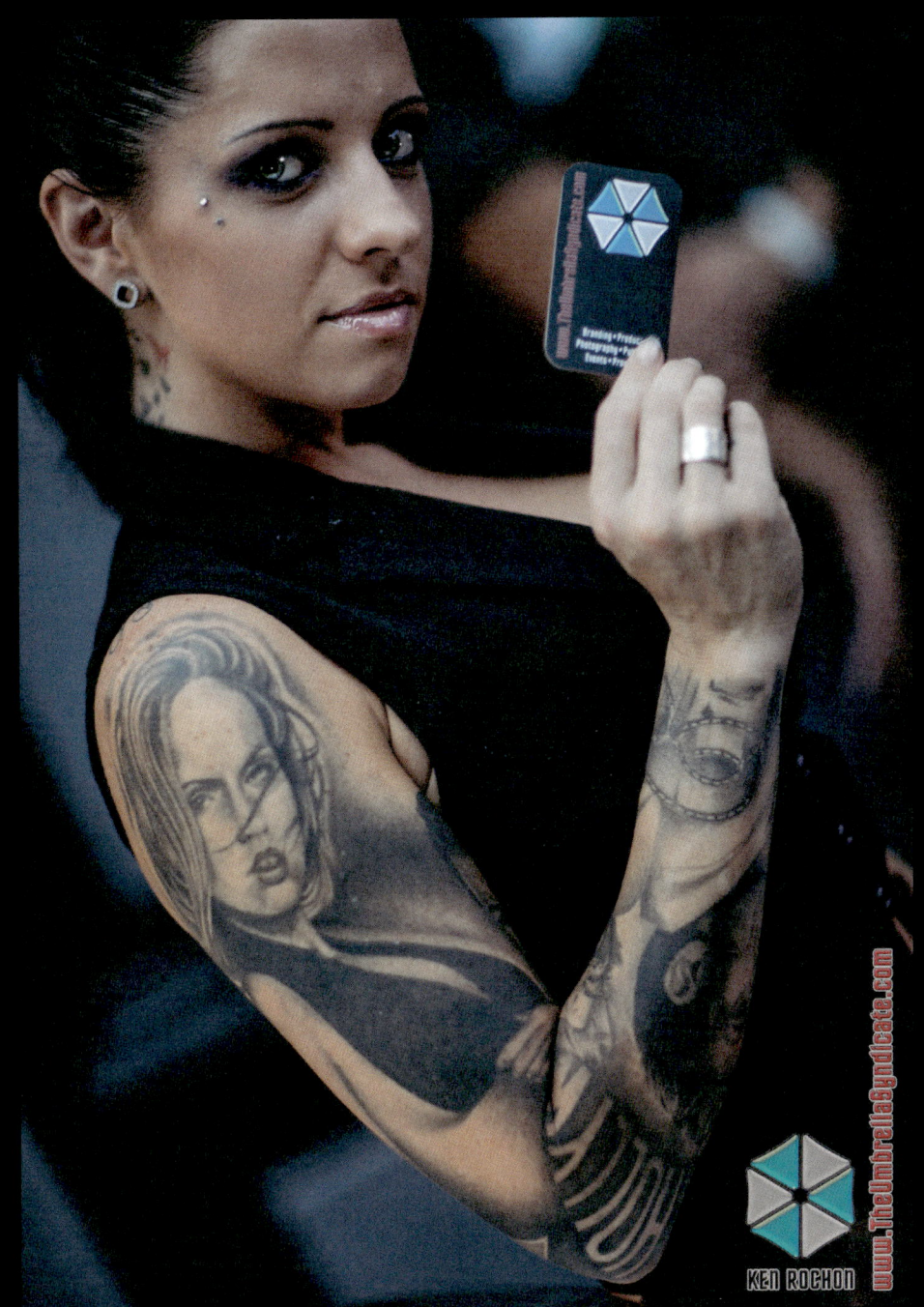

Tattoo Umbrella Girl

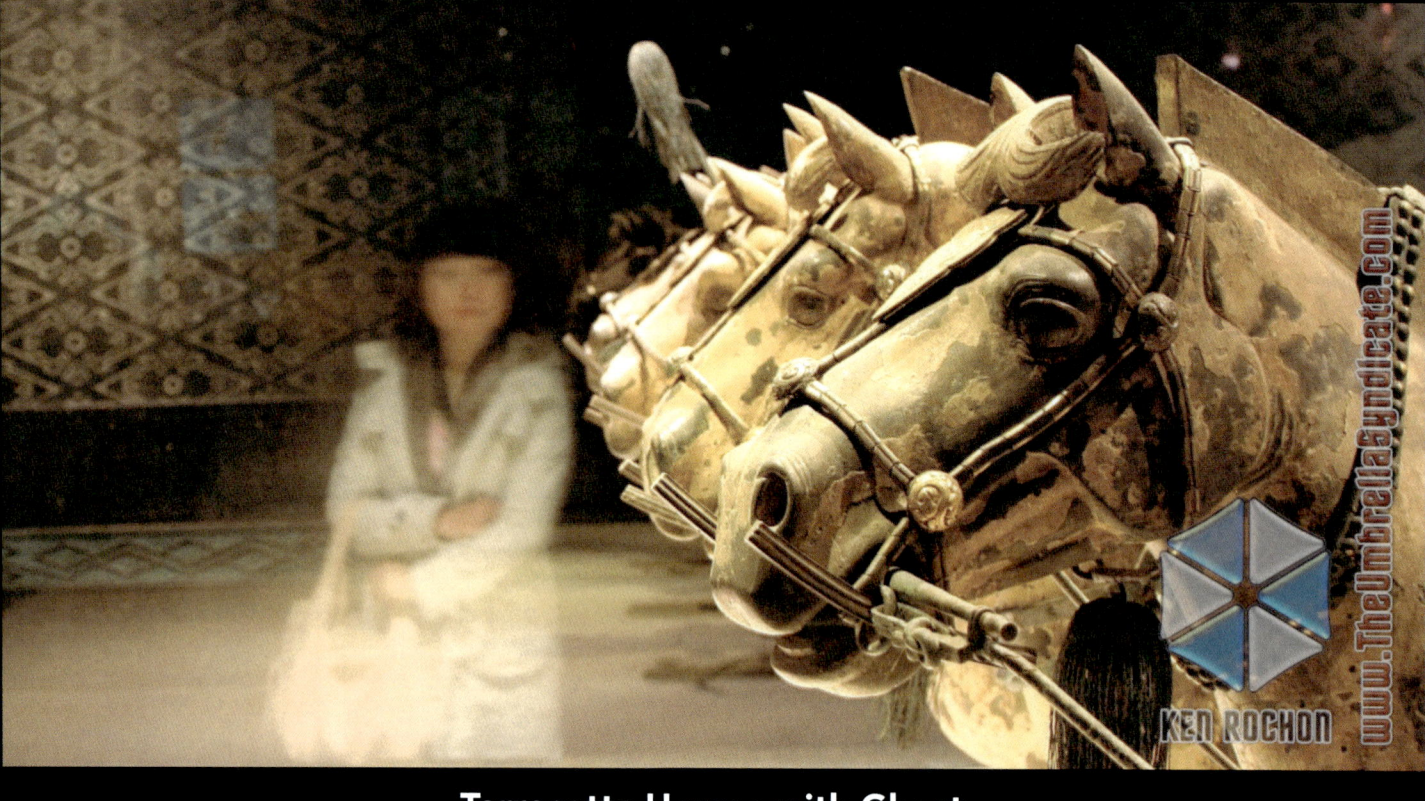

Terracotta Horses with Ghost

www.TheUmbrellaSyndicate.com

KEN ROCHON

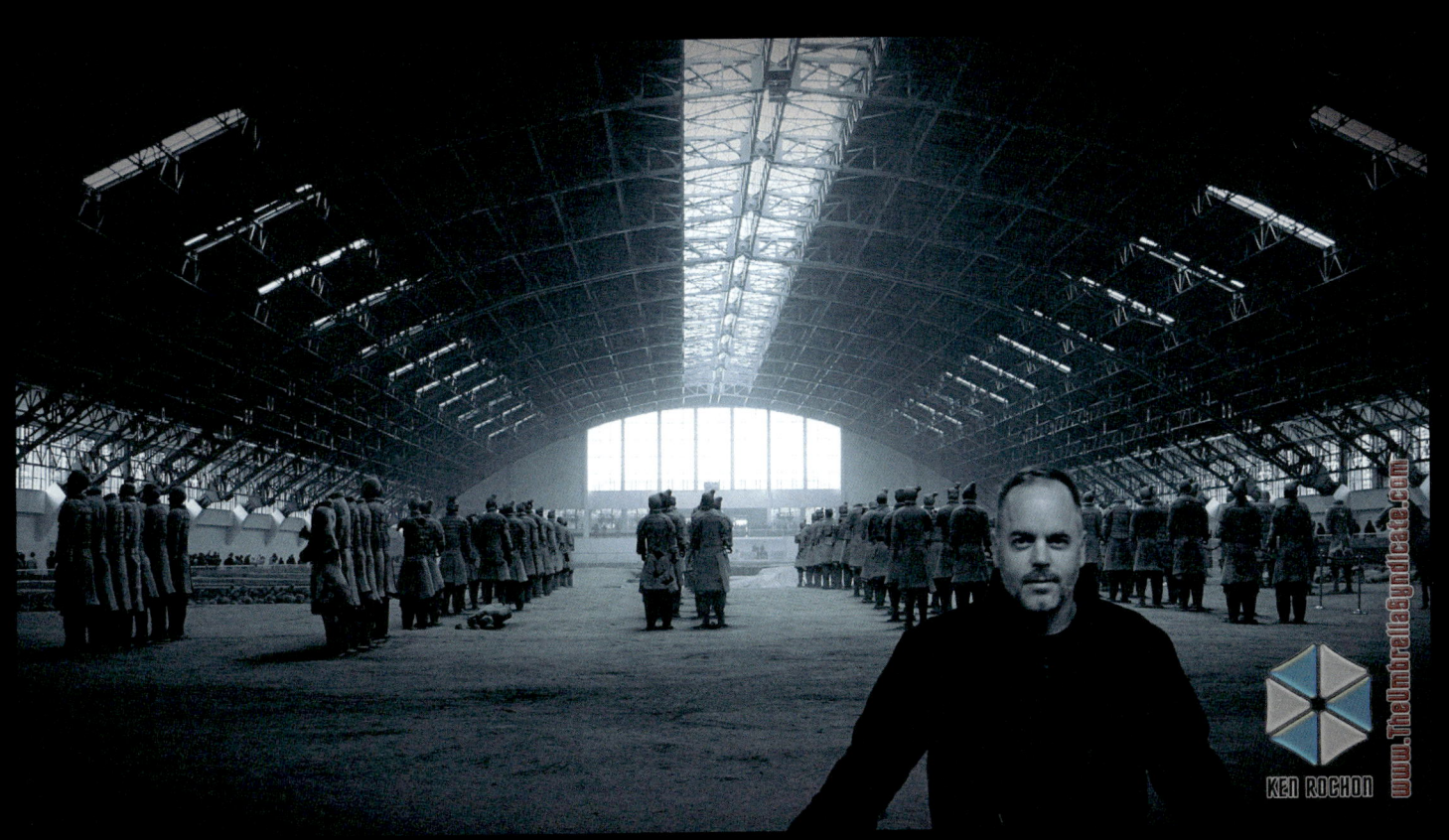

Terracotta Warrior Xian

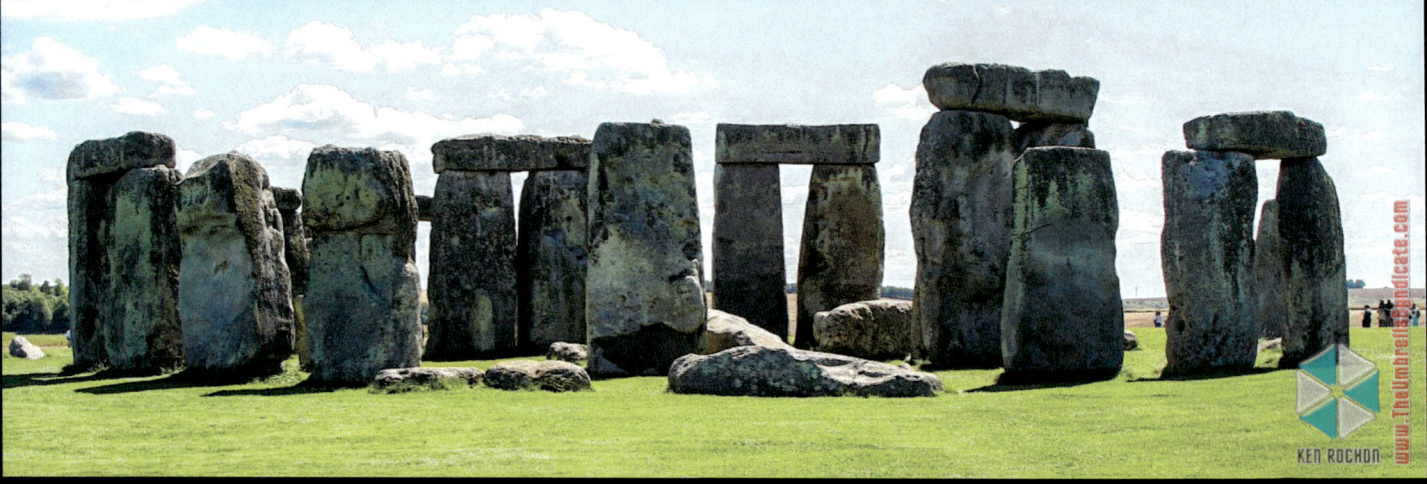

Stone Henge

KEN ROCHON www.TheUmbrellaSyndicate.com

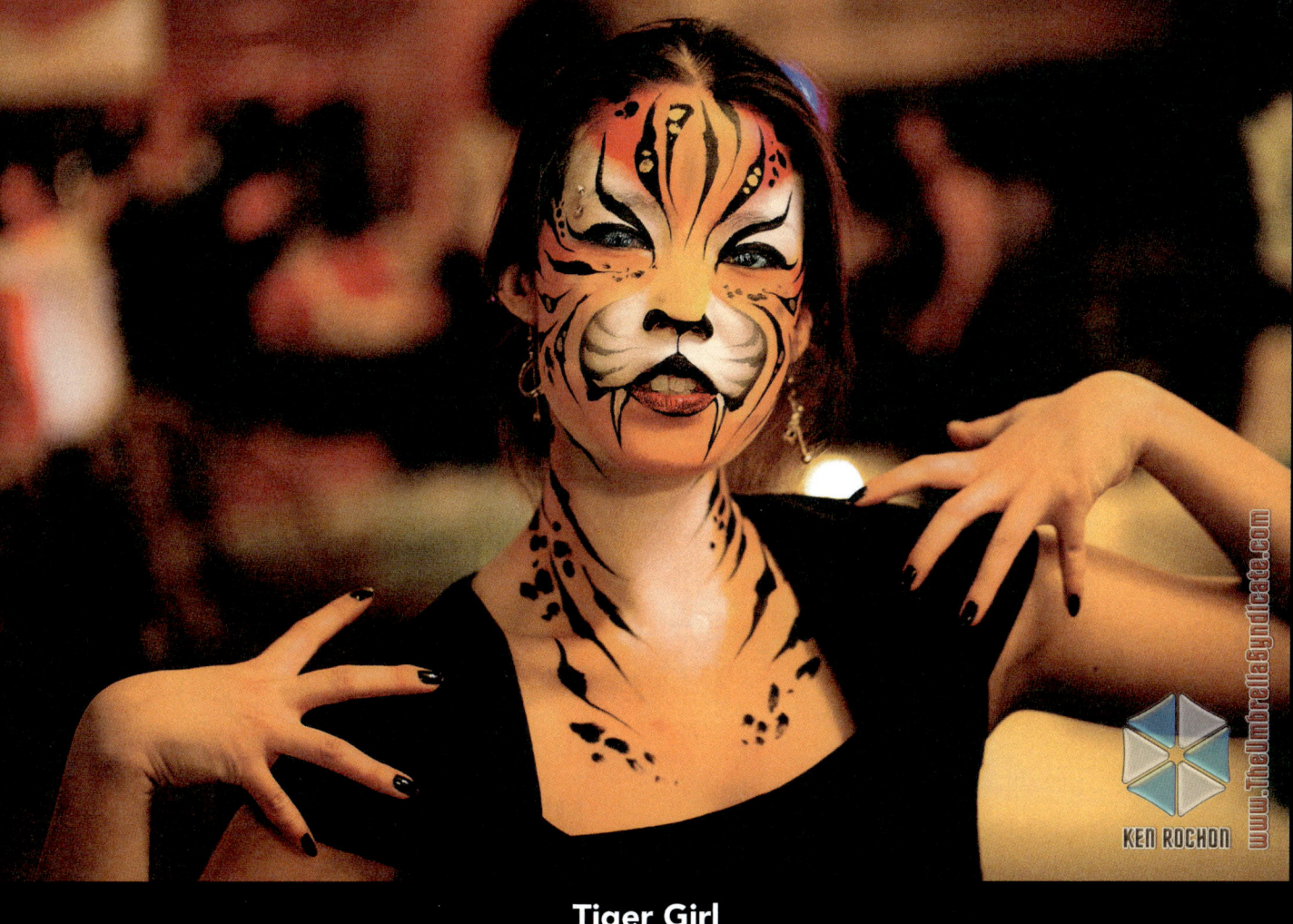

Tiger Girl

www.TheUmbrellaSyndicate.com

KEN ROCHON

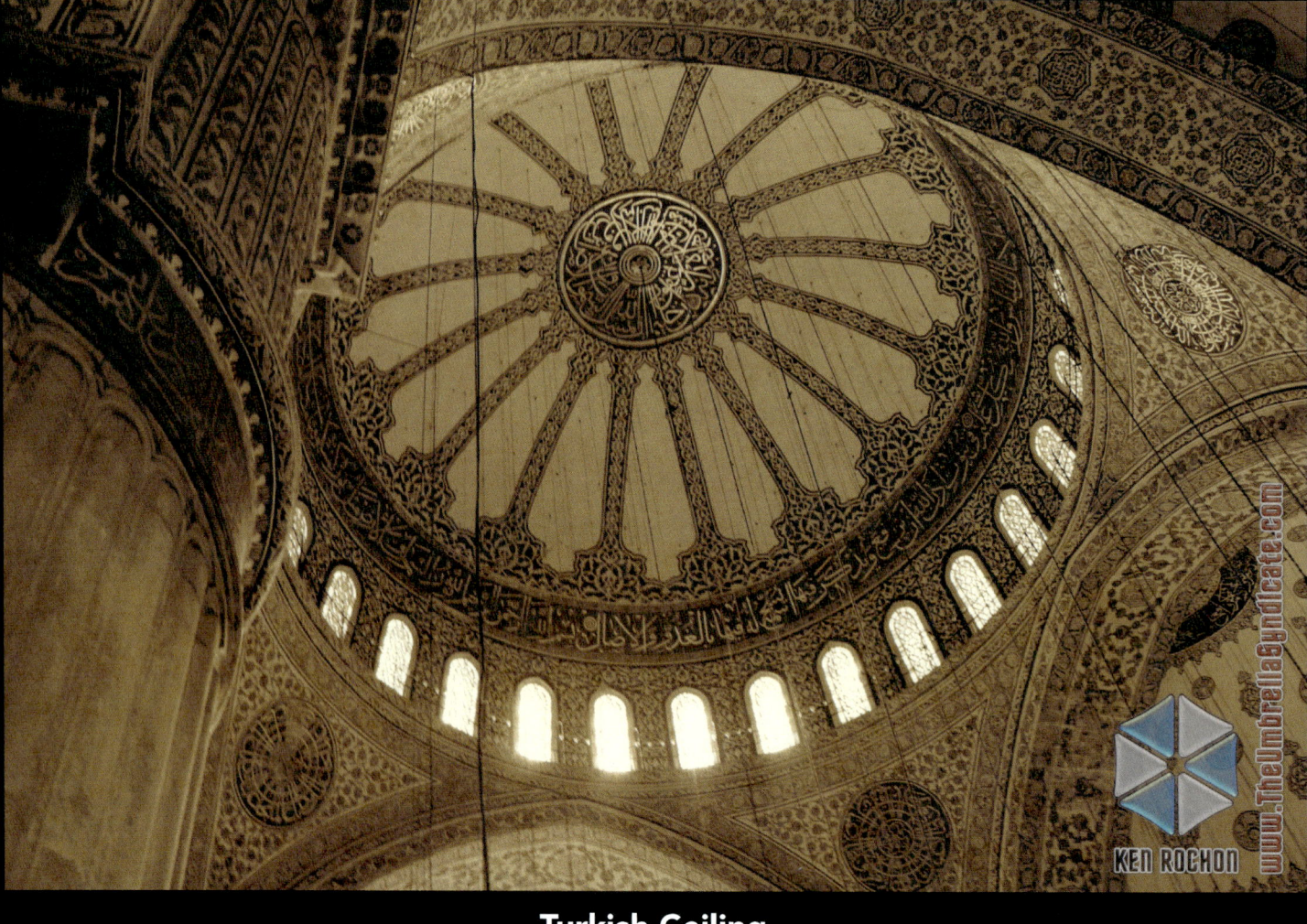

www.TheUmbrellaSyndicate.com

KEN ROCHON

Turkish Ceiling

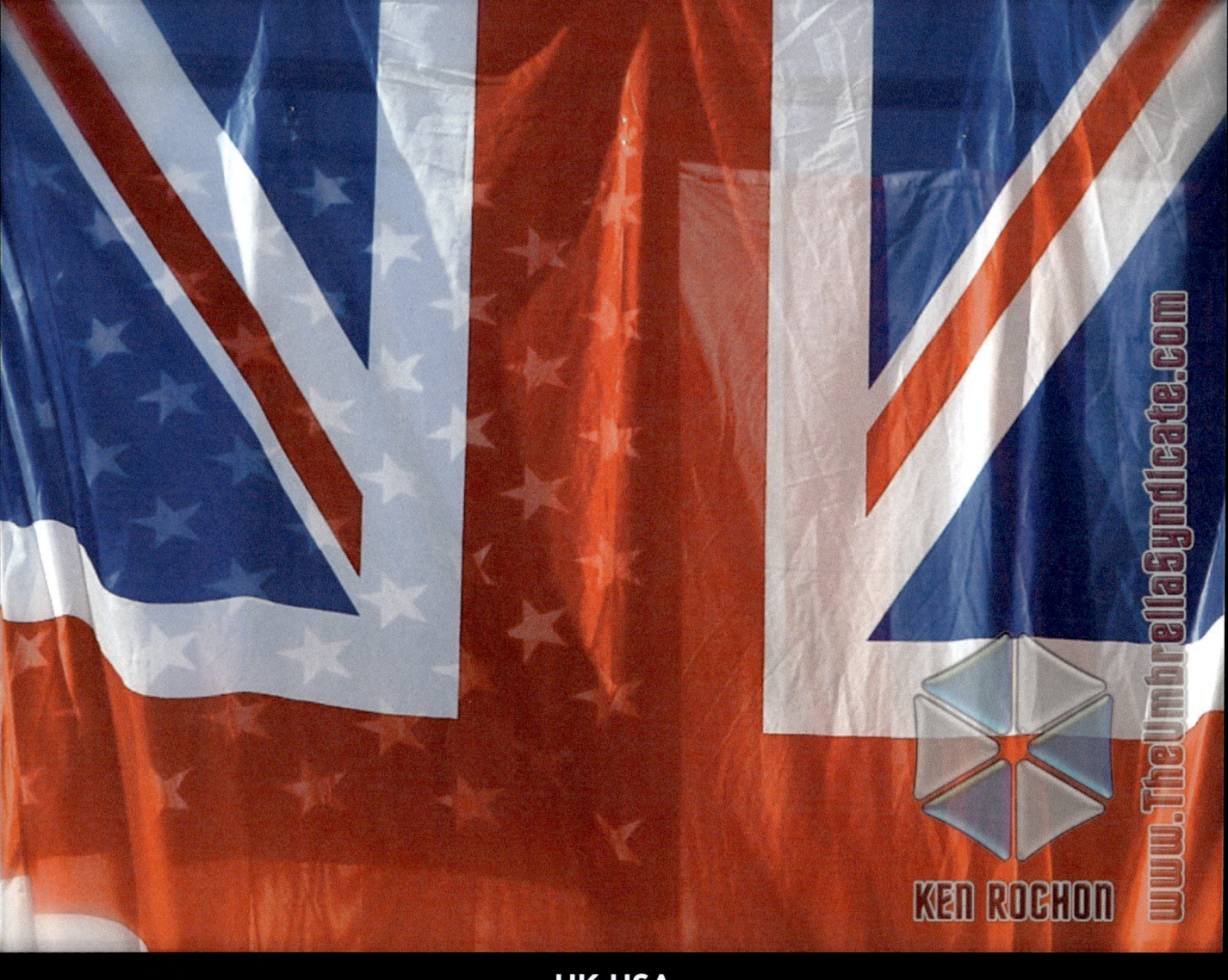

KEN ROCHON

www.TheUmbrellaSyndicate.com

UK USA

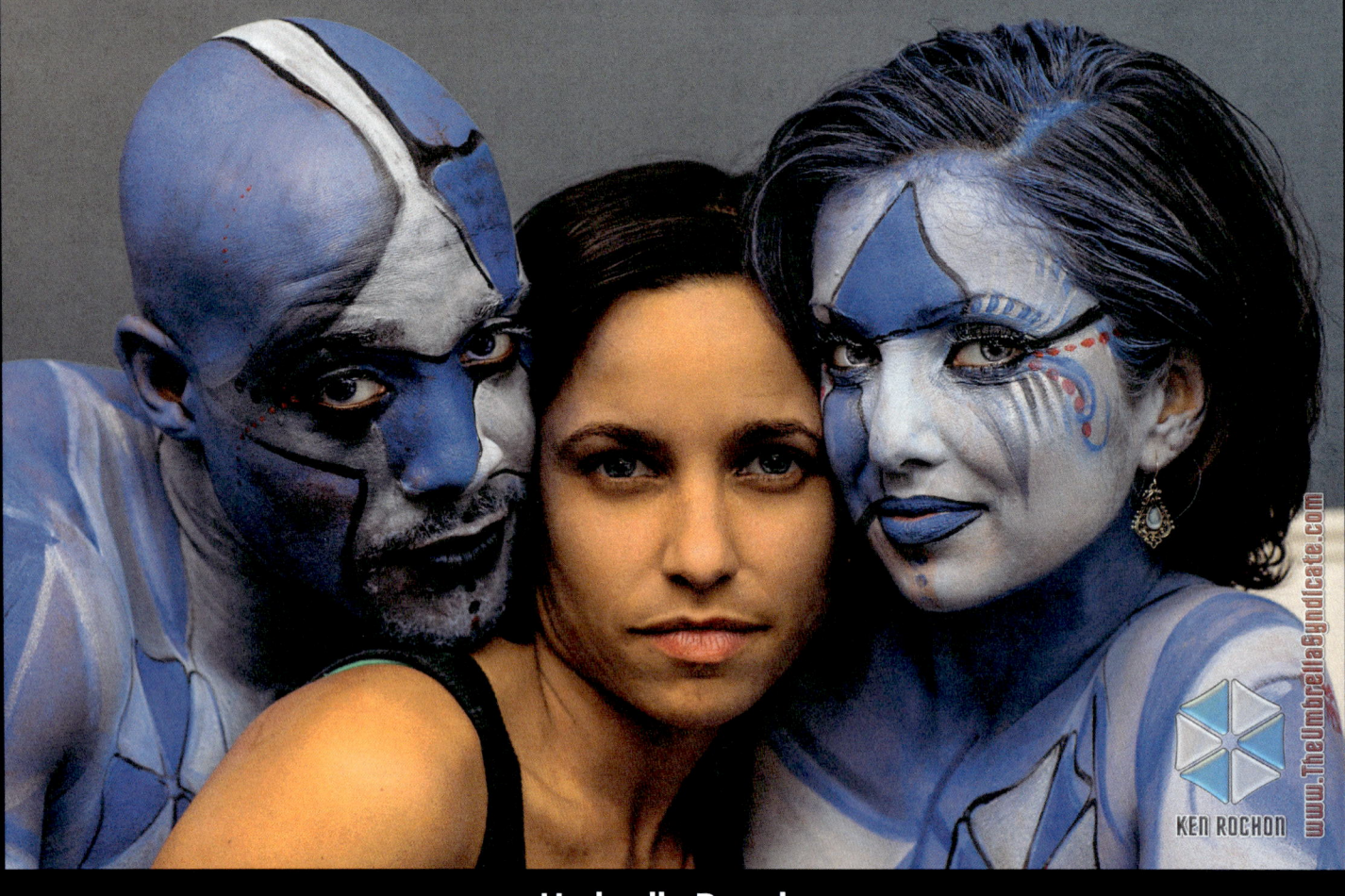

Umbrella People

KEN ROCHON

www.TheUmbrellaSyndicate.com

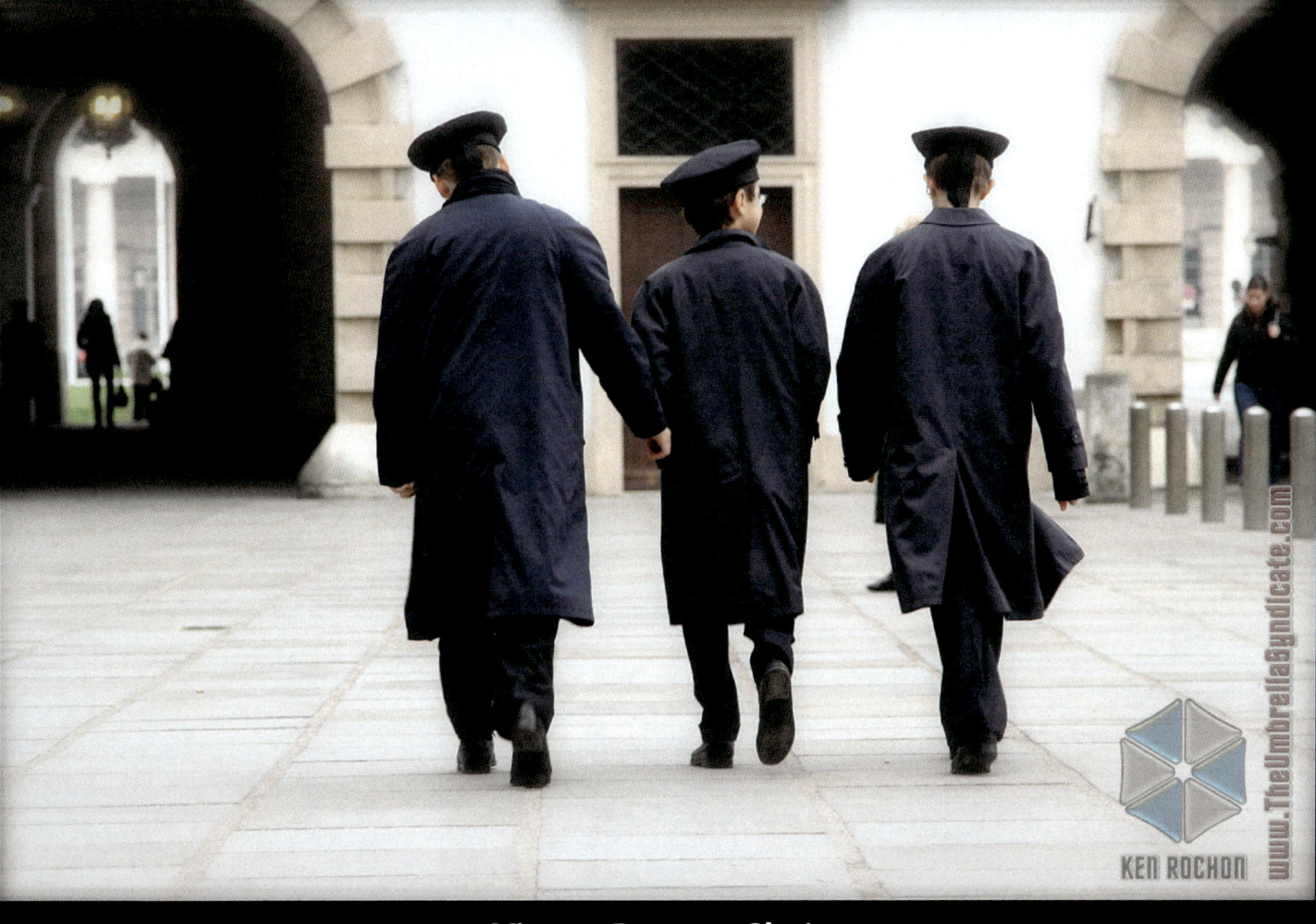

Vienna Boys to Choir

www.TheUmbrellaSyndicate.com

KEN ROCHON

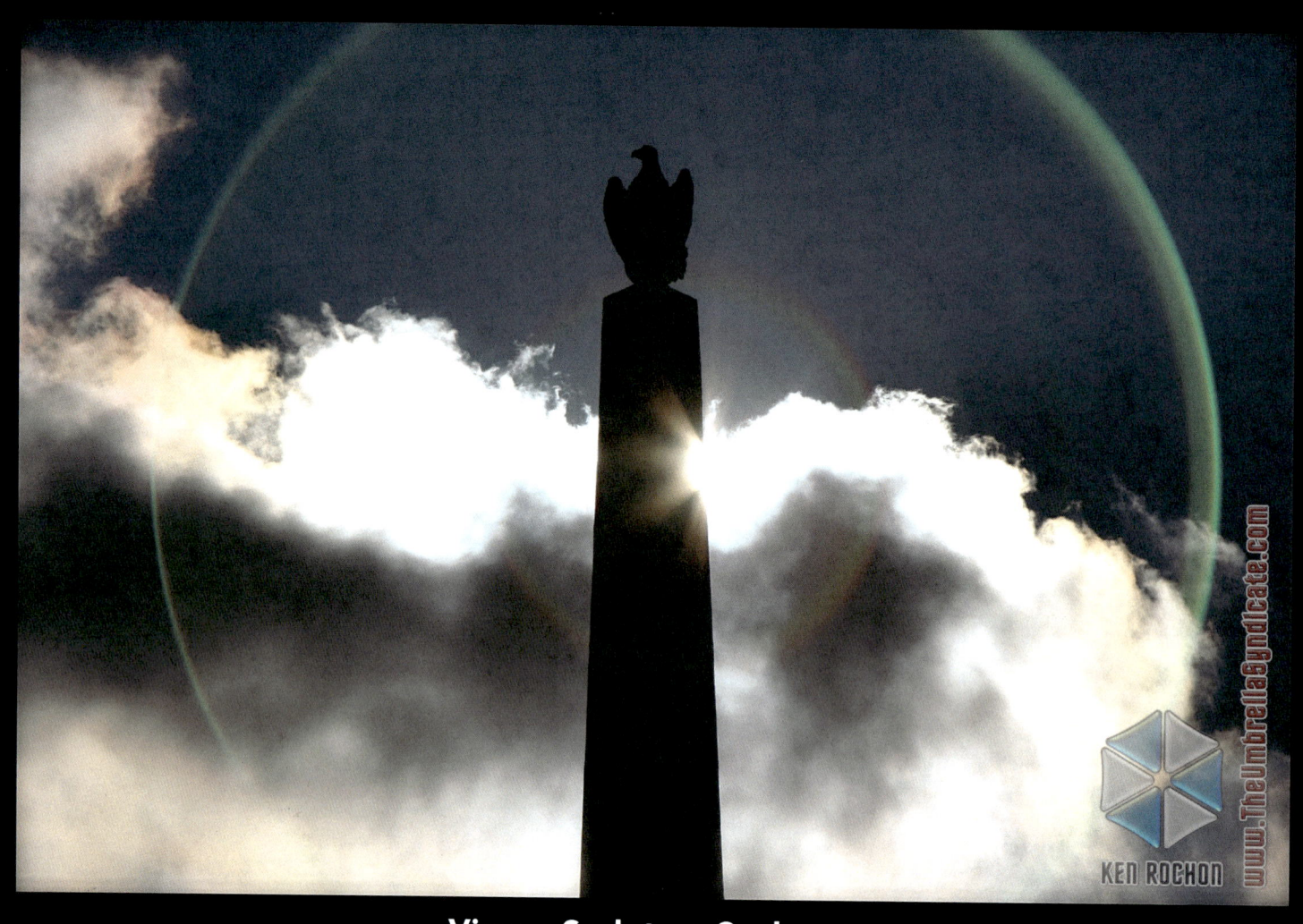

Vienna Sculpture Sunburst

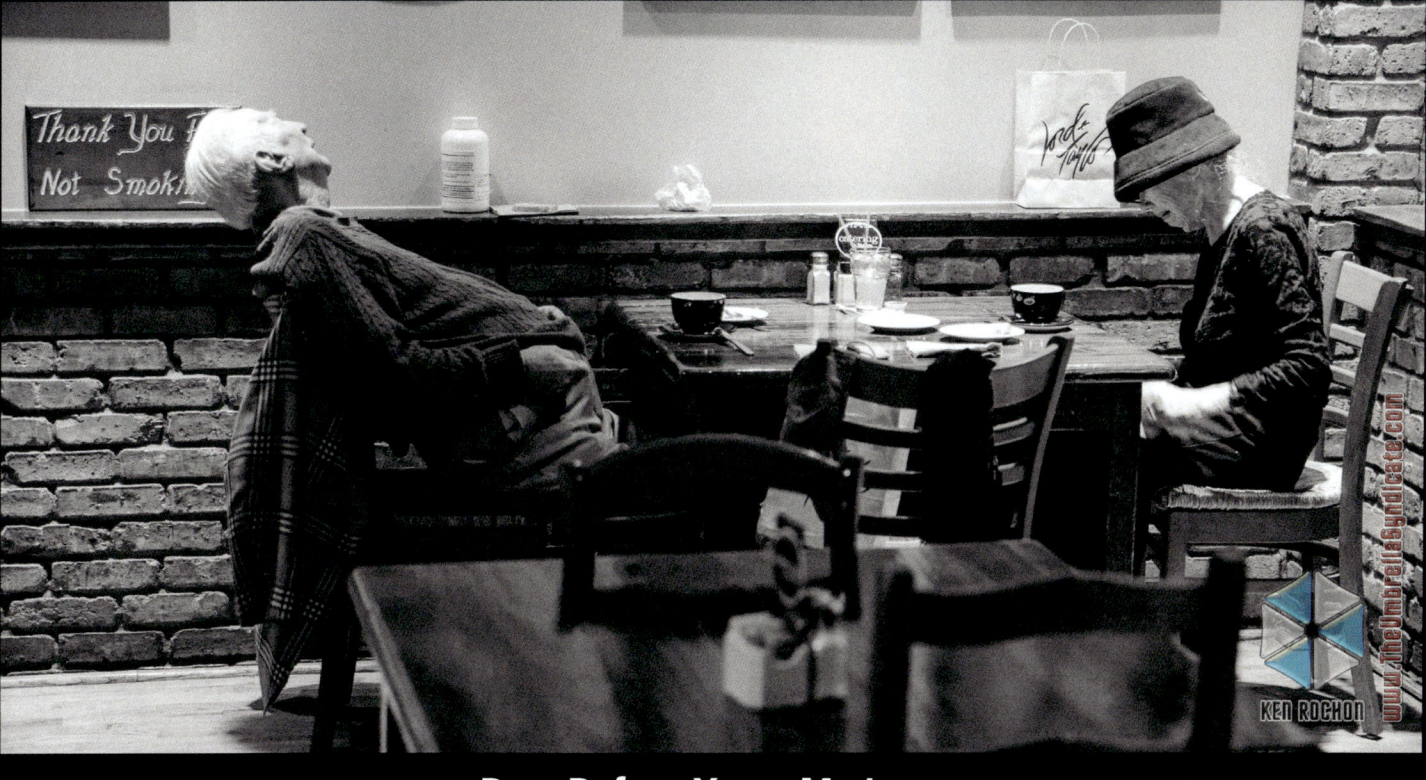

Pass Before You... My Love

KEN ROCHON

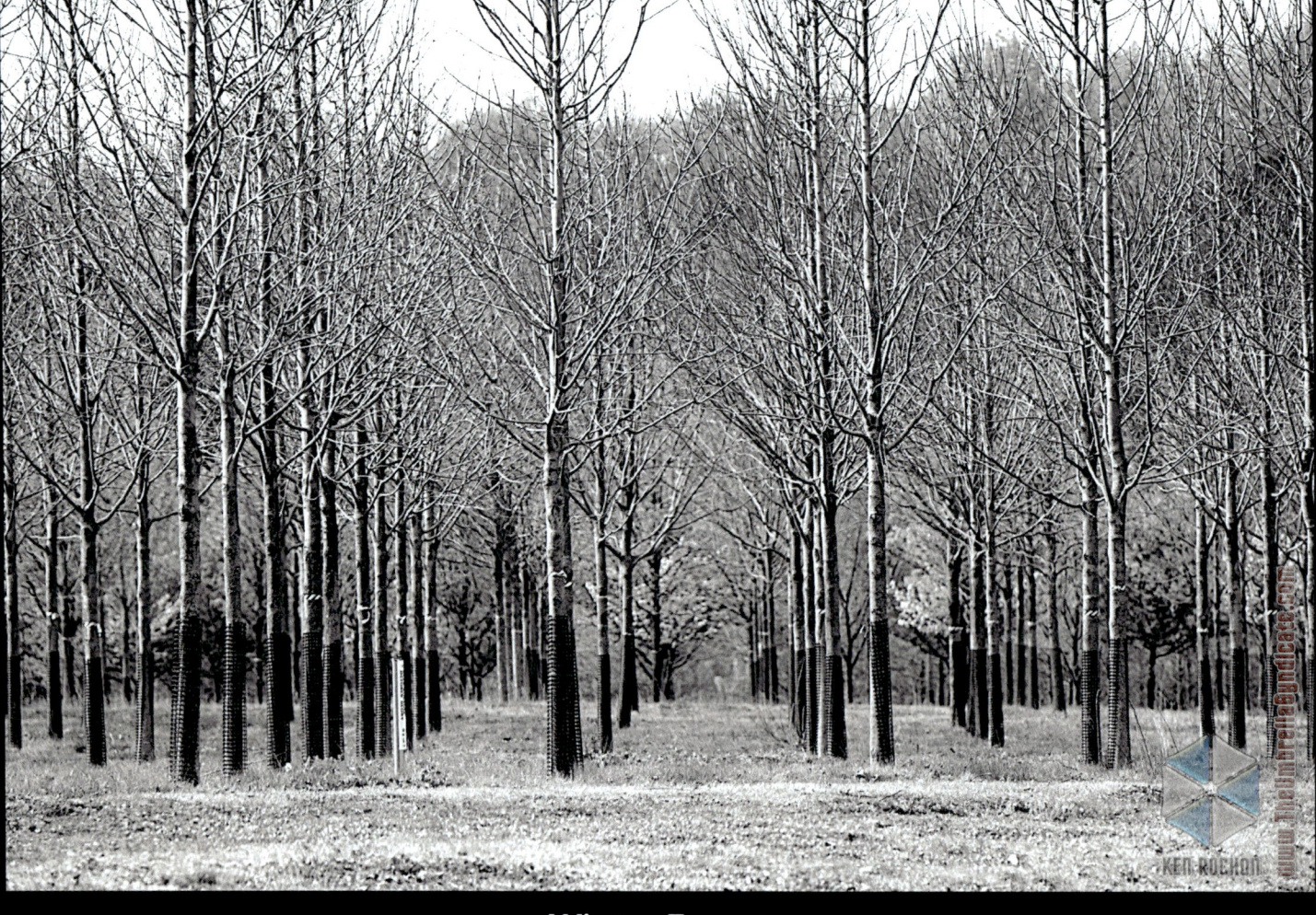

Winter Forest

www.TheUmbrellaSyndicate.com

KEN ROCKON

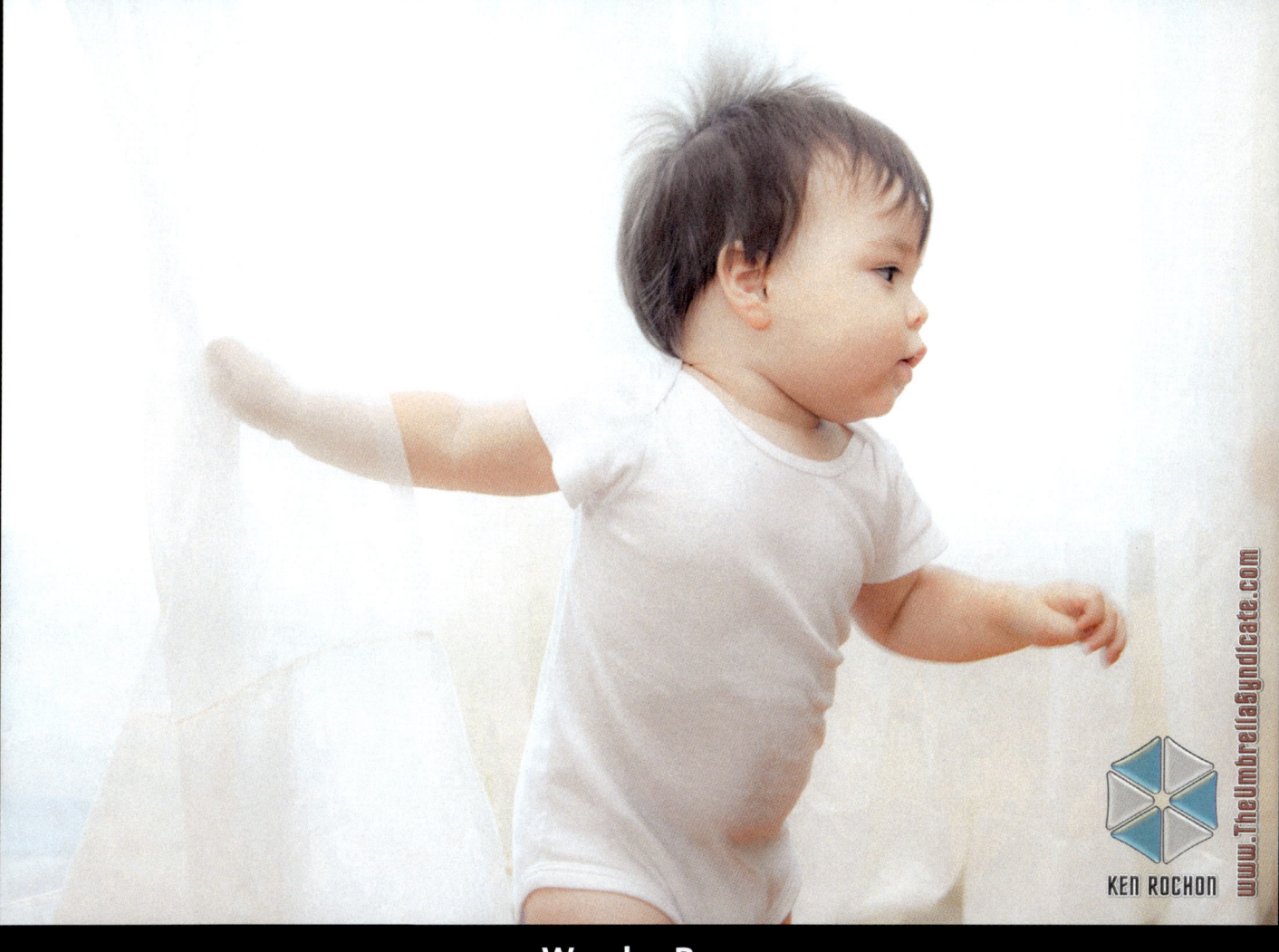

www.TheUmbrellaSyndicate.com

KEN ROCHON

Wonder Boy

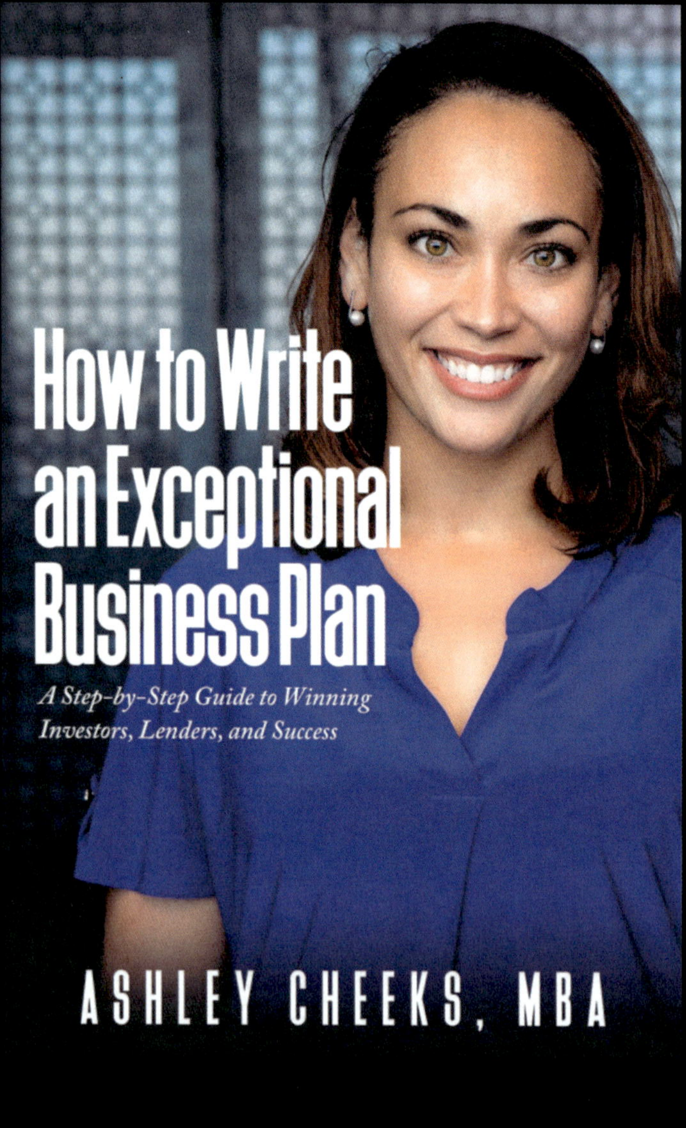

How to Write an Exceptional Business Plan

A Step-by-Step Guide to Winning Investors, Lenders, and Success

ASHLEY CHEEKS, MBA

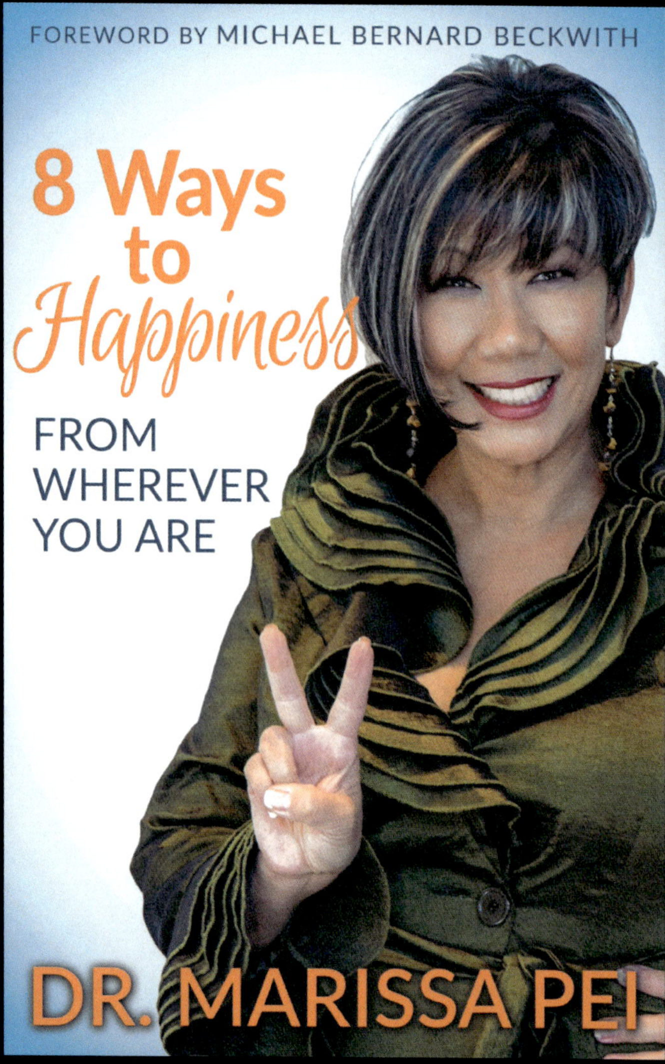

FOREWORD BY MICHAEL BERNARD BECKWITH

8 Ways to Happiness

FROM WHEREVER YOU ARE

DR. MARISSA PEI

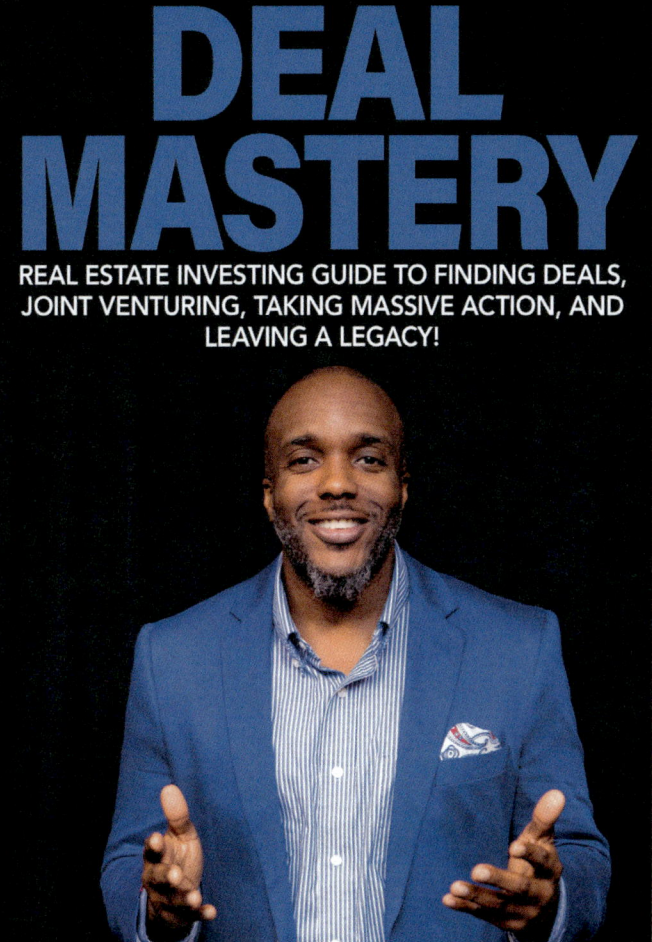

DEAL MASTERY

REAL ESTATE INVESTING GUIDE TO FINDING DEALS, JOINT VENTURING, TAKING MASSIVE ACTION, AND LEAVING A LEGACY!

ANDRE JOHNSON

Foreword by Best-Selling Author – Steve Farber

SOFT AS STEEL

QUALITIES OF LEADERS AND EVERYBODY ELSE

DENNIS D. DORAN

MICHELLE ROBINSON & FRIENDS

TEXAS
Sweetheart
COOKBOOK

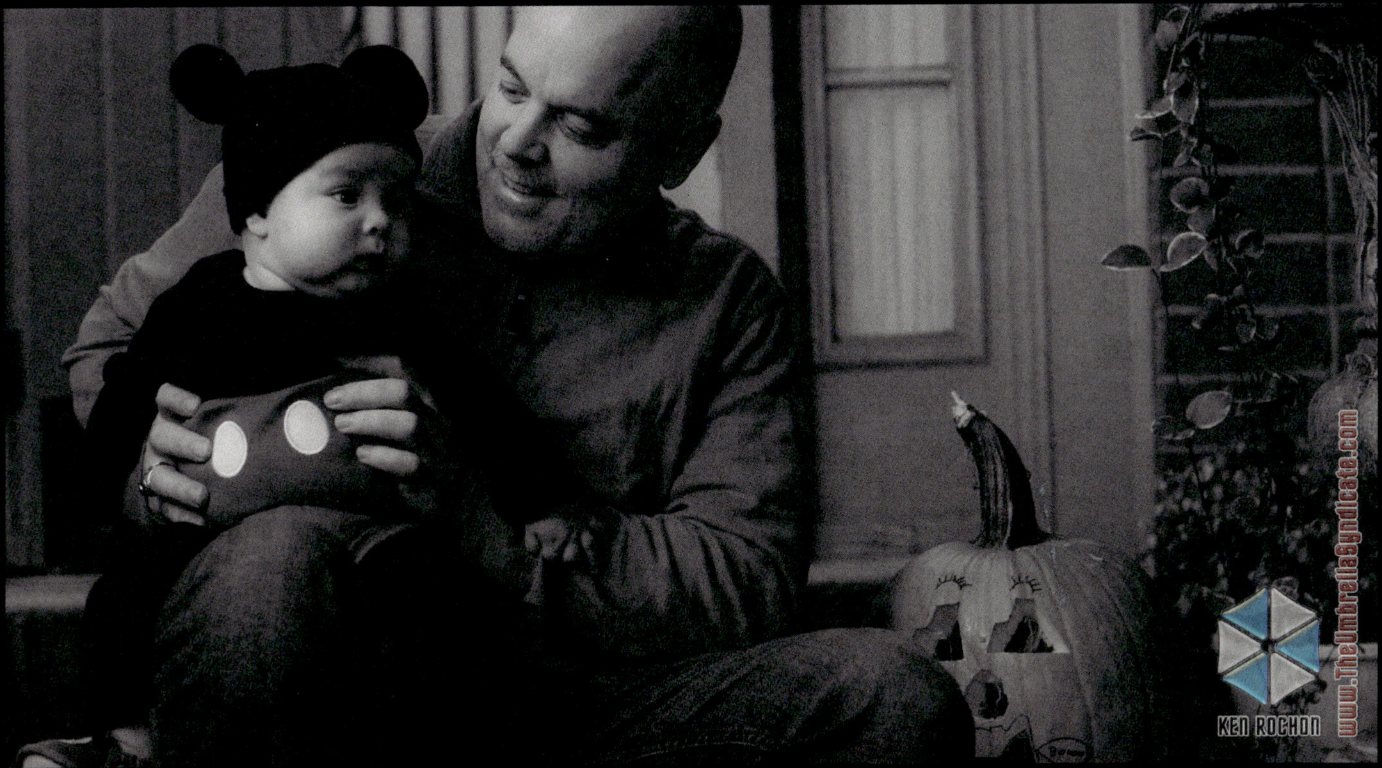

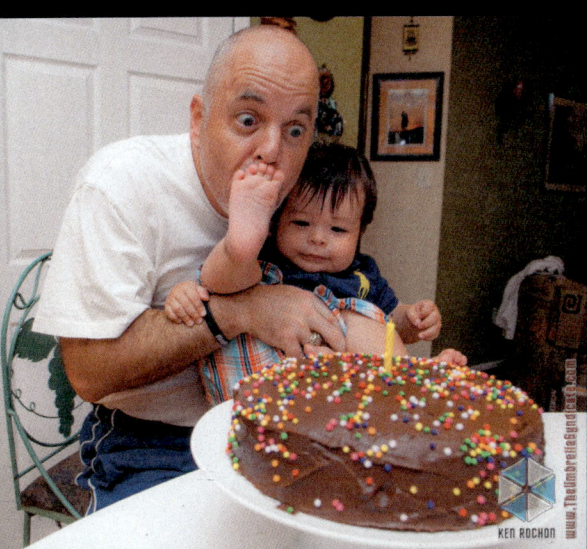

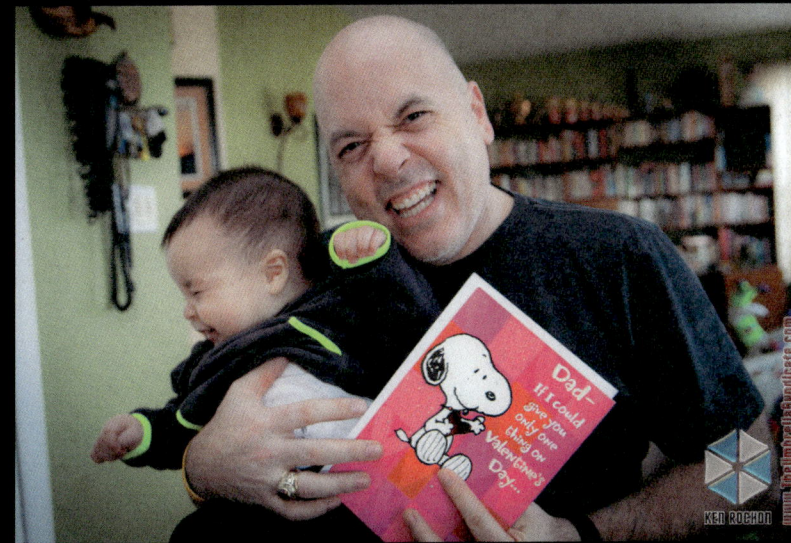

About Ken Rochon Jr.

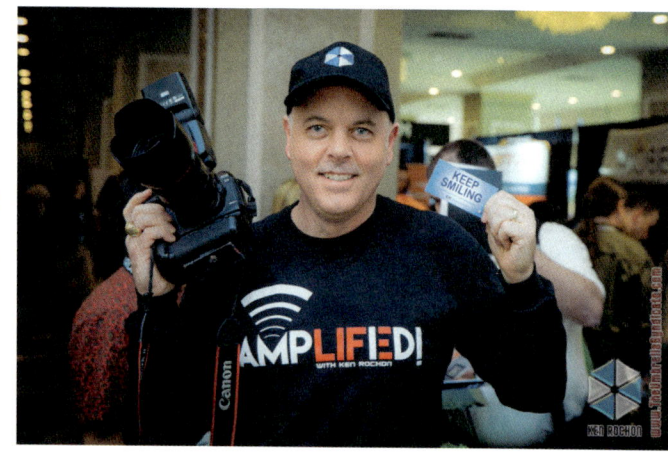

Ken Rochon, Jr. is an internationally recognized dynamic speaker, author, social media expert and connector. He is a renaissance spiritual leader, who loves the arts, sciences and people.

After losing his mom to Alzheimer's disease in 2008, he searched for the ultimate meaning and purpose for his life. He prayed for a sign that would allow him to dedicate his life to service and utilize his skill sets to amplify leaders making a positive impact in the world.

Ken's ability to capture and captivate the human spirit at live events, on the radio, through speaking, photography and writing are highly recognized as evidenced in the multiple hundreds of reviews and recommendations. His love for his mom cause him to take more actions, which resulted in the sign he prayed for. His evidence was the avalanche multiple hundreds of 5-Star reviews and recommendations. Ken is creating a dynamic positive impact and building a legacy for himself and other leaders. He is Internationally recognized as an influencer that uses his gifts and creates platforms and systems to amplify the messages of leaders that desire to change the world.

"Ken Rochon is a master at creating social proof. He and The Umbrella Syndicate team are fantastic with guests and really know how to connect everyone in the room. He consistently produces fantastic work and we are always so happy to have him speak and photograph at our You Will Change The World summits and masterminds" Peter Anthony Wynn, Founder of 'You Will Change The World'

The Umbrella Syndicate (TUS) was created, by Ken, with six elements represented by each segment of the umbrella that strategically and synergistically move the vision of a leader beyond their own minds eye. He studied strategies of leveraging like-minded and like hearted audiences to create these epic social proof campaigns for the leaders he chose to serve. Ken has created a formula that captures and catapults the message that wakes the world up with a positive frequency that inspires people to learn more.

"Ken and the Umbrella Team are probably the most proactive, positive and professional media I have ever seen. If you want viral videos and photography, creative coverage and incredible insights into your event, brand or persona, they are the top of the food chain." Dave Crane

Ken is lifetime entrepreneur, starting in his teen years, founding and delivering excellence with the award winning company Absolute Entertainment. He continues as a visionary and leader with companies and movements such as; The Perfect Networker, Live Loco Love Studio, The Perfect Publishing Ken has authored 17 books on diverse topics; children, linguistics, marketing, networking, and travel. He has published over 50 solo and compilation books. His current book 'Keep Smiling Shift Happens!' has caused a movement of celebrities and leaders t to join in helping remind the world positivity, with just a simple smile, attracts positive power.

"At the end of the day public relations, marketing are about communicating a story. The "HOW" is identical: Get customers. Move product. Drive revenue. Our WHY is what positions us to change the world." I love to travel because I learn so much about myself and others. I recently accomplished becoming a Centurion Traveler by experiencing over 100 countries. My favorite place to travel is back home. My son Kenny is the light of his life and a moment by moment inspiration of my purpose in life." Ken Rochon, Jr.

202.701.0911 • Ken@theumbrellasyndicate.com • www.BIGeventsUSA.com

Other Books by Ken Rochon

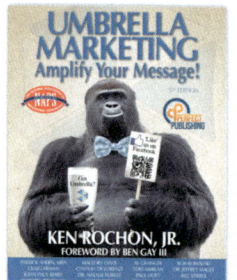 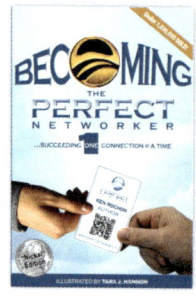 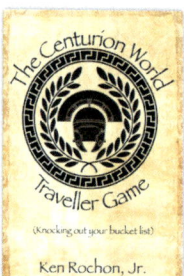 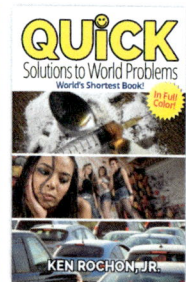 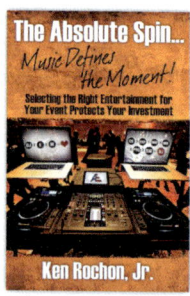 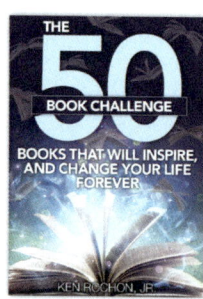 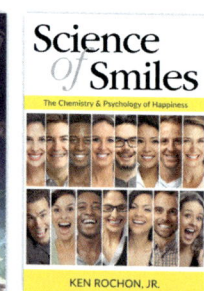

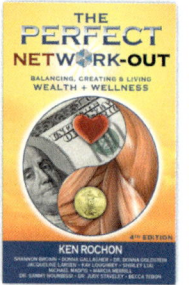 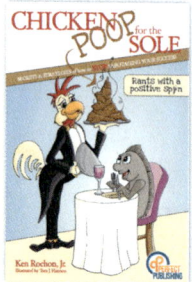 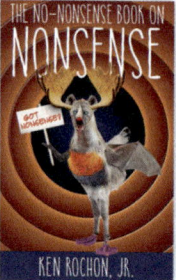 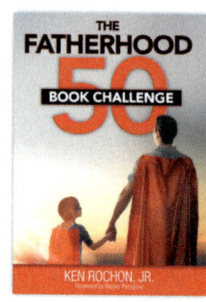 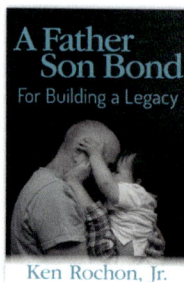 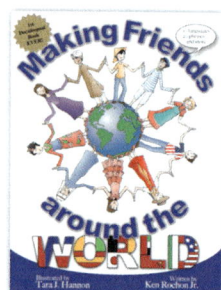 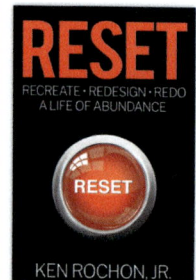

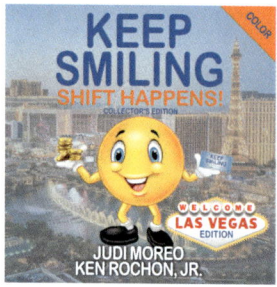 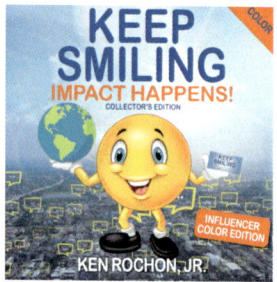 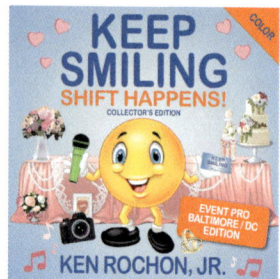 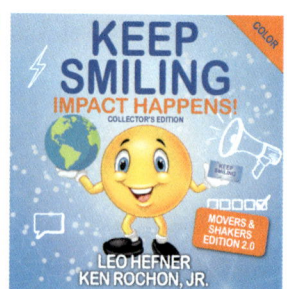 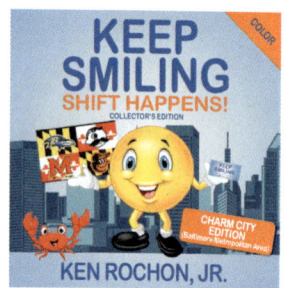

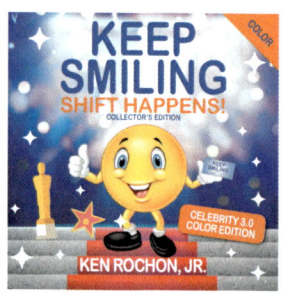 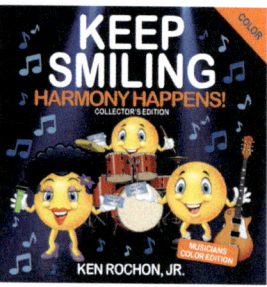 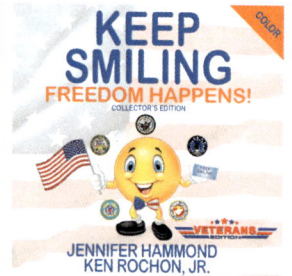 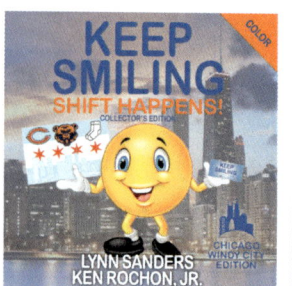 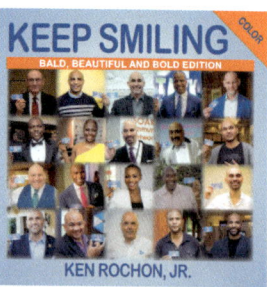

Made in the USA
Middletown, DE
24 March 2022

63129144R00069